THE AMERICAN ECONOMIC REPUBLIC

Other Books by Adolf A. Berle

THE
AMERICAN
ECONOMIC
REPUBLIC

ADOLF A. BERLE

HARCOURT, BRACE & WORLD, INC., NEW YORK

To

BEATRICE BISHOP BERLE,

Baccalaureate of the University of Paris,

Master of Arts in History,

Doctor and Teacher of Medicine,

Ambassadress of the United States,

whose skill and hearth and heart

have been open alike to the high and the

humble of many lands,

this book is dedicated, in admiration,

friendship and love.

FOREWORD: GUIDE FOR THE READER

THE UNITED STATES has worked out an organization and framework of economics, commerce, and business peculiar to itself. Its system differs widely from the descriptions usually given. I have ventured to call it "The American Economic Republic."

This organization is not built around a doctrine. It is not "capitalist," "socialist," or "communist." It is built around a process—the process we call "democracy." Specifically it has integrated the democratic process by which we operate our politics with visible or indirect controls of the private decisions by which we work our economics. These last run all the way from decisions made by a woman buying groceries at a supermarket to those governing great plants like General Motors in manufacturing and selling automobiles. They include policies adopted by United States Steel as it produces iron and steel and decisions by the Department of Agriculture affecting the western plains in raising wheat and food. The decision-making includes department-store policies in granting credit to consumers, as well as policies of great banks in taking deposits and making loans. The sum total of all economic operations creates and distributes wealth and income, and feeds, clothes, and supplies the United States.

The achievements of the American economic republic are outstanding.

Why should we regard the American system as different? Briefly, because it has left nineteenth-century "capitalism" behind. In doing so it has modified property, capital, and the "free market" system. All this occurred somewhat gradually. Modern technical organization silently battered property into its component fragments. The cruelty and irrationality of unrestrained free markets forced their modification. The conduct of banking and finance proved too important to leave to individualist bankers and financiers. Great areas of business had to be taken out of the free market altogether. Many remaining areas had to be put under various kinds of control, stabilization, or restraint.

The nineteenth-century system continually left great numbers of people in distress. Some could not accumulate wealth sufficient to meet their needs in old age or in times of sickness, unemployment, or other conditions of distress. Accordingly a compulsory system of gathering wealth for them had to be worked out. Others were victims of circumstance or misfortune. They had to be provided for. Measures were taken; these in aggregate make up the "Welfare State."

Coming up is a new development we still do not understand. Modern science—which never interested itself in private property or cared much about private capitalism—is pushing inward and outward into every area of life. Most of its advance comes from research in private, university, and government laboratories, chiefly financed by the government. What it will do next, no one can now tell. Its economic application need not follow any known rules. Whose is the Telstar in the night sky? Whose is the formula for Salk vaccine? Whose are radio waves and nuclear energy? Where are cybernetics and automation taking us? An unmapped space stratum of economics is being explored, in which all of us are destined to move.

The reader will find himself in this book, probably a good many times. He is in this republic because he buys and consumes goods, also, because he receives pay, or has a Social Security number, or is covered by a pension trust. There is a preponderant chance that he "owns" some productive wealth (be it more or less) through an insurance policy or a mutual fund or a savings-bank account, if not through direct ownership of stocks or bonds. In any case he is in it because he is a citizen of the United States. He has a vote. He can express an opinion.

He can help make the political state do a better job of causing the economic republic to do what it ought to do.

The study is in three parts.

The first part deals with the dissolution and regrouping of old conceptions—conceptions on which the American economy was operated when I was young. They dissolved because they no longer described or corresponded to what really was happening. As will be seen, property changed its nature. The supposed "free market" began to do unexpected things as great corporations replaced individuals. Money and banking stopped being an affair of private moneylenders and became a national credit currency system. Capital (whatever that is) remained more or less the same, but new power groups settled where it should come from, and how it should be used. The decision-making owner capitalist in large measure disappeared.

The second part of the book has to do with the major institutions we now maintain, accompanied by brief notes as to how they are working; for example, wealth—and how it is distributed (rather badly), and income, and how it is distributed (not too badly by comparison with most systems, though far from ideal). Ours is a government of laws. I have tried to sketch the structure of the system, as it appears in our legislation and our political and governmental organization. It is derived from a tiny nucleus of provisions in the Constitution of the United States, from a few statutes attaining almost constitutional dignity, and is made real by government institutions whose work in the economic republic is almost as well defined as the work of the Supreme Court of the United States is defined in our legal and political system. Some of this law is unwritten—yet nearly as fixed and important as the written law. This will not surprise anyone familiar with Great Britain, whose very well-defined constitution is almost entirely unwritten.

Part Three describes a new economic theory—the theory of the "transcendental margin." It is my conviction that philosophic drive adds to the economic energy of a civilization. The word "drive" is used advisedly. Philosophy here means an impulsion. In America it developed historically from what is called the "Protestant ethic." Increasingly, the evidence convinces me that no economic system is successful unless it includes motives beyond those of individual profit or advantage. Such motivation derives impetus from philosophical convictions.

PREFATORY NOTE

COMPARED WITH the system of any other great nation, the American economic republic is the most successful in the modern world. It has done more for all of its population than any other, without ignoring or glossing over its deficiencies, its omissions, and its problems.

Because of its success, Americans repeatedly are requested by foreign students, teachers, businessmen, and others to recommend a book outlining the theory and practice of the American economic system as it actually functions. They mean, not the system classic or reformist scholars plead for, or theorized about by economists in terms of past conditions, but the system as it works. I have been unable to find such a volume. The monograph by Professor Gerhard Colm and Professor Theodore Geiger, published by the National Planning Association, entitled *The Economy of the American People,* comes closest. In any case, such a book seems needed for most Americans. Immense indeed is the gap between what we say about our political-economic system and how we really operate it. In a mood tinged with desperation, I have here attempted a sketch of its theory and practice.

This is, let me emphasize, an outline, not an encyclopedia. It deals, especially in Part II, with the main governmental framework, without going into detail of the structure. That could require a multivolume work with various parts written by specialists. Spare parts exist now, though not brought together in the frame of a single systematic study.

Part of this material has been presented in the 1963 W. W. Cook Lectures at the University of Michigan. The theory of "The Transcendental Margin" was presented in 1961 at "Prospectives," a research group working with the Ecole des Sciences Politiques at the University of Paris.

I am indebted to Mr. Pierre De Vegh, who has checked my figures, though he is not to be held responsible for my views; and to Miss Margaret Poole, who has worked on the manuscript and to whom I am grateful for unlimited patience.

ADOLF A. BERLE

Columbia University

CONTENTS

THE AMERICAN ECONOMIC REPUBLIC

INTRODUCTION: THE AMERICAN
POLITICAL-ECONOMIC SYSTEM

1.

THE AMERICAN political-economic system, judged by its total achievement, is the most successful in the present-day world. By the same standard of judgment, it is more successful than any in recorded history—though there were civilizations like that of the Inca and the Maya of which we have no adequate record. Its outstanding success has been, first, a level of production never attained by any other large population, and, second, distribution to a point at which only a fraction of the American people have any fear of catastrophic want. Most of them have no acquaintance with poverty, in the sense that poverty exists over great areas of the earth.

This does not mean the system is ideal. Its shortcomings are many and obvious. Its problems and injustices properly engage the attention of many Americans and incite the criticism of students. Yet, I must add, no ideal system has anywhere been proposed, let alone achieved, partly because no two philosophers have ever agreed even on the basic goals or outline of such a system. If today such agreement were had, the sights would be lifted by the next wave of thought. Any perfection conceived by this generation would be overpassed and restated by the ideas of the next.

No adequate description of the American political and economic system as it presently operates is now extant. Only the superb statistical material gathered and collated by the government of the United States and by institutions like the National Bureau of Economic Research and other academic institutions tells the tale. These statistical services give a reasonably fair picture of what has happened. They rarely, if ever, attempt to tell how and, especially, why the results occurred. Most commentators who do make the attempt assume motives and describe processes as these were assumed or thought to have existed many years ago. Their assumptions are chiefly those worked out at the end of the nineteenth century or in the first decade of the twentieth, from which most of our current political-economic thinking is drawn. Their relevance to the processes of today is increasingly limited.

There are, fortunately, an increasing number of studies of specific parts or functions of the American system not thus limited. These are the product of observers who attempted to note and state what the system was doing in their particular areas of study. That is, they dealt with facts and left theorists to harmonize their conclusions and evolve a general theory. No such theorist has arisen in the past generation. The great economic theorist at the close of the nineteenth century, Professor Alfred Marshall, remained virtually supreme in his field until in 1935 the late John Maynard Keynes wrote his book *The General Theory of Employment, Interest, and Money*. Accepting most of the premises of Marshallian economics, Keynes introduced a set of new conceptions. Most of these were based on his cold observation of the way the British and allied European systems operated after the close of World War I. Keynes was—and still is—a controversial figure. Controversy is supposed to rage around his monetary theories. But I suspect the reason for continuing attack on him lies deeper. Keynes challenged the comfortable nineteenth-century *laissez-faire* men who condemned any attempt by the political state to interfere with results of unhindered economic operations by businessmen. In doing so, he challenged a power group—challenged it so effectively, in fact, that no economy in the civilized world is now left merely to financiers or businessmen. Academic economic controversy dies down. Changes in power structure, on the other hand, are never forgiven as long as they live by those whose power is diminished.

Obviously Keynes did not do this all by himself. It is arguable indeed that the processes he described and the emergence of planned or guided economy were under way before he wrote. But he, more than any other in the Western World, rationalized and gave basis for the doctrine that an organized state—possibly a group of states—could stabilize, stimulate, and direct the course of its economy *without* resorting to dictatorship, and *without* superseding a system based on property by a system based on naked power, as the Russians have done. In doing so, he re-created the conception that economics and politics are indissolubly united. This is the practice of the entire modern world today. It is also the reason why in this volume we shall call the American system a system of political economy—not merely an economic system.

We must here demolish a rarely stated, but prevalent, notion. A system of political economy is only an instrument—a means to an end. It is not an end in itself. Nor is it a "civilization," though its processes powerfully affect civilization as we understand it. Primarily, its function is to supply the jobs, materials, goods, and services from which a civilization is built. Secondarily, its task is to establish these jobs, create these materials, and offer these services under conditions and on terms which offer the greatest opportunity for civilization and development, as the evolving morals, perceptions, and dreams of the population may conceive civilization, and thereby give outlet for human endeavor. A political-economic system does not by itself create either a good life or a good society. It can offer the materials from which men can realize and expand their individual conception of the good life. And, because human life (good or, indeed, bad) can only be lived in the framework of the organization we call "society," it must be the instrument for meeting the material needs of that organization as it attempts to realize the "good society."

Part, perhaps, of the current confusion about the American system lies in failure to understand this distinction. The habit of thinking that life is primarily economic is an old one. Probably it rises from the fact that when there is not enough to go around, when want is chronic, when most of a population asks "Can I live another year?," men do live chiefly on the economic plane. That condition of chronic want was certainly the case throughout the entire world until well into the twentieth century. It is the situation in Asia, Africa, and considerable parts of South America today. Professor J. Kenneth Galbraith pays pungent tribute to the fact in his book *The Affluent Society*. He notes that nineteenth-century theorists not only assumed the fact, but also, thanks to Malthus, demonstrated that it must always be the fact. Malthus had explained that population must always outrun production—which led Scrooge in *The Christmas Carol* to reject a request for charity because, if the proposed objects of it starved, it would help reduce the surplus population.

Worse yet, the reformers, the humanitarians, the justly angry men of the nineteenth century accepted the premise that man's whole problem was economic—though in their case it was perhaps excusable. The Socialist and Communist movements, as indeed most of the welfare movements not based on socialist doctrine, took this view. When all human beings were reasonably provided for, were reasonably housed, their problems would be over. Then civilization on a newer, happier, more human pattern would result. What else might be involved could be left to that time.

It remained for the Communist experiment to teach a bitter lesson. An economic system does set up the conditions under which men work and produce and distribute. It does powerfully affect the lives of the individuals composing it. It is thus a formative influence of great power. But it remained for Lenin and Stalin to prove to the twentieth-century world a terrible thesis. When the economic instrument is primarily used to form life, the compulsions, the cruelties, the limitations, physical and moral, the injustices, the resulting personal agonies transcend any oppression yet known. Statistically, it kills, imprisons, exiles, and otherwise torments more of its population than any existing modern system. This is why, for example, the number of prisoners in concentration camps in the Soviet Union has steadily been greater than the entire number of men and women unemployed in the United States save perhaps for one brief period during the Great Depression. The correlation is not accidental.

The important point is, therefore, that a political and economic system is a means to a greater end—an entirely good society. That goal (it will never be reached until the human mind stops developing) is not, as we shall see later, determined primarily by economic considerations. When the attempt is made by economic means alone to reach the good society, the economy falters, and may break down. This fact is outstanding. It is perhaps the greatest single difference between the operation of the American political-economic system of today and the nineteenth-century systems whose shadows still obscure the understanding of the remarkable economic and social achievements (even after allowing for all defects and failures) attained in the United States.

It also explains the problems, moral, social, and esthetic, and some of the economic shortcomings evident on the American scene. As an instrument, our system is obviously capable of doing anything the American public consensus really wishes it to do. It provided both guns and butter for America and a number of other nations during World War II—perhaps the greatest war in history. It could—and one day will—build cities as splendid in beauty as they are now in strength. It has not done so—but this is not the fault of the economic instrument. When the American value system demands stateliness, beauty, and repose as well as consumer goods, fast transportation, and great armament, the instrument can and will provide them, and that within a relatively short time.

2.

OUTLINING the American system would, probably, have been impossible twenty-five years ago. It was then emerging from the nineteenth-century theory of the free market and automatic balance. Its peculiar characteristics were developing, but obscure. Their emergence was the occasion of the bitter political struggle known to history as the "New Deal controversy," which raged over specific measures and detail. Only in the decade following World War II did its integral structure reveal itself as an established fact.

More important, perhaps, there was nothing with which to compare it. Today it can be contrasted to the structure of Soviet organized Communism. The fact is salient, for no system can be described or analyzed in terms of itself. Until the Soviet structure emerged, the economic and political systems throughout the civilized world claimed the same theoretical base. In practice, to be sure, they differed in considerable degree. The twelve imperial systems ruling most of the earth's surface (outside the Western Hemisphere) until 1919 had their own forms. Essentially, nevertheless, these were all premised on classical capitalism. It fell to the Soviet Union to construct a political system on a different base. This it accomplished during the period of Stalin, so that at the advent of Khrushchev in 1951 a different structure existed, serving as basis of comparison.

Analysis of the Soviet Communist system is not the purpose of this volume, and only a brief note of the chief differences between it and that of classical capitalism need be made. Classical capitalism of the past was based on private property. Specifically and importantly it assumed that property intended to produce goods (and not for mere consumption) would be created and operated by individuals impelled to do so by hope of individual profit. Karl Marx's assumption (it was not too far from likely fact when he wrote *The Communist Manifesto* in 1848) was that productive property would be monopolized by a small class; that this class would continuously and inexorably become richer and extend its monopoly, and that it would control conditions under which labor would work and would be paid. The private-property right and the profit motive, key to this system, were therefore anathema to him. The class he assumed to exist was the ruling oligarchy, automatically the oppressor of laborers (called "wage slaves") and exploiter of consumers.

The Communist system by the time Lenin died, and increasingly so under Stalin's guidance, merely substituted for this assumed monopoly of property a new monopoly—the monopoly of power. By transferring all productive property (and a great deal of consumer property as well) to the state, and by talking abstractions such as "ownership by the people," the emerging Communist royalty became a centralized, dictatorial power over all economic activity. It was wielded by a dictator, through an oligarchy of state officials, buttressed by an unparalleled spy and secret-police system. Economic power, political power, and military power were thus merged. To these was added monopoly over information, education, and intellectual development. Under this power system of its own devising, the Communist states have undertaken to bring about capital formation, to organize production, to allocate distribution.

Under the old system the individual inducement to gather capital, to enter production, and to distribute the product was hope of profit and accumulation of wealth. To move up in the bureaucratic pyramid, to acquire more power, and incidentally more consumer comforts and appurtenances as he ascends, provides the incentive for any individual under the Soviet system. Ascent, as in all power pyramids, depends in its earlier stages on the favor of the men above. As one reaches the higher ranks, it turns on capacity to mobilize support and influence through intrigue or control of men. At the apex of the pyramid certain individuals may indeed mobilize so much support that the dictator must conciliate some, cautiously neutralize some, and destroy others, and balance forces as dictators have had to do since the dawn of history. It is merely one more of the grim ironies of twentieth-century idealism that the attempt to destroy what was assumed to be a monopoly of property replaced it by a more ferocious mechanism based on the monopoly of power. The limited and relatively manageable profit motive as incentive to a human individual has been replaced by the uncontrolled and apparently uncontrollable urge for personal position and power.

This is the elementary comparison between the two systems. Obviously it is oversimplified. Human motives are usually mixed. As we shall see, the profit motive under the American system was never the only—perhaps not even the primary— cause of American economic growth. Probably, when evidence unavailable now can be gathered as to the Soviet system, we shall find a similar mixture of motive operating in the Communist pyramid. Very possibly many of these men, while struggling for power, also are struggling to increase the growth, might, and prestige of Mother Russia, to strengthen the kind of nationalism and imperialism familiar to every student of the age of Louis Quatorze or of Catherine the Great or the Napoleonic era. Or perhaps individuals in the power structure are touched in some part by messianic motives. The men who served the sixteenth-century Spanish empire lusted for power and gold, but also quite sincerely proposed to impose the Catholic faith on the vanquished in sincere desire to save their souls from hell. Both in structure and in method (including methods of subversion and seizure of other countries) there is a singularly close parallel between the Spanish imperial system under Philip II and the Communist imperial systems today. Unlike the Spanish empire, however, the Soviet empire has preoccupied itself with the organization of its economy. The contrast, therefore, is between results obtained by the American system of political economy here to be examined, and the simplicist power system erected in the Soviet Union and China, though the Chinese experiment, being only a decade old, has not yet revealed its permanent structure.

Now it is clear that a power system can form capital, can produce, and can distribute. Power can be substituted (within limits) for what we loosely call capital. It can build, man, and operate plants, factories, transport by land, sea, and air, and create distribution systems. It can crudely allocate its production and distribution. It can, I think, eliminate want and poverty, though the Soviet system has not done so yet and Khrushchev holds out to his subjects the hope that in another decade Soviet production (he says little about distribution) will "catch up" with that of the United States. It is fair to note that the Soviet Union has made substantial progress in production and some in distribution. Considering that the Soviet system has been in existence nearly half a century, and that its difficulties through war and disturbance have not been greater than those suffered by other countries, notably those of Western Europe, it is about time for the system to begin to demonstrate results. Yet it is to be noted that in the same period (say from 1921 to the present) both the American and the Western European systems of political economy have been able almost to abolish the "proletariat" in their areas. The Soviet workman and peasant still live under conditions Americans would consider unacceptable for a civilized people. The major achievement of the Communist system has been construction and organization of a vast armament, accompanied by a costly though effective imperialist expansionism.

The second salient difference between the two systems lies in the relation under each between economics and politics. The American system has in wide degree separated its means and methods of political action from its means and methods of economic operation. Americans regard politics as a means by which purely economic operations can be modified, directed, and, when necessary, controlled. But they are careful not to admit any economic machine, whether publicly or privately owned, to the control of their politics, and they are equally cautious about permitting politicians to enter economic operations.

This point ought to be emphasized, because a good deal of nonsense, some of it malicious, has recently been printed on the subject. Professor C. Wright Mills's *The Power Elite* was an interesting but singularly inaccurate and unimpressive attempt to manufacture an interlocking oligarchy in the United States controlling, respectively, finance, business, the armed forces, and its government. The fact, of course, is that in America, as in most countries, individuals of demonstrated capacity in any field are frequently called upon to change occupation and work in other fields, but they are not allowed to carry their influence in one sector of work into another. A businessman called to a Cabinet office in Washington is marked for certain destruction if he is suspected of using his government connection to assist his former business connections. A political figure called to the presidency of a great company receives the coolest reception when he knocks on the door of his former department to ask special favors. In both cases these men are held under the most rigid scrutiny by press and politicians.

Political doctrine calls for the separation of powers—executive from legislative, and legislative from judicial. An unwritten constitutional rule prohibits the use of political power in business administration, and vice versa. Even where the American state itself carries on an economic function (as in the case of the Tennessee Valley Authority), any serious tampering with this line of division forces immediate penalty—political and sometimes criminal. Retribution is equally swift where there is political interference with an American corporation, or where an American corporation incautiously induces a political officer to betray his trust in its favor.

A third outstanding difference completes the list. This is the relative decentralization of American economic power. It is only relative. Factually, concentration of economic power has been slowly and steadily growing in the United States over the past fifty years, partly through growth of large corporations and partly through the steadily increasing proportion of industrial production and decreasing proportion of agricultural production.

It is frequently (and erroneously) said that the degree of concentration of American industry has not increased significantly in the past fifty years. By this it is meant that a few hundred corporations have continuously produced about two thirds of the American industrial product. This statement conceals the fact that industry as a whole has steadily increased its proportion of national product, while the proportion of agricultural product has equally steadily decreased. During the past half-century, the proportion of agriculture (traditionally carried on by individuals or on a small-scale basis compared with industry) declined from 17.3% of national product to 3.8%.[1] The number of men engaged in agriculture has also steadily declined and is continuing to do so. Between 1950 and 1960 alone, a million farm-operating families left agriculture for industrial employment. Meanwhile, industrial production soared. The economic power position of the 500 or 600 corporations which account for two thirds of the industrial production of the United States had steadily increased, measured by the share

1. The notes are on pages 219 to 238.

of national product they produced. That increase is continuing.

It is debatable whether the 500 or 600 corporations which produced two thirds of American industrial production in 1947 produce much more than that fraction now—though there is some reason to believe that they do. But two thirds of industrial production in 1962 is a substantially greater proportion of the national product of the United States than it was in 1947, and far greater than in 1912. The strength of the few hundred large corporations thus has necessarily increased. Perhaps it had to increase.

Yet the fact was, and is, that centralization of industrial economic power to a point where it could dominate the political state has been avoided in the American political system. It is not at present a major threat. In the one period when such concentration did become dangerous—the decades beginning in 1870 and ending in 1910—American political reaction was quite sufficient to prevent the great corporations which were predominant in production from becoming masters of the state. By 1960 few, if any, sane administrators of American corporations would dream of attempting a political adventure of that kind. Had any done so, his business career probably would have ended with speed and drama. In any case, the facts would have frustrated such ambitions. There is no high factor of unity when several hundred corporations in different lines of endeavor are involved. There is still less when a substantial degree of competition prevails among them. Dominance by them over the political state in major matters is not a present possibility. Decentralization is one result of the American system, and it has been jealously maintained, insisted upon, enforced. "Monopoly capitalism" is strictly a Communist phrase. When applied to America, it is merely a Communist myth.

Power monopoly, which also includes control of capital, does in fact exist in the Soviet Union. The Communist system indeed is pledged to it. Their theorists base their claim that the Communist system will eventually prove superior on that fact. Through a power monopoly, they say, the Communist state can plan its productive operations, can allocate its resources, can control its distribution. It can maintain economic stability, can avoid waste of materials and of men through unemployment, and can create a higher civilization. This capacity, they assert, does not exist in the American system. This, of course, is an echo of Marx's "Theory of Crises"; he assumed wrongly, as the American event proved, that monopoly capitalism, by increasingly drawing income into the oligarchy of wealth, would restrict purchasing power, diminish mass markets, and cause the system to break down.

The end, of course, is not yet. On the record, the Soviet Union has thus far been unable to produce enough food for its people (in production it has conspicuously failed by modern standards), or to house its population. It may attain these ends in time. The American system has, on the other hand, succeeded in modifying depressions to the controllable level, has, since 1933, avoided substantial depression, and has maintained a large population (now 185 millions) in substantial safety and comfort, save for a few, steadily diminishing, areas whose elimination is a primary target of American policy. Only the future will tell whether the Communist power-monopoly system can produce to a point of affluence and can distribute to the point of accomplishing a measure of social justice before it destroys itself (and possibly the world with it) in a Hitler-like plunge for world domination or disaster.

3.

THE TWENTIETH-CENTURY American economic republic in its present form could come into existence only because of the conjunction of two conditions.

First was the fragmentation of concepts on which nineteenth-century American economics had been built.

The conception of property had been battered in several directions. Intellectually it was under attack, chiefly from European thinkers. Functionally, it was hammered by the growing need of collective, large-scale organization. Physically (if one can use the word), property was being split into a whole range of diverse elements, some as intangible as scientific experience and know-how, others as tangible and inert as bricks and mortar and land. The whole range is called "property," but few elements in it are useful except in combination with others. Most elements are not useful at all apart from organizations of men, themselves diverse in interest, training, and equipment.

"Capital" became fragmented. Originally conceived as an entrepreneur's tool, it increasingly became divided in source, kind, function, and ownership. Increasingly, elements of it— for example, intellectual capital—could scarcely be reduced to conventional ownership.

The "free market" increasingly ceased to be more than an abstraction. In any event, its behavior changed.

The second condition was the really remarkable capacity of the American political state to enter and deal with the economic field with a remarkable combination of courage and restraint. No better vindication, perhaps, of the American democratic process (irritating as it often is) can be found than the history of the past thirty years. It nailed its flag to no dogma. It evolved instruments adapted to problems. It met situations pragmatically —in the sense that it has been flexible in the choice of alternative means to reach the ends. It never deserted its primary premise of a free society designed to permit free men to realize themselves. It sought economic conditions fostering such a society.

Hence the division of this study into two parts. The first part deals with the passing of the concepts of the old order, and the new conceptions emerging from their recombined fragments. The second part relates to the evolution of the political state and its accommodation to and use of nonstatist institutions, of which the American corporation and the American labor union are the two most important examples.

The result is the American economic republic as we know it today, evolved but still evolving. Consciously it faces problems of adaptation in the next generation greater than those of the past. Its demonstrated capacity for adaptation gives reason for sober optimism.

Meantime, "capitalism," as that word is classically understood, and "Communism," meaning Marxism in any of its current organized forms, are both obsolete. They belong in museums of nineteenth-century thought and culture.

PART ONE

Theory

CHAPTER 1 THE FRAGMENTATION

OF ECONOMIC CONCEPTS: PROPERTY

IN ANALYSIS[2]

1. The Attack

THE YEAR was 1839. Pierre Joseph Proudhon presented to the French Academy of Moral and Political Science a memorandum entitled "What Is Property? It Is Theft." (Later he deleted the "It Is Theft" clause from the title—but left it on the first page.) His thesis was that property, by which he meant property which produced income for its owner, was essentially illegitimate.

The proposition upset nineteenth-century France. For a generation, the resulting storm of controversy raged in French intellectual circles. It survived the Revolution of 1848 and the establishment of the Second French Empire.

On December 20, 1865, Pierre Larousse, presenting to the world that paragon of encyclopedias, the *Grand Dictionnaire Universel,* concluded his majestic introduction with a final paragraph—a lament for the death of the "boldest and most profound thinker" of the nineteenth century, Pierre Joseph Proudhon. Larousse quoted a letter to him from his late collaborator:

When you come to the articles "God" and "Property," let me know. You will see by a few words of explanation that there is no refuge from the paradox in these propositions: "God is evil," and "property is theft"—I maintain these propositions in their literal sense, without on that account endeavoring to make a crime out of faith in God, still less to abolish property.

Yes, illustrious philosopher [adds Larousse], when we come to these two phrases so terribly misunderstood, which have raised so many traducers of your memory, all the shadows so hypocritically spread will be wiped away.

19

Honorably, when the title *"propriété,"* was arrived at by Larousse and his fellow editors, the pledge was tenderly redeemed, and the discussion reviewed. Sainte-Beuve had taken a hand in it. A point made by François Quesnay and the French physiocrats a century earlier, when property as we know it today was less well established, had been reasserted. Property was a social institution by which men could become free of the tyranny of the state. L. A. Thiers participated. Larousse noted that he had "devoted himself almost entirely to defending individual property, and this constant preoccupation led him to struggle against economic facts whose force and effectiveness it is today [1865] impossible to deny, notably associations [corporations] and the application of the cooperative system."

Proudhon in defense had asserted with characteristic dogmatism, "The principle of property is ultra-legal, extra-judicial, absolutist, egoist to the point of iniquity. By its very nature, it must be so. As a countervailing force it has the 'raison d'etat'—absolutist, ultra-legal, illiberal, and statist to the point of oppression. This also must be so." Yet, in Proudhon's view, though property is nothing but sanctified egoism, it has this use: In the defense of liberty against statist power it becomes a mighty fortress—as indeed statist power might be opposed to the absolutist and oppressive use of property.

The politics of Europe had moved against Proudhon. A young disciple, Karl Marx, had swallowed the first part of Proudhon's contention whole; much of its influence appears in *The Communist Manifesto.* But the Revolution of 1848 entrusted the Second French Republic to the not too tender hands of Prince-President Louis Napoleon Bonaparte. He in due time converted it into the Second Empire. Bismarck, in Germany, crushed radical as well as republican ideas. The revolution in Austria, while it displaced Metternich, became political rather than economic in character and was defeated. Marx became an obscure exile in England. The philosophical discussion abated, aside from minority groups of revolutionists.

Meanwhile, throughout the nineteenth and early twentieth centuries, the institution of private property had, one observes, done rather well. Too well, perhaps. It had become a social fact—a fact so well established that few of us in the twentieth century remember that private property, except as a favor of the state, hardly existed until the middle of the eighteenth century. In England, and especially in the United States, whose history and geography removed it from European philosophical struggles, private property and private ownership of capital were assumed to be as natural and unchangeable as the solar system. The subversive influence of corporations, and perhaps co-operatives, noted with unusual perspicacity by the French encyclopedist and struggled against by Thiers, went unremarked and unnoticed. Marx with his *Communist Manifesto* undertook to destroy property altogether. Corporation promoters and managers, without any manifesto at all, and without the slightest preoccupation with social institutions, were actually changing the nature of the beast.

This perhaps is why the philosophical discussion languished. And why, resumed today, it presents an entirely different set of issues. The form of property thrown up by the corporate system, while by no means wholly new, is nevertheless entirely different in its human as well as its productive connotations. It is not the property attacked by Proudhon as stolen goods, and by Marx as the nucleus around which a bandit's protective association called the state has been organized. The largest part of productive property (industrial property) does not answer to either description. In fact, it becomes increasingly difficult to distinguish between property in production (Proudhon let consumptive property alone) and property designed to provide for individual wants.

Both Proudhon and Marx, both Adam Smith and our contemporary Ludwig von Mises, treat of property as a rather simple element around which complex philosophical, economic, and human processes flow, and upon which complex theories might be built. The twentieth century finds property itself a singularly complex and unstable affair.

The half-century following the publication of the Larousse encyclopedia was, without question, the half-century of property *par excellence*. It may have been the fruit of crime and a continuing crime, as Proudhon suggested, or a gift, if not of God, at least of natural law, as the classical economists believed. But in any case it was a social fact. Philosophers might mumble about it—and did, as Marx had done, laboring in the British Museum in London. Economists might find justification for it, and did, as Ricardo had done. The so-called "liberal" (*laissez-faire*) school accepted it as a major tool of economic progress, and desire for it as a major motive. In any case, everyone wanted some of it. The peasant wanted land, the laborer wanted pay, a home, and a bank account. The small merchant or manufacturer wished to enlarge his business, his shop, his plant, his working capital, and his profits. The dreams of the larger entrepreneurs grew. Great bankers, like the Rothschilds, went further; money was power, and they were learning how to use it.

There was not then enough production to meet need—a fact reflected in the sea of poverty which included most of the population of Europe and a substantial part of the population of the United States. The entrepreneurs who organized and the capitalists who dominated production were therefore the elite of the system. Whatever their faults (they were many), they did bring into existence railroads, communications, mines, steel and metal plants, as well as lighter forms of fabrication. The Industrial Revolution was rolling, and desire for profits and property was its motivating force. Speculative profit—that is, wealth acquired without appreciable contribution—was condoned on the theory that it helped capital-gathering. In any case, the always beneficent gods of the classical free market would eventually make the best possible allocation of human endeavor. As for equality of humanity—well, that was a revolutionary idea and also, so far as property was concerned, an impractical one. Malthus had made that clear: population would always expand to the uttermost limit of production, even though most human existence was lived at the bare level of subsistence. To keep the productive machine going, some group of men had to be on top of it and directing it.

That last idea persists today. It will be found, admirably explained, in Walt Rostow's *Stages of Economic Growth*. He considered that in the capital-accumulation phase, the organization of modern means of production depended on an elite of driving, powerful men who knew what they wanted and got it. What they thought about while they were getting it was of little importance. It would probably have shocked both Marx and Lenin to have been told that the dictators of the proletariat they were planning would be (and indeed later proved) close analogues and imitators of the Morgans, the Goulds, the Vanderbilts, the Rockefellers, of the American plutocratic era, exploiting to the limit the labor of the people they dominated in order to gather capital for the heavy-industry plants they created. It would have been still more surprising if, while Lenin was still a revolutionary in Switzerland, it had been pointed out at a meeting that he and his friends proposed to do through political power exactly what the Rothschilds and other buccaneer capitalists had done in the nineties through economic power. No doubt the meeting would have exploded if the perfectly true statement had been made that the Lenins, the Trotskys, and the Molotovs were obsessed by desire for power in precisely the same way that Western European and American capitalist organizers were obsessed with desire for profit, if, indeed, as one approaches the extreme of profit, as typified by a Carnegie or a Vanderbilt, there is any real difference between their emotions and those of the Russian revolutionaries who sought and got despotic power in Russia after 1917.

Not being as self-assured as Proudhon, this writer is not prepared to pass moral judgments on the past. In social fact, the plutocrat capitalists of the late nineteenth and early twentieth centuries did collect capital, did create a vast capital plant, did set it going. The human cost cannot now be reckoned; still less, the human cost which might have occurred had they not set it going. The Lenin-Stalin regime did the same job for the Soviet Union. The Khrushchev regime is passing the same moral judgments on Stalin and the human cost of his operations that the public of the United States at one time passed on the tycoons of her plutocratic era. Perhaps, in this latter half of the twentieth century, we can excuse ourselves from such judgments. Let Saint Peter do his own work and let us deal with the results.

2. "What Is Property?"

DURING ALL THIS, Proudhon's question went unanswered. What is "property"?

Until relatively recently this question got little attention. There were, of course, certain rough categories generally agreed upon. Property was divided by the law into two great branches: real property, that is to say, land and buildings and other works constructed on it, and personal property, that is, movables. About all this meant was distinguishing property which could be carried off and property which could not.

Horizontal division of these two kinds of property was also made. Some property was devoted to productive use, that is, "capital" use—designed to produce goods or services necessary to or wanted by other people. Another sector of property, both real and personal, existed or was maintained for the purpose of satisfying the owner's needs, wants, or whims—a home, a set of furniture, a carriage and pair, or, more recently, a motorcar, a television set. This was property "in consumption."

In the personal-property sector of property at work, there were "claims," including pieces of paper representing someone's promise to pay, such as promissory notes and longer-term promises to pay (bonds), and, as the system came into maturity in the nineteenth century, shares of stock in a collectivism called a corporation.

These, and more especially bonds and shares of stock, were expected to have two qualities which distinguished them. They could pass from hand to hand without difficulty—they were "negotiable" as the law merchant says—and they were supposed to be "liquid"—that is, capable of being converted into cash on short notice. This liquidity was a very desirable attribute. It meant that the holder of them could, by selling or borrowing on them, turn them into money and do something different. He could detach himself instanter from any relation to the enterprise which had issued the bonds or stock. If these pieces of paper fluctuated in value on the exchanges, he could speculate in them. To the enterprises which issued such paper, liquidity was highly desirable, because, in their early stages, investors were far more likely to buy such paper, and thereby contribute to the capital of the corporation. Nobody thought of this as anything but a highly useful financial device. That it might be a crack in the surface of property itself—worse yet, a quality forcing the political state into the picture—then occurred to few, if any, analysts.

Property examined under a microscope turns out to be unlimitedly complex. This is because property does not exist unless there is at minimum a relation between a man or an organization of men and a thing or aggregation of things. A piece of rock has an owner. If the owner is a sculptor, the rock is in passage toward becoming a work of art. The subjective factor is the chief element. A piece of Chinese jade has an owner—perhaps a collector. It is a thing in being, objective, lying quietly on a display shelf. The owner neither adds nor subtracts; he enjoys. The less a thing is susceptible to being worked with or upon, the more objective it becomes.

But then property turns a corner. At the extreme of objectivity—for example, hoarded gold—it can become, not a thing in itself, but a claim on the goods, the services, or the labor of other men at the will of its owner. At this point, surprisingly, its significance once more becomes almost entirely subjective. Its owner can cause events to happen by selling this purely objective property, or perhaps by drawing and spending the dividends or interest realized from it, but he cannot otherwise affect the property whose prime characteristic is "liquidity." To accomplish this liquidity, it is necessary that the property (thing or claim—for example, a share of American Telephone & Telegraph stock) have no relation whatever to its owner *except* that relation arising from the owner's capacity to transfer it. Nothing can be liquid if any value assigned to it depends upon the capacity or effort or will of the owner. Marble would stop being readily salable if its value depended on having the sculptor transferred along with it.

And now we find ourselves involved in a range of companion problems.

Any community rapidly develops needs and desires which can only be satisfied by things, assembled or fabricated by men. It must have capital. Owners must devote some things to produce others which will satisfy these needs and these desires. Otherwise the community suffers, or, in extreme cases, breaks up. The owners may have individual ideas and subjective wills about their property, but enough of them have to agree on using part of their property to produce the things desired and needed to satisfy community demand. Any motive which produces adequate allocation of property to capital suffices. Fear of secret police, hope of profit, desire to gain favor with the tribal gods, devotion to an ideal of humanity, or any mixture will do, provided the economic result is achieved. To assemble capital or organize enterprises, ruling groups have used all these motives at one or another time in history. Modern civilization, which must take care of vast populations by assuring sufficient capital to make possible the mass production it requires and has developed, demands a very high mobilization of the will of property owners—where it does not invoke power and wipe out owners altogether.

Naked power can in fact be substituted for property mobilization. When that happens—as it has happened in Communist countries—the problem, though it appears different, merely changes form. Mobilizing human sentiment so that it crystallizes in and causes men to accept a power mechanism is, if anything, more difficult and less satisfactory than mobilizing the desires and wills of owners into the degree of co-operation required for mass production.

Under the property system, this mobilization of property was accomplished by the profit motive. Certainly this has been true in the nineteenth and twentieth centuries. It is an economic fact that such mobilization produced results. Through corporations, the will of owners was energized by the prospect of increasing their property, though co-operation entailed loss of decision-making power. The price they paid was abandonment to the corporate management of their capacity to decide, each for himself, what their individual property would be or do.

In return for relinquishment of an active role in working with their property, most owners wanted, sought, and got, a new variety of property—stock or bonds—which was highly liquid. Being liquid, it was completely passive. This form of property —securities and peculiarly corporate stock—now probably represents (or at least purports to represent) more than half of all individually held property in the United States at the present time. (Hereafter we shall, from time to time, call it "wealth.") In theory, all of it can be converted into money on a few hours' notice through the machinery of the securities markets. None of it can be worked at, changed, or in the slightest degree altered by anything its owner does. So far as that quality of property is concerned, the owner is out of it. On the other hand, the owner has absolute, immediate, whimsical power to convert it into cash, with which he can buy or secure any and all kinds of goods and services available in our society. If he has enough passive property, he is as mobile, and as free to act or not act, as a man can be. But that is all. His "property" affords him no job, presents him with no mission, assigns him no function. He must, within himself, or, in any case, aside from it, develop whatever reason he may find for cluttering up this singularly puzzled planet.

Whether he knows it or not, he is now at the mercy of the political state. Liquidity in the long run depends on the functioning of the banking and currency system; and in the twentieth century, banking and currency systems are peculiarly and typically the province and prerogative of the modern state. I do not here repeat the argument I made in *Liquid Claims and National Wealth* (1934), for which Miss Victoria Pederson was the consulting statistician. Liquidity on any large scale (which means, in practice, in any industrial civilization) is artificial. To have it, there must be currency or bank credit and also a method of expanding the supply of currency and credit to meet demand for it. There must be reserves of one kind and another to maintain its value. These depend on the will of the state. Given adequate banking and currency mechanisms, it is possible to maintain, with at least acceptable stability, supporting institutions for liquidity like the New York Stock Exchange.

All liquidity systems depend on a calculation that everyone

will not wish to convert all of his passive or liquid property into cash at the same time. That, in fact, only a small percentage of individuals will wish to do so at any given time, and that these will be balanced by other individuals wishing to convert their cash into passive property. So, markets for passive property—the New York Stock Exchange and similar institutions—are in reality like great banks. The seller of securities is seeking payment in cash at the paying teller's window. His expectation of payment is justified on the assumption that there will be buyers for stock, paying cash into the equivalent of a receiving teller's window. As long as these balance, there is "liquidity." When they do not balance, in theory, a change in the price level of any particular stock or all stocks, or of any particular interest-bearing bond or of all such bonds, will rectify the situation by inducing more buying at the lower price or more selling at the higher price. In case of real difficulty, the government, through its banking system, induces more buying and makes it possible by permitting bank credit (currency of a sort) to be used for that purpose; or, in the reverse situation of a speculative boom, where buyers are plentiful and sellers few, by withdrawing bank credit so that buyers find it harder to buy and the price is either stabilized or diminished. The Federal Reserve System watches and endeavors to influence these markets so that they shall continuously be liquid; it is not the least of the tasks the Federal Reserve has to perform.

It shocks the American financial community to be told that the New York Stock Exchange is one of the most highly developed statist institutions we have. But there is no escape from the fact.

Probably the fact would not have disturbed the philosophers who discussed property in Paris a century ago. They, thinking through the institution of property, had come to one conclusion: Any kind of property, whether you like it or not, depends on a system of social order and has to be protected by a system of law. Both depend on the state. This fact, indeed, led one branch of thinkers into the revolutionary movement. If you assume that property is theft or stolen goods, and you assume that it can only be maintained by the state, then the state becomes the instrument for the protection of thieves and ought to be over-thrown. That reasoning, carried to its ultimate, was embodied in Lenin's dictum requiring violent revolution as an essential precedent to reorganization. Only victory and conquest in a shooting class war will produce that result, and results produced in any other way, according to the Leninist school, are immoral. The theory is loose on the continent of South America today: one can only hope it does not produce as much slaughter as it has produced in the Soviet Union, the satellite states, and Red China.

Beyond question, liquid property in large supply was what the twentieth-century United States wanted. Liquid property constituted about 15% (calculated at market value) of the gross national wealth from 1880 to 1890. It climbed steadily to 24% in 1920, thence to 40% in 1930. The stock-market crash and deflation unprecedented in history knocked the per-centage down to 31 by 1933; whereupon it started to climb again. In 1962 the aggregate market value of the bonds and stocks assumed to have liquidity was probably more than half the entire individually owned wealth of the United States. Total individual wealth was rather more than a trillion dollars. Ex-cluding bonds of all kinds, the aggregate value of stocks alone, listed on the New York Stock Exchange and other national markets, was on the order of $450 billion—fluctuating, of course, as stock prices rose and fell. The figure does not in-clude bonds, cash surrender value of life insurance, and bank deposits.

Hence, a curious result: The more completely the individual property owner is divorced from subjective relation to the under-lying things constituting the productive mechanism of the coun-try, the less contribution he can make to the actual process of production and the more "liquid" his wealth becomes. Super-ficially, perhaps, this is more desirable. While his will no longer has significance in production, it has almost complete play in consumption. If all this wealth were evenly distributed among all American families, we would be very far toward realizing the earliest, simplest dreams of the forerunners of Marxian Communism.

From such a situation the age-old question of "legitimacy" fairly shrieks for solution. What is the philosophical, moral, or economic justification for this sort of property? In more practical terms, why should the state not only protect it, but erect financial mechanisms so that its assumed qualities of liquidity shall be maintained? Let us, for the moment, leave that question for later consideration. Here we have been trying to discover what property is.

3. Property as Enterprise. Power Holders

MEANWHILE, we must go back to our tangible things. We left them behind when the owner deserted them for pieces of paper with liquid value.

They, in fact, are in obvious existence, smokestacks and all, visible anywhere and everywhere, organized for all manner of production and use. They are office buildings and apartment houses, they are shops and garages, they are railroad and truck lines, they are small factories and large factories, they are grouped factories connected with transport facilities leading to forests and mines. And in each case there is a man or a group of men—possibly a very large group of men—taking care of them, combining them with labor, operating them, producing from them, marketing the product. There is a relationship between men and things. But the men are not the owners of the things where any really large-scale operation goes forward. Somewhere between a quarter and a third of industrial product may still come from the aggregation of things brought into existence or operated by their owners. Individual ownership of productive process still does exist in the United States. But much of this proprietorship is plainly destined for ultimate haven in large corporations, if, indeed, it is not destined for ultimate liquidation.

This is not to say that private-enterprise property—meaning thereby personal proprietorship in industrial production or commercial operation—will disappear; far from it. It means only that the existing small proprietary enterprises will either find their way into large corporations or will disappear through the owner's death, liquidation, bankruptcy, or otherwise. As they disappear, a new army of proprietors or entrepreneurs with new enterprises will probably occupy their place—marching anew toward an ultimate organization in which the ownership will have become passive, while agents or deputies ("management," in fact) will impose their will upon the things in place of the bygone owners. And a new generation of individual owner-entrepreneurs arises in its turn.

Now, however, our unit of "property" begins to outrun the simple trajectory of ordinary arithmetic. The larger the aggregation of things, the bigger the corporation, the more elaborate the organization of men combined with them to make them productive, the less the result can be valued by simple addition. The value of the productive whole is not equal to the sum of the parts. It is either a great deal less or a great deal more. Two elements of this divergence can be detected, though there are probably a number of others.

The first element arises from the intangible but extremely real (and costly) factor of "organization." A plant, with its equipment and its connections, is a dead thing—almost worthless—if and while it stands still. Brought to life by a management and a labor staff which has been shaken down to a smooth-working operating routine, shaken up by an effective research-and-development crew, and shaken out by continuous introduction of new processes, machines, and methods (not excluding automation), the whole becomes a productive mechanism. Its value, by any test, is far greater—or perhaps far less—than the appraisal of any particular set of things and of contract relationships between the men comprising the management and staff. It will grind out goods which perhaps can be sold at large profits. It may, equally, grind its way into a deficit and eventual destruction of the enterprise. It develops emotional relationships not unlike those which prevailed when the owner was really there, and really managed the show. A district manager will refer to "my plant" though he may be eighth-echelon down in the General Motors or the General Electric hierarchy. Individual workmen will develop an attachment, analogous to affection, for a particular assignment to a particular aggregation of real estate and metal—as old railroaders were passionately possessive of their particular stretch of difficult track and obsolescent rolling stock. Operating property takes on a new dimension precisely because of the mobilizing minds and egos which make it go. The collection of things has given them opportunity to make go and make do. They have put the collection of things into motion, producing goods or services. The combination introduces another coefficient, the coefficient of motion or, in slang phrase, "turnover."

Crudely, this coefficient affects the market value of the piece of paper held by the passive owner who bought it on the stock market. It makes him rich or loses him his stake, though he knows little or nothing about the throbbing entity itself. Vaguely, moving from one inexact calculation to another, the market arrives at a purely romantic estimate of what a share of General Motors or General Electric is worth. It imports all sorts of considerations, which have little to do with the company itself, and arrives at a price which buyers are willing to pay, more or less continuously, for its stock. The "property" (with which must be included the management and organization, which is not, and cannot be, owned) is the theoretical basis underlying the liquid value of the passive property, which, nominally, represents its "ownership."

The other discernible element of divergence relates, not to the things themselves, or to the organization which makes them go, but to the place or niche an enterprise holds in the social-economic aggregate known as the United States. Here I diverge from some of the current theory. Assumedly, enterprises have value more or less proportionate to their success in producing goods or services the public wants badly enough to pay for. As they do this, and as the public pays for the goods or services, they make a "profit" or "loss." I here suggest that there is no way of knowing whether any enterprise in the United States, taken by itself, makes or loses money, and that the utility or nonutility of the goods or services it produces or provides is not necessarily the factor determining the profit. I believe that the profit-and-loss statements made up at the end of the year really reflect whether the enterprise holds a favored or an unfortunate niche in the whole aggregate.

I suggest that the "cost" of their operation reflects, not its real cost, but only the cost paid directly by the enterprise. All around it are services provided to it for which it does not have to pay, or, if it does, for which it pays either more or less than the full cost. The plants are located in these and these communities; to them, they pay property taxes. They may pay more than their fair share, or less. They employ a community of laborers. These must be permanently available. When the plant shuts down, their savings and the Social Security allowances support those laborers and keep them available until conditions permit the plant to start up again. Part of the cost of the whole operation is then borne by the federal government, or by the community, or by the individuals, or by all three together. The opening of a new thruway or the erection of a plant which buys their goods—neither having been brought to pass by the management—increases their market and their take, therefore their "profit." The converse may throw them for a loss. Change in the federal policy of agricultural price support may make—or break —great concerns designed to supply farm machinery. One can multiply illustrations.

The point is simply this: Every American enterprise today takes a position in a highly organized world which it did not create, and—necessarily—takes as it finds it. Presumably it takes advantage of all favorable factors it can find. It assumes risks of governmental or social action it cannot foresee or affect. It adjusts prices in accordance with the conditions it finds. It closes the year with a profit—or a loss—on the basis only of those costs it has paid, and the price it has received.

There is no objection to this. Short of going into business on a Robinson Crusoe island, any enterprise of any kind, public or private, capitalist or Communist, starts from a historical base building up ever since the Stone Age. The objection is to making the assumption that a profit statement can be taken as any measure, or, at least, any exact measure, of its utility apart from the social and economic structure in which it works. Presumably if it had no utility, that is, fulfilled no need or want, it would fail. If it does satisfy a need or want—an economic "demand"—its product will sell. But the price has only an oblique relation to all components of the actual cost of production. The price merely shows what the producer can get, and the producer's cost merely shows what he had to spend, after taking advantage of all possible factors in the civilization he found when he decided to go into the business.

Some day we shall have true "social cost accounting," which will show not merely what it cost a producer to produce—that is, what he paid out—but also what it cost society to produce. The technique of social cost accounting has yet to be invented. All we can say, now, is that the value of the aggregated things and organizations, in motion and in use, depends in part, perhaps in very large part, on their strategic position in a highly organized society.[3]

Two added dimensions of things organized into productive use thus appear.

Here are plants, railroads, airlines, small garages and grocery stores, supermarkets and chain stores, dredging and construction organizations, the whole congeries of enterprise. They produce goods or render services needed, desired, or, at any event, used in American life. They have a dimension given by motion, as the combination of materials, technique, and labor roll the productive machine forward. This motion transforms the collection of things constituting the small garage or the great plant from dead objects into value-producing (and valuable) economic instruments.

They also have a dimension produced by their strategic position in an economic world their enterprisers never made. The garage is in a quiet town; a thruway is constructed nearby. The garage leaps from a modest community-service enterprise into a substantial facility assisting the stream of traffic—and the enterpriser's fortune is made. Or a technical discovery is made in a distant laboratory. A little-known element, beryllium, of no particular significance, suddenly becomes useful in the manufacture of heat-resistant steel. The little plant which formerly made a modest living supplying a limited market suddenly finds its experience, its know-how, and its familiarity with sources of supply an immensely valuable asset; its importance in the economic complex leaps overnight. Or the enterprise is an oil-drilling affair, whose owners derive a profit because our complex tax laws allow deduction from income (and correspondingly from income tax) of a large percentage of its receipt for depletion and depreciation. That item makes the difference between an attractive and an unattractive profit.

Both these factors, motion and strategic position, in large measure lie beyond the control of the enterpriser, be he a village garage owner or the General Motors Company. For him, the continuity and speed of economic motion is like the weather—he can talk about it, but do little. The strategic position of the enterprise is like a fact of geography—a fact, perhaps, which induced the enterpriser, person or corporation, to choose the particular type of activity he engaged in and the particular place where he organized his enterprise. Property in production, once organized, becomes a social fact. The active result is registered in the record of operations of the enterprise. The wealth result is registered in a quotation for shares of stock—passive property—on a securities market.

These are the faces of "property" in the twentieth century. To accord with them, the concept of property itself had to change.

Property is active and productive—but is so because it is organized and administered, not because it is "owned."

It sets up passive, exchangeable wealth, thanks to surrender by the wealth holder of owner's power, and to state-fostered mechanisms giving liquidity to this wealth.

Its usefulness depends as much on position in an organized economy as on its physical characteristics: this is a phenomenon of culture.

Its value depends, not on itself, but on the flow of economic life, that is, on motion and turnover. Stop the motion, and its value disappears.

What quality of it can fairly be called "private"?

CHAPTER 2 CONCEPTS IN TWENTIETH-CENTURY FISSION: POWER AND PROPERTY, A PROBLEM OF PHASE

1. The Power-Property Transition

THE PRINCIPLE that power and property are different phases of the same social phenomenon has been suggested above. It comes to this: Power, fragmented among many (or many millions) of individuals, tends to become possessory property. At one extreme, property is static. The miser sitting on bags of gold, the frightened owner maintaining all his holdings in liquid cash in a bank but fearing to use it, or the land speculator merely maintaining ownership has reduced property to its exclusive or negative sense. He excludes others from using it—and does not use it himself.

Property, as it is aggregated and put to work, increasingly sets up power. Its owner or owners must find other men to work with it or on it, and must find ways and means of giving direction and orders to these men. Capacity to give such orders is power. Aggregated to the point required by great industry—for example, an integrated steel enterprise—the factor of power outweighs, though it has not fully overcome, the property phase.

At the extreme, a power system blanks out all, or almost all, the property phase within the area of its scope. The absolutist power systems constructed under Communist theory are examples.

The power-property process obeys certain laws analogous, perhaps, to the laws which prevail in physical bodies. Though observation of these forces is still in infancy, certain of these laws may be stated here with reasonable assurance.

1. The power-property interchange is never static. Through-

out its range, at all times and at all points, there is a tendency to transition. Any aggregation of power tends to become fragmented, moving toward the possessory-property phase. Any aggregation of possessory property tends to move toward the power phase. Human motivation is the obvious reason. Human beings, and their relation to things and to organizations, are an integral part of the process. While human motivation is complex, certain results of it are clearly predictable. The tendency of motion from one to the other phase is therefore also predictable.

Specifically, bodies of possessory property tend to accumulate. Holders desire this, and work toward it. Any system which permits collection of interest, rent, dividends, or other profit permits such accumulation. There is nothing either moral or immoral about this. It is right or wrong, moral or immoral, depending on the conditions society exacts from the receiver in return for the privilege. Marx was right in posing the possibility, and outlining the danger, of indefinite accumulation of property—the danger that more and more property would accumulate in fewer and fewer hands. He was wrong in assuming that accumulation could not or would not be controlled.

Power, like property, also tends to accumulate in fewer and fewer hands. To be effective, or to have wide impact, it must be capable of being delegated. But it will be delegated only on condition that the result of the delegation yields more power to the center of delegation. The principle of delegation of power increasing the power at the center is entirely familiar. It is used in every army in the world, and has been used by every empire in history. Less dramatically, it is the principle by which every large American corporation maintains effective organization. Power has a tendency to increase itself; any holder of it desires to increase his power and his importance.

2. But as either power or property becomes concentrated, a counterprocess sets in. With greater accumulation, there comes a marginal phase. As accumulation continues, it reaches a point at which the accumulation is itself destructive of that function. It then begins to reconvert itself into the opposite phase. Accumulated power begins to fragment, and moves toward the

property phase. Accumulated property moves into high organization, and thus toward the power phase.

If not checked, accumulation either of property or of power becomes destructive, and finally self-destructive. Power centralized to the ultimate becomes absolutism, losing any function save its defense and self-perpetuation—the phenomenon evident in the last years of the late Joseph Stalin and dramatically described by Shakespeare in *Macbeth*. Property, accumulated to the point where there are too few possessors of it, ceases to be capable of effective use, and produces the kind of crisis foreseen by Marx. Probably also the extreme phase of either property or power tends to destroy the individuals involved. They become removed from reality—or go mad. In any event, they cease to be capable of dealing with the situations created. Medical and behavioral science will, one day, give us better explanation of this human phenomenon. It is not accident, I think, that signs of mental disorder have appeared in a high proportion of the dictators of our time—Hitler and Stalin are examples. Illustrations on the side of undue accumulation of property are not as easily found; this is probably because possessory property without becoming power cannot reach the extreme point of accumulation. As it approaches extreme accumulation, it becomes modified; dealing with it increasingly compels transition into the power phase.

3. The most efficient or productive (that is to say, socially useful) phase within the power-property range occurs when there is balance between the propensity toward possessory property and the propensity toward power. "Efficiency," "productivity," "social usefulness" are determined by the prevailing culture, and by the social philosophy dominating it.

Balance—the right point in the spectrum between the extreme of possession and the extreme of power—is determined by the function performed. Certain functions are most effectively performed by individuals working with possessory property—for example, maintenance of a home, carrying on of a craft activity, or operation of certain kinds of farms and agricultural production. Other functions require a high content of organization and power—for example, the production of steel or electricity. The power principle is not absolute in a large steel plant, any more than the principle of possession is absolute in a homestead. Both are modified by the claims of the surrounding community, of society, and of the prevailing culture.

Attempt to force any function into the mold either of possessory property or of power organization—away from the optimum mix—entails loss of productivity, less effective fulfillment of function, or, in extreme cases, breakdown. The Chinese Communist attempt to force steel production through back-yard furnaces into a mold of individual possession (whatever the property theory held by the Chinese Communists) turned out to be a ghastly failure. Soviet Russian attempts to conscript all agriculture into a power-organization mold have been so unsuccessful that their agriculture compares unfavorably with agriculture generally in the developed world. Attempt to force American industry, accustomed to large-scale operation, into individual possessory-property operation would at once reduce its productivity to minimal proportions.

No method of determining the ideal "mix" of possessory property and power is presently in existence. The United States, empirically, has arrived at a solution more satisfactory than any other country. It has evolved a range of personal possession, of small, personally owned possessory businesses, of larger businesses including both elements, and of large-scale businesses in which power overwhelmingly predominates while property is relegated to a purely passive position. Far from perfect, the results are, nevertheless, reasonably satisfactory in the culture and under the philosophy prevailing in the United States. It does not follow that the same system would necessarily produce equal success in other cultures, or where a different philosophy prevails. Nor will the norm presently arrived at continue to be equally satisfactory as philosophy develops and as American culture makes other and perhaps greater demands, or shifts its emphasis. In the United States, as elsewhere, the picture of an ideal life and an ideal society continuously changes. Such changes occur slowly. As they occur, they are likely also to change the power-property relationship in any given function.

2. Social Implications of Productive Property

THE QUESTION here discussed is anything but new. Nineteenth-century Socialism, notably in Great Britain, drew a sharp distinction as to property which ought to be "socialized"—classified, loosely, as "productive" property. On the other hand, "personal" property, from one's toothbrush to one's home, was excluded from the Socialist process. In crudest form, this thinking reflected the principle we are endeavoring to set out with more exactness here. Now, when the line between personal or consumptive property and productive property is no longer considered clear, the instinctive division of the old Socialists requires refinement.

An automobile, for example, as a rule is personal property. It is consumptive in the sense that it gives convenience and pleasure to an individual. But it also carries a large part of the transportation of the country. Automobile traffic into and out of any large city performs much of the work handled by railroads a generation ago. Up to a point, apparently, given the engineering device of a motorcar, widely distributed personal possessory property in the form of automobiles can perform a substantial part of the function formerly performed by common carriers, apparently to the greater satisfaction of the community. In the highly unlikely event that manufacture of steel could be carried on by any individual with a kit of machinery or tools available at moderate price, the steel industry would change in the range of which we are speaking. In the more likely event that one day electricity can be generated by tiny units of household size from, let us say, sunlight or atomic capsules, the electric-power industry would immediately change position in the power-property spectrum. The functions of the electric-power industry that now must be performed by large, highly centralized electric companies, in which the power factor is overwhelmingly great, could then be performed by individuals holding possessory property.

The socially satisfactory use of the power-property phase is

tested by its results; results, that is, judged by the public consensus of the society in question as to what it wants. If, as is
true in the United States, the public consensus really wants
something approximating President Franklin D. Roosevelt's
famous "Four Freedoms," these criteria would form the basis
of judgment, not only of the property-power system as a whole,
but also of the functioning of each economic activity within it.
In aggregate, the American political-economic system exists to
provide the fullest practicable freedom from want—adequate
production, adequately distributed, and freedom of personal
development unhampered by undue restraint, whether from
grinding poverty or from arbitrary governmental interference;
freedom, in a word, economic and intellectual, offering the widest
practicable scope for self-realization. Maintaining proper balance in the organization of the community as a whole and in
respect of the many varieties of economic operation within it
is a function of the state.

But, in the American sense, the "state" functions in two
ways. So far as possible it works informally. Yet there is a
public consensus. Men in respect of personal possession, or of
the power they may be wielding, are expected to observe the
standards laid down by that consensus without compulsion. The
state may also move to require their observance directly through
government. Through its police function, its task is to prevent or
to remedy undue concentration or undue abuse either of possessory property or of organizational power. The American antitrust laws are a striking example of this kind of police function.

Also, and perhaps more important, the state has a function
of guidance. Though Americans dislike the term, this is state
"planning." One of the major problems of state planning is to
assure that, in respect of any given operation, there is proper
balance between the property function and the power function.
American theory does not say that the state does this. American
practice, nevertheless, empirically does this. The antitrust laws
outlaw monopoly. This is intended to restrain undue power—
though the words used are "restraint of trade" or "limitation of
competition." But in determining how much competition is
possible, American courts and the Department of Justice in

many situations accept a high concentration of economic power —division of an entire industry, say, between two, three, or four very large units. Organization of power is necessary for productive operation. Therefore the units are large. Their combination into a monopoly would overemphasize the power principle. Therefore there is division. Because we do not yet know what an optimum size is, a rough approximation is reached. Unconsciously, rather than consciously, endeavor is made to strike the best practicable balance.

3. Legitimacy of Economic Power

AS IT CHANGES, the power-property phase nevertheless changes the basis upon which holders of power, or of property, are justified in having either. This is particularly evident at present. Functions formerly carried out by property holders are now carried out by power holders—that is, by corporation managers who determine policies and give orders. This is the present condition of most American industry. On the property side, what used to be possession of things has become purely passive, represented by a bond, a stock certificate, an insurance policy, a share in a mutual fund, a claim on a pension trust, or the like.

In both cases, a question is raised—has been raised throughout all history. Why should this man or group of men hold power instead of some other group? Why should these individuals have passive wealth any more than anyone else? At its crudest, the question is individual—why Nym instead of me? Why Bardolph instead of my brother? Why Pistol instead of my son? Why are the respective positions of the power holders and the property holders "legitimate"?

Libraries have been written about "legitimacy." For the purposes of this study, "legitimacy" is taken to mean merely that the holders of power are considered by the community to be justified in their tenure of it, and that the community considers the holders of property as justified in having it. That is, the system conforms to the general consensus on a moral base. The word "moral" is used advisedly. In its classic sense, morality means that the situation conforms to the accepted customs of the community, which, in turn, approximate the current public consensus on what is right and fair and equitable.

[The moral base of power, clearly, is not the same as the moral base of property. At bottom, tenure of power is considered moral and "legitimate" if acquired in customary form, and if it performs acceptably a more or less defined function. This is true of both governmental and extragovernmental power. Many a usurper has seized a throne immorally, though he usually did his best to manufacture a claim of legitimacy. He invented a descent from a previous king or he got a coronation certificate from a complaisant pope, or he pushed through a rigged election, or the like. This would satisfy no one unless he also proved an efficient and satisfactory king. If able to do that, after a period of time his legitimacy had established itself: his power was legitimated by his performance. The managers of American corporations who hold power, though it is extragovernmental, satisfy customary requirements by a paper vote of stockholders. But they justify themselves by running their corporations well according to prevailing standards. If they do this, few people ask whether the fiction of a corporate election amounts to much. The telephone company is well run; the steel is well made and in adequate supply; the conditions of production are decent; the price is acceptable.]

When it comes to property, especially of the passive variety mentioned, such as stocks and bonds, the situation is not so clear.

4. Legitimacy of Passive Property

THE OLD BASIS for justification of property was straight enough. The community needed capital. People who could accumulate wealth by thrift and industry and who invested it in productive enterprise were entitled to it—and entitled to pass it on to their children. Even owners of large aggregations of capital (the plutocrats of the late nineteenth century) had their justification. They aggregated enough capital to undertake and carry through

great projects which lesser individuals could not, though theirs
was a passing phase. Yet America also imposed on them an
overriding moral trust. In *McGuffey's Reader,* nineteenth-century American school children were taught that God permitted
men to become rich so that they could assist the poor. This
was an aspect of the Protestant ethic: men were required to
glorify God with every capacity they had—including property.
And in any case property was assumed to have proceeded
primarily from some form of work or activity the community
considered valuable.

Passive property, such as stock certificates, obviously does
not pass this test per se.[4] The rewards or losses derived from
it bear no necessary relation (if any) to work done, or risk
taken, or the usefulness of the aggregated property. None of
the old answers suffice. Both the original moral base (reward
for capacity and thrift) and the original pragmatic function
(need for individual skill in applying capital) have pretty well
disappeared.

Then why is passive property "legitimate"? What justifies its
existence? What justifies me in having it? Or you? Is it necessary
—or, if not necessary, useful?

Before attempting an answer, it is well to examine what this
avalanche of paper wealth really accomplishes. It channels a
portion of the income stream of the United States into the
hands of its holders. Interest and dividends paid out annually
transfer currently a small fragment of gross national product
directly or indirectly to many millions of individuals. Total payments received by individuals from interest and dividends in
the year 1960 aggregated $40 billion or almost exactly 8% of
the gross national product for that year. (Gross National Product for that year was about $504 billion.)[5]

And it allocates wealth, as common stock outstanding increases or changes in value. Logically, it should increase in
value in proportion as the industrial plant and organization
increases its holdings of actual things and its capacity to produce
and make itself useful in the prevailing economic weather and
the social niche of its situation. Great enterprises generate
their own capital up to about 60% of their needs (and borrow

from the currency system another 20% of their needs). This is reflected, more or less, in additions to plant, in modernization, and in enlarged facilities. These automatically add to the value of the equity stock of the corporation.

In addition, as population grows and wants increase, a reasonably successful enterprise will "turn over" more rapidly—that is, be more in motion. It will also be endeavoring to improve its strategic position in one way or another. The American industrial plant taken as a whole has fairly steadily increased in productivity, year by year. Appraisal of this increase is made, erratically, by quotations on the New York and other stock exchanges of the stock of the component corporations. Lopsided, emotional, unpredictable, illogical as these are, they do represent a variety of estimate of the increase (or decrease) in the wealth-producing capacity of the enterprises whose names appear upon their shares. In this fashion, they give the holders of the passive paper, in accordance with their terms, a passive claim on the increase in value of the enterprise itself. The holder of shares of equity stock cannot go and get any part of this actual increase. But he may sell his shares and receive it from a buyer, through the liquidity mechanism of the securities markets.

In the year 1961, the value of all the shares listed on the New York Stock Exchange was $306.9 billion at the beginning of the year, and $387.8 billion at the year's end.[6] The increase represented some sort of an estimate (not to be taken seriously in any exact sense) that the worth of the productive enterprises whose shares were listed on the stock exchange had increased during that calendar year—at all events, enough buyers of passive property thought so to permit those holders of passive property who wished to sell to receive the higher price. Behind all the froth and fiction, and the complete impossibility of relating the increased price to any real increase in value, there was undeniably a substantial increase in their worth. In that year, the gross national product ($504.4 billion in 1960) rose to $521.3 billion.[7]

Allocation of wealth, so far as I can see, is what passive property does—and almost all that it does. Purchase of securities on the stock exchange by a buyer is not "investment" save in a folkloric use of the word. The one certain fact is that the price a buyer of stock pays to the seller never goes near, never was near, never had anything to do with, the enterprise whose shares are thus bought and sold. No one has ever found out, when Nym buys from Bardolph, what Bardolph does with the price. Psychologically, of course, these transactions have an effect. For some strange reason, when the securities markets are boiling, people are more willing to spend money. When they fall, propensity to spend tends to shrink. To a minimal extent, when the market is high, a few individuals are more likely to invest (using the sense in its accurate meaning) in new enterprises, by contributing directly to the capital funds of such concerns. In respect of two types of industry—regulated and stable public utilities and communications corporations and a small group of new and wholly untried enterprises—a high price for stocks enables them to sell more common stock and attract true investment. But these are almost the only types of enterprise which now regularly raise capital by selling common stock; and all the "new" common stock (which may be assumed to represent real "investment") sold in any year is minimal in amount. The year 1961 just missed being a record year for sales of new common stock: the amount sold was slightly over three billion dollars—against total expenditures for new plant and equipment by all business of about $35.7 billion—that is, less than 9%.[8] This is hardly, one would think, an adequate justification for maintaining values of and liquidity for stocks (let us leave out bonds) in the United States amounting to perhaps $450 billion.[9] Adequate justification ("legitimacy") of the social institution has to be found elsewhere.

Passive property is, of course, wealth, useful to and servant of the individual holder. Nothing in itself, it asks of him that grave and agonizing question rapidly becoming the central question of our time: "What do you want, what do you want to do, what do you want to be? I have no answer. I am not a house in which you dwell. I can give you the means to buy or build, but only if and as you choose. I am not a reward for a task fulfilled—you must find that for yourself. I can perhaps enable you to find the task without regard to the pay you receive.

What do you want to have? I can, up to the amount of me you own, enable you to have it if it can be bought. Ask me for no more."

This is wealth whose worth is subjective: it responds to the consumptive will of its owner—nothing else. Consequently, if it is to be justified, we must look at the owners, actual and potential, and the degree to which in satisfying their probable wants the interest of society is served. Put differently, we may ask what society ought to expect owners or potential owners of this liquid wealth to "want"—what direction they should give to the privileges conferred by this property. In doing so we are, of course, jumping several squares on the board. We cannot ask each individual what he is all about, or who he is, or tell him what kind of man or woman he or she should propose to be. Only a totalitarian society would endeavor to do that, and there is yet no proof that such society succeeds. Nevertheless, within narrow limits, we can ask what society expects of a man, and what contribution passive property makes toward enabling him to fulfill the expectation. From those questions we can discover certain bases partially justifying this strange form of wealth, multiplied in such profusion by the late twentieth century.[10]

Five categories of expectation come to mind. All take as premise the American insistence that individuals shall be free and are primarily responsible for their own self-development but that they also share responsibility for the progress of society.

First, men are expected, so far as possible, to provide for themselves and their families. A reserve of liquid property can provide for those periods of life in which the individual is helpless. This is far and away its greatest use—provision for children during their infancy, their youth, their education, and their launching; provision for periods of illness, periods of unemployment or maladjustment; provision for widowhood and old age. If the individual does not make this provision, and a property system does not make it possible for him to do so, the task has to be done by society. Unhappily, society does not do these things well. (Perhaps they never were done well—I do not know.) There is little, if any, question that individuals can do better for themselves, their children, their parents, and their dependents than any social-welfare arrangement yet devised. So much so, that the welfare system in force in the United States, and indeed in most of the Western World, is really a system coercing individuals into providing a small wealth-reserve for themselves, to be translated in due time into money, affording them the means to deal with these problems.

Second, this type of property can afford to its owner an added margin of economic resource for his own self-realization. Plainly stated, this means that his life is not entirely dependent on his pay or salary check. He can, for example, enter with comfort on an occupation whose commercial rewards are low —for example, be a teacher in a primary school. He can divert (as this writer has been doing) from commercial practice of law to a measure of noncommercial teaching, research, and writing. He can make himself comfortable during the long lean years of medical internship and apprenticeship. He can put in eight hours a day in the factory and still indulge in travel, or motorboating, or stamp-collecting, or heavy preoccupation with his Masonic lodge. He can run for the legislature, or accumulate a good library, or support a camp in an accessible wilderness. He can, in a word, extend his personality. Like all individuals, he can make of his life a temple, a palace, or a warehouse. He can do any of these things more effectively if he can command an added margin of goods and services.

Third, passive property makes possible the existence of an untrammeled leisure class. In the United States it does not do so. In the social norms of American life, leisure is no longer considered a creditable way of life. The real luxury, as Americans see it, is having an interesting job, preferably one which enjoys the regard and esteem of the community. The son of a multimillionaire could loaf his life away without economic difficulty; but those who do are disliked by the community, and perhaps because of that (as well as for other reasons) are desperately unhappy. He therefore seeks, according to his taste and capacity, a job as university instructor, or in the diplomatic service of the United States, or in a museum, or in a publishing house, or in politics, or running a country newspaper—unless he wishes to go into a business or a profession for the primary reason of achieving a financially unnecessary commercial or professional success. But because the American social system has, and does not hesitate to express, a low opinion of a leisure class in general, and men of leisure in particular, this does not mean that the possibility can be entirely discounted. There have been countries where, and periods in history when, leisure classes were not only tolerated, but esteemed—and when they turned in a substantial dividend intellectually and esthetically.

(I doubt that we shall have a leisure class in the United States in the foreseeable future. It gave a bad account of itself in the famous Mauve Decade. The real and growing shortage in the United States is the shortage of available needed work, not merely work of any kind, but work which entails real participation and sense of achievement in the ongoing stream of life. One can imagine without difficulty a civilization to come in which everyone's wants and comforts are provided—*except* adequate opportunity to participate in significant tasks. Then, the intriguing, the use of influence, the wangling, and the throat-cutting competition will be addressed toward getting and holding jobs which have and give this sense of participation. Wealth will seek such jobs. The "lower class" will then be, not a class in poverty or want, but a class in meaningless comfort.)[11]

Fourth, passive property can be used—is now used—to provide resources for those activities which are not, or should not be, carried on commercially. Endowments for universities, schools, and hospitals and operating funds for philanthropic foundations are already large and growing takers of this paper. Foundations, universities, and hospitals alone held about $20 billion in 1960. There appeared to be general agreement in the United States that these and similar activities ought in fact to be more heavily endowed than now they are. This goes deeper than mere philanthropic sentiment. It rests on the assumption that education of all kinds, scientific and medical research, and (more vaguely) the enrichment of the cultural heritage of the country must be a charge on its continuing progress because, indeed, they are causative factors in it. Because there is danger in any purely statist system, nonstatist institutions must always be in existence to pace them, and to avoid the deadening hand of bureaucratic monopoly. By consequence, private institutions are not beggars, but claimants. Because they cannot, or certainly should not, enter the field of direct management of commercial enterprise, passive property is almost made to order for their needs.

Those needs will multiply. The necessities of education alone will quadruple in the next decade or so. On the economic side, they clearly can be met. Whether their needs in terms of men of dedication, creativity, wisdom, and conviction can be met so easily is another question. This is the area of the "transcendental margin" later examined in this volume—the margin of economic activity, progress, and profit detached from personal advantage or gain and devoted to a larger ideal.

Fifth, the institution of passive property makes possible collection and application of taxes, notably on inheritance, on gifts, and on capital gains, which otherwise would be impossible. This is no small factor. Taxgatherers in the early nineteenth century always ran the danger that their collection would impede the tangible and material processes of production. Earlier civilizations found greater difficulty. Wealth did not mean necessarily ability to pay. In point of fact, it is now standard practice for individuals who have retained control of things—who have been real entrepreneurs—to convert their enterprises into corporate form, to place their shares on the market and obtain liquidity thereby, precisely so that their inheritance taxes may be met without undue sacrifice. From gift taxes, inheritance taxes, and capital-gains taxes, the United States annually collects $4 billion, without seriously impeding processes of production.[12] As wealth is increasingly transformed into liquid passive property, the state is increasingly enabled to levy, collect, and apply the taxes needed for the national welfare or the national defense.[13]

This tax justification will not appeal to some people. They are, of course, wrong. It is not accident that, despite the high level of taxation in the United States, individuals annually attain a level of income unknown before, so that every American has a reasonable expectation that, a decade hence, his real income (after due discount for inflation) will be about 30% higher at the end of the period. A great and populous country requires a substantial level of public-sector activities. As it grows in density of population and in complexity of operation, public-sector necessities rise. A simple, rural community can do with relatively little of this. A great city must do, governmentally, a great many more things than the rural town. If it does not, life becomes first uncomfortable and then unlivable. In different emphasis, this is true of national life.

If these are the real justifications for passive property—the representation of somewhat more than half of the national wealth of the United States—how does the performance of the institution respond?

5. Distributed Wealth and Personality

IN RESPECT of the first two points—passive property as giving to individuals resources of wealth to meet years of helplessness, illness, disaster, or old age, and as giving to individuals added margin of resource to develop themselves according to their likes—the test must be distribution.

Not equal distribution: the American democracy is not equalitarian. It is true that the Declaration of Independence proclaimed that all men were "created equal." But by that was meant that all must be regarded as equal before the law, should have equal opportunity for self-realization, and in any case that the American system did not presume to be judge of inequality. Neither the Founding Fathers nor the American economic system was so stupid as to assume that men should remain equal through life. The industrious should go farther than the idlers; men of integrity should outpace rascals. All, through their own efforts and in accordance with their own moral and intellectual capacity, should settle their inequality by achievement and result. So the ideal has been to set a threshold of material welfare and security, below which the individual is protected either by the state or by the community; beyond it, he can go as far as he can and as he likes.

Leveling, but to a limited extent, does happen at the end of each generation. This is the inheritance-tax system of today. Rightly or wrongly (I believe rightly), the leveling is not complete. No system, no state, whether based on property or based on power, will ever prevent most parents from endeavoring to bequeath to their children some inheritance of use to them in this world or the next: a good name, a presumption in their favor by their father's friends, a kit of skills, economic tools. I know of no civilization ever maintained on a completely equalitarian basis. The Communist civilizations certainly have not done so. There the individual who has scored some advance in the bureaucratic pyramid takes the greatest care to pass on to his son such advantage as he can. A dissident Yugoslav Communist, Milovan Djilas, has written of this in *The New Class*. Accurately apprehended, the problem (it is not simple) is to maintain a society in which every individual is born free, and has, so far as possible, equal opportunity; in which every individual is encouraged to make the most of himself and to attain reasonable reward; and in which too much violence is not done to the elementary and age-old human emotional attachment of parents for children.

We do not have adequate distribution of passive property in the United States. I think that the rapidly developing institutions may be beginning to achieve the result. It is, I think, possible to foresee that a reasonable distribution will have taken place at the end of the next generation, that is to say, by about 1990.

Estimates of holders of common stock listed on the New York Stock Exchange range from the exchange's own calculation of 17 million to a smaller figure of about 12 million. Since there is no census of property in the United States, either figure is a sophisticated guess. The reality is probably nearer the larger figure. In addition, there are some 3,200,000 holders of shares or participations in investment companies including the so-called "mutual funds"—aggregations of stock of all kinds, each shareholder having a participation proportionate to what he paid in the value of the aggregate. (Obviously, the holder of shares in a mutual fund may also be the holder of shares of common stock, so there is duplication. The Stock Exchange estimates that 2.2 million investment-fund shareholders do not hold stock in other corporations.) A fair guess (it can be nothing more) suggests that between 15 million and 19 million people in the United States hold listed stocks or shares in mutual funds, or both.

There are about 45 million families in the United States. If one individual in each family held stock or investment-fund shares, this would mean distribution of this form of property among about one third of all American families. One cannot make that assumption. More likely, several members of a prosperous American family will hold this form of property. A sophisticated guess might be that five to six million American families—slightly more than one tenth of the total—between them hold all the individually owned shares of outstanding stock and of investment funds.

If we knew the actual distribution of shares among these several million (we only have indications), we should find a less reassuring picture. We know enough now to state, with some certainty, that by far the greater part of the holdings are heavily concentrated in upper brackets. A million adult individuals, more than one of whom are in the same family, probably own well over one third of all the publicly held shares of stock and of mutual funds. Distribution has been gradually going on; this wealthy stratum has grown and is historically larger in proportion to the whole population than has existed in any other known non-Socialist civilization. More important than that, the transformation of property from an active role to passive wealth has so operated that the wealthy stratum no longer has power. But it cannot yet be said that distribution has reached a point where passive property can claim to have justified itself adequately by that route.

Having said that, it should be added that the wealth-distribution process nevertheless goes steadily and implacably forward. Taxation, especially inheritance taxation, is perhaps the most powerful influence toward it. Absence of primogeniture in the American system means division of the parents' holdings among several children. The steady and remarkable rise of real income in the middle- and lower-income groups makes it increasingly possible, as economic practice makes it increasingly fashionable, for the less wealthy to acquire a stake through passive property in the worth and product of the American industrial complex. The federal government can adopt policies, implemented by its tax system, which will speed this distribution. For example, it could exempt from income taxation the income (and possibly the capital gains) received on shares of stock by every individual up to the point where his holdings of stock had a total value of, say, $5,000 or $10,000.

Indirectly, meanwhile, there is a different and far wider distribution of this form of wealth. It is being realized through the device of the pension fund. Some 59,000 such plans were in operation in 1960. These are "private" in the sense that they are not statist; they must be distinguished from the Social Security funds administered by the government of the United States (whose policy has been to invest only in government bonds). The policy of most pension-fund managers has been to seek to divide these funds, amounting to about $45 billion now, equally between stocks and bonds. These funds are held for the ultimate benefit of workers, to whom in the end they will pay old-age pensions and corresponding benefits. About 55 million American workers are now enrolled (usually through the action of their unions) in such pension arrangements. Thus far, these funds are on the way to accumulating 4% or 5% of the total stock outstanding. This percentage is bound to grow as the pension funds themselves grow. They are expected to level out, in twenty years or so, when their total assets have reached $125 billion. The figure is probably on the low side. If they then have half their assets invested in the stock of American corporations, they would control between 10% and 15% of the shares of corporate stock (calculated at current market values) now in circulation. One must expect, however, that the amount of stock will also increase, probably not as rapidly as will the pension trusts, but rapidly enough so that the percentage holdings of these funds in the total will remain low.

Forecast that these funds will eventually own about 10% of all American industry (as represented by the value of its stock outstanding) may not be too far out. But it will not be realized for a number of years. And it must be recalled that workers covered by pension funds also have enough margin to permit them to buy stocks directly, if they will—as a good many of them do.

Indirect distribution of passive property also goes on through the development of insurance, and notably life insurance. Life insurance companies are the great collectors of personal savings in this country. They are the chief investors in bonds. They also buy stocks, but only in extremely limited degree. (The maximum investment in common stocks usually allowed to a life insurance company under prevailing law is about 5% of its assets; most insurance companies do not avail themselves of this form of investment up to or anywhere near their allowed maximum. They like the greater security and certainty of income afforded by interest-bearing bonds.) It is estimated that 80% of American families—eight out of every ten—hold some form of life insurance. In the total account, the American public is thus the greatest bond-holding class in the world. Through this insurance, they also have a tiny, though appreciable, stake in the equity securities, whose dividends and worth reflect the present, as they will inherit the future, appraised value of the American system.

The conclusion must be that the need for wide distribution is clear; that the process is going forward; that it has not gone far enough—far enough, that is, to bring about those results which, when attained, will be full justification for the existence of passive wealth. On the other hand, distribution is on its way, and moving forward (historically speaking) with some rapidity. The institution of passive property as presently organized shows that the thing can be done, and gradually is being done; is, in fact, making possible a distribution of wealth never before achieved in history, save at the price of intolerable loss of individual liberty and individual capacity for self-realization and of disrupting production as distribution goes on.

Distribution will go forward with much greater speed as individuals increasingly desire to realize themselves, and increasingly know how to do it. This is, in effect, saying that the higher the education and the moral and cultural capacity of a population, the more it will want wealth, because it will know how to use it. The American system has taught one fact with incontrovertible force. Men do not seek better education and a higher standard of living and of life because they are prosperous. They become prosperous because they seek higher education, more developed personality, and because avenues to and means of self-realization become apparent to them as the level of their cultural awareness rises.

The fourth category of justification—use of passive property to support enterprises and activities which by their nature are not commercial and therefore do not pay their own way out of the price they charge—is a justification of real substance and importance. Here, passive property makes it possible for an individual, a group, or an institution engaged in noncommercial activity to receive income, and to own wealth which leaves them free to pursue their noncommercial calling, or to assist others in doing so.

Endowment of philanthropic, altruist, or noncommercial institutions is anything but novel. The history of the Catholic church, and of the religious orders and specific institutions sponsored by it, is a sufficiently striking example. The famous hospice at Beaune, in France, still holds in its ancient endowment glorious vineyards from which come that benison of Burgundian sunshine, the Hospices de Beaune wine. But, to modern minds, that sort of endowment has a catch in it. The hospital must supervise the vineyard. Until relatively recently, that wealth could not readily be transferred into the form of a building or a laboratory. Administrators of most American hospitals would feel that they had difficulty enough running their institutions, and would prefer to shed the direct responsibility toward things, land, and people involved in direct management. A million dollars' worth of General Motors stock would be, in all respects, more convenient and more apposite.

At all events these nonprofit, noncommercial philanthropic institutions have become and now are very substantial holders of passive property and, recently, of equity stocks.

There are, in the United States, about 13,000 foundations,

exempt from income and capital-gains taxation because they are philanthropic. Their aggregate endowments are estimated at a total of $13 billion.[14] The writer knows of no good estimate as to the proportion of their funds invested in bonds—interest-bearing securities—and in equities—that is to say, common stocks. In the past few years the tide has run heavily in favor of stocks. The probability is that nearly half of these endowment funds are so invested. These are only a part of the philanthropic organizations holding this form of property. Private colleges, from Amherst, in Massachusetts, to Yankton, in South Dakota, and Pomona, in California, have endowment funds, some running to very large amounts. A rough estimate would be five billion dollars. Government-supported universities also have such funds. The fact that they are supported by state government does not prevent their admirers, friends, and alumni from adding private gifts. Private secondary schools must be included; growing awareness of their crucial position in the educational system has led to increased private gifts to them. Technical schools and institutions of all sorts, from the Rockefeller Institute, in New York, to important, though less-known, organizations on the Pacific Coast. Thereafter the list comprises hospitals, great and small, and organized activities more specialized in function or more limited in the area served, down to modest funds established to support a town annual symphony concert or maintenance of Salvation Army shelters. A rough estimate of the aggregate endowment of these institutions, great and small, might be close to $40 billion. A fair guess would be that one half of this consists of investment in common stocks.

Sociologically, this use of passive property has produced some piquant results. Most of the passive property representing the appraised worth of the Ford Motor Car Company is in the Ford Foundation. As that foundation sells the Ford shares, it buys other shares. A somewhat similar condition persists in the case of the Great Atlantic and Pacific Tea Company (Hartford Foundation) and the Campbell Condensed Soup Company (Dorrance Foundation). A number of other major industrial and commercial corporations are, in effect, "owned" (so far as passive property constitutes ownership) by such foundations.

These usually endeavor gradually to diversify their investment. Typically, the funds of foundations, universities, and philanthropic institutions of all kinds are diversified. Most do not wish even the limited degree of responsibility resting on the holder of a large enough block of stock to elect the management of the corporation.

This use of passive property is, in broadest sense, nonstatist socialization of a part of the income and liquid worth of the American industrial system. Its great significance is that this fragment of the income stream and the possible exchange value of the shares are devoted to activity designed to protect or to increase human potential. The trustees of the various institutions devote a great deal of time and thought in endeavor to reach these results. They have, of course, all manner of success —and failure. The Rockefeller Institute and the Rockefeller Foundation virtually eliminated yellow fever as a factor in human development, and have contributed mightily to eliminating malaria. The Guggenheim Foundation has liberated the literary, artistic, musical, and academic genius of many men. Endowments of the small academy in Vermont, the library in a California town, not to mention orphan asylums, child-care agencies, or the snug harbors for retired seamen were, as the founders of these institutions saw it, salvaging, maintaining, or forwarding human individuals and the human resource. This, one may say, with fair assurance, is one of the things property ought to be for.

This outlines the case for the American passive-property system as it has emerged out of the American industrial system. It would not be a good enough case from the point of view of Proudhon. But he was dealing with a different concept of property. It is not an ideal case from the point of view of those French revolutionaries who believed (or claimed to believe) in perpetual and continuous equality. But they had never heard of the power-property phase. It is a respectable, if not a good, case from the point of view of the historian. Its results compare favorably with most past eras. Inequalities of property distribution are far less striking, galling, and oppressive than are inequalities in distribution of power, which is the currency in which Communist systems are registered. If the classic justifications have faded to minor account, newer justifications have appeared. Though all their criteria have not been realized, at least there is visible motion in the right direction.

Most important of all, while progress is being made toward justice, a tolerable, not to say comfortable, situation exists for nine tenths of the population of the United States. Even the bottom tenth is better taken care of and has more opportunity than most of the population of the world.

CHAPTER 3 SOURCES OF CAPITAL AND
SHIFTS IN DECISION-MAKING POWER

"CAPITAL" is a basic concept in all economic systems. Never exactly defined, it includes that body of tangible and intangible goods set aside or used, not to satisfy current needs and wants, but to produce other goods and services. A bloc of reserves used for production must exist at all times. As industrialism and technical development increase, as population piles up and its needs become more intricate, the resources allocated to production steadily grow, both in absolute amount and in proportion. They must be added to each year—which means that part of each year's production must be "saved," rather than consumed, for current needs, and "allocated" or invested to increase production. Socialists and Communists have accepted this; their quarrel is not with "capitalism," but with the location of power which control over capital resources undoubtedly gives.[15]

The technical world, however, quietly and ruthlessly dealt with the conception without benefit of theories. Increasingly the tangible things—plants, machinery, and so forth—were flanked by a growing body of technical knowledge, or "know-how," accumulated through abstract research, application of scientific principles, accumulated experience. These are reflected in libraries, in laboratory records, in scientific formulas, in the heads of men. They are sometimes called "incorporeal" capital. They are far harder to re-create than a physical plant. If, for example, all the tangible property of General Electric were destroyed tomorrow, but its staff, its records and research, its libraries, and its organization remained intact, the plant could be reproduced within a relatively short time and productivity could be restored or perhaps even increased.

Increasingly this incorporeal capital has ceased to remain confined as private property, or indeed as property at all. Knowledge rapidly becomes available to those who desire it. The scholarly world by tradition makes its discoveries generally available. Research is increasingly the result of government or philanthropic effort—two thirds of all research in the United States is now paid for by the federal government. Experience can, of course, be cornered by hiring all or most of the men having it; but in a free country men can always go elsewhere. Organization is more capable of being held within control either by the state or by private corporations—but then, no one has a monopoly over capacity to organize. Increasingly, therefore, resources allocated to more production, rather than to consumption, include a body of continuing human and intellectual effort, and the recorded results and these human and intellectual resources—undoubtedly capital in quality—escape from the conception of "property."

This was less apparent in the nineteenth century. The French Revolution had had a dim view of science. "The Revolution has no need of chemists," said the judges who ordered their greatest scientist, Lavoisier, to the guillotine. During most of the nineteenth century, capital was considered as plant—factories or railroads or the money accumulated to provide them. In mid-nineteenth century a proposal was made to abolish the United States Patent Office on the ground that all useful discoveries had already been made and there was no further use for it. Sensible people knew better; but the ascendancy of abstract and applied science and of technical engineering skill, and the recognition of their worth in the productive picture, are essentially products of the twentieth century.

However the nature of capital may be described, one point was and is clear. The power to secure capital (of all kinds and however defined) and to accumulate and to apply it and to allocate its use is the power to maintain and to direct the current and future economic development of the country. It is also a major factor in assuring stability. The smooth, even, and increasing accumulation and flow of capital goes far toward avoiding depression and cyclical crises.

It is hardly surprising that the twentieth century formulated two major questions. Who can and should make the decisions that control of capital implies? What rules govern the amount of capital to be accumulated and the method and direction of its allocation?

Power to make these decisions is power to decide the economic present and future of a highly industrialized society. Not unnaturally, the American economic republic here has developed its own approach and answers.

1. Capital Formation—and Resulting Power

THE NINETEENTH CENTURY sanctified the capitalist as creator, or damned him as a thief, or both. The assumption was that individuals "saved" and thereby accumulated capital, that they organized enterprises and put it to work, and that this work was productive. Therefore they were entitled to praise. They also controlled the capital for the purpose of making a profit out of consumers' needs. So, they were exploiters, "bourgeois," enemies of the masses. Remnants of this debate go on today. In it, ownership and power over capital are still, wrongly, equated.

Capital, meanwhile, as a social and economic phenomenon was quietly changing its habits. Its origins and sources changed —it was differently accumulated. And its content changed. The first change eliminated most of the decision-making "capitalist class" so dear to Marxian socialists, and simultaneously changed the locus of power determining how capital should be used. The second expanded the impact of capital, and probably limited the capacity to use it, to an extent we scarcely understand even now.

Most capital, in the first half of the twentieth century in America, ceased to be "saved," at least consciously. It was conscripted.

The greatest source of capital—at present—is the price of goods, sold predominantly by large corporations and paid by consumers.[16] From it, cost of production is paid, but there is also a charge for depreciation and depletion—replenishment of past capital—and for profit. Some of this profit is paid out to stockholders as dividends. But an undistributed balance—between 30% and 40%—of profit (37.4% in 1960), along with the depreciation allowances, accumulates in the treasuries of the corporations. These accumulations are available for "capital purposes"—that is, for investment by the corporations in replacing or expanding existing plant and facilities or for organizing new projects. The accumulations are still called "savings." Obviously, they are not voluntary. Nobody asks the buyer of an automobile whether he wants to pay some additional money to General Motors so that General Motors will have increased funds to set up a new plant or go into the air-conditioning business. The buyer pays the price, and General Motors takes part of it for capital purposes.

A second substantial source of capital exists in the Social Security fund and in the many billions of pension trust funds. Both funds result from out-and-out conscription: the individual is not asked, but required, to contribute. The state adopts a law directing that everyone paying and receiving wages or salaries shall pay a stated percentage into the Social Security fund. (In 1963, it will be 7¼% of a worker's pay, though one half is contributed by the employer.) In addition, a bite is privately and less observably taken out as "employer's contribution" to the company's pension trust fund if it has one—as most companies do, and as most labor-union contracts require. Both the Social Security fund and the pension trust funds have to pay out benefits. But they must continuously accumulate more funds than they pay out, because they will need these for later distribution. They thus conscript savings, most of which are available for—indeed must be devoted to—capital use.

Third, the state itself also directly exacts savings through taxation, chiefly on incomes. Most taxes pay for current services. But part of the taxes pay for roads, plants, technical research, and other improvements—that is, they are used as public-sector capital.

Fourth, there are the voluntary savings of individuals—the slowly vanishing "capitalist class."

These were considerable. There is some trouble in finding out how much of them can be considered "additions to capital." [17] Economists have never quite decided whether when individuals save to buy motorcars or houses the savings thus used constitute "capital" or consumption. I take the view that they are essentially consumption. Certainly they do not directly increase production. They increase the comfort and capacity of the individual laborer or worker—a quite different thing—and I exclude them as capital.

Individual savings spent in making payments on nonfarm homes and on "consumer durables" (motorcars and other machines) amounted in 1960 to $62.7 billion.

Aside from that, individuals that year saved about $20 billion. They spent $12.7 billion on farm buildings, farm machinery, and small business construction combined. (The new barn, the roadside restaurant stand, the two-man garage were probably paid for out of this—true capital investment by individuals, probably self-employed.) The remainder, individuals saved in cash. Most of this went into insurance companies, savings and loan institutions, and savings accounts. It represented true disposable capital.

Excluding savings for homes and cars, household machinery, and the like (here taken as a form of consumption), personal accumulation used or capable of being used as "capital" for productive uses amounted to slightly less than two fifths of "gross capital accumulation" in the United States in 1960. This is the contribution of individual savings to national capital formation.

Capital, it seems, now is formed less by individual choice of men and women than by required charges levied on the production of the economic machine, including the productive agencies of the political state. The change in source and in the place of accumulation is crucial.

Power over capital naturally changes as its sources and the

places of its accumulation change. Managers of corporations dispose of the savings their companies accumulate. Banks managing pension trust funds and public officials managing the Social Security fund direct where the capital these funds accumulate shall go. The Congress of the United States and the state legislatures settle what capital gathered through taxation shall do.

Finally, there is the individual, rich or poor. He, of course, can settle how to apply his personal savings. He usually knows enough not to try. So he commonly puts it into life insurance, or savings institutions, or their equivalent. Managers of these institutions, usually guided by a good deal of state regulation, put these pooled savings to capital use. They lend them on mortgage to build homes and hotels. They buy bonds of light and power and perhaps manufacturing companies, and they finance airline purchases of jet planes. Rarely, if ever, does the individual accumulator and presumable "owner" of savings appear in the transaction. He may—and usually does not—read about them in an annual report of his insurance company or savings bank. Public officials, professional administrators of financial institutions, and the managers of corporations—these are the real holders of economic power proceeding from capital. The nineteenth-century warfare between Socialists and private-owner enterprisers—"capitalists" —thus becomes increasingly, if not wholly, academic in the twentieth century.

More exciting, the possibilities of capital as such have explosively proliferated. We familiarly reckon annual accumulation of capital in dollars—in the United States, on the order of $100 billion to $125 billion annually. This is mere abstraction. Put to work—"invested"—the mathematical amount represents accretion of every known kind of asset, some as static as idle land, some as active as nuclear protons. Concealed in the dollar figure are physical assets, such as plants or stretches of thruway. Also, there are incorporeal items, for example, additions to the whole body of research and present recorded knowledge relating to nuclear physics. One item of investment is static, a second productive, a third in furious unpredictable motion. A single piece of capitalized research, like that which produced the Salk vaccine, or that which curbed syphilis, or that which (someday) will enable man to convert salt sea water into fresh water for human use, may outweigh, in economic effect, billions of dollars spent on transcontinental highways.

Capital is not dead. It is as live, as active, perhaps as unpredictable as the imagination and the capacity of the men who use it. The greater the body of developed talent in the United States, and the greater the opportunity for all possessing talent to bring it to bear on the use of annually formed capital, the greater will be the range and quantity of productivity. Dully, the results will appear in the figure for gross national product in ensuing years. Yet the figure will conceal, rather than reveal, a vast drama—a drama which annually runs the whole gamut from the epic of Prometheus taming fire to the niggling calculations of speculative real-estate operators.

Growth of the American annual product only tells a little about the actual impact of its capital. Who can measure the gains drawn from near elimination of tuberculosis or polio or the results, plus and minus, derived from release from drudgery brought about by automation? Audit, to be real, becomes matter of philosophy. There was a time when mankind was supposed to progress through the experience of disease, pain, and suffering. Some hold even now that release from the toil of manual labor weakens, rather than strengthens, the citizenry. Economic measurement can tell only one thing. The gross national product, and its annual increase, merely reflects the fact that Americans wanted certain goods and certain services and certain results— and brought about the allocation of capital needed to get them. In the United States, allocation decisions of this kind spring fundamentally from someone's estimate of future popular demand.

Few in the United States have wasted much time on theories of capital allocation. The American economic system is nothing if not practical. It was well described a generation ago by an Italian theorist, Professor DeVitti de Marco, who was not thinking of the United States at all. His book, a little inappropriately entitled *Public Finance*, concluded that in the twentieth century there was no great economic distinction between a governmental (socialist) operation of a function and a private (capitalist) operation. Where the function could be performed more cheaply and efficiently by government, let the government do it. Where the governmental machinery is too ridden with politics, or too inefficient, leave it to the private sector.

So, in fact, it is working out in the United States. Americans want the result, not the process. If their desire is for more electricity, they do not greatly care whether they get it from a government-owned or a privately owned enterprise—provided the price is acceptable and the service good. New York City is not commonly believed to be a socialist city, nor do New Yorkers feel great concern about the relative merits of socialist or capitalist theory. Emotionally, they are, if anything, predisposed against "socialism." Yet their port, their transport to and from Manhattan Island, their underground railways, their air terminals, and a large per cent of their housing are operated either by government-created and government-owned corporations (the Triborough Bridge and Tunnel Authority, the Port Authority of the City of New York, to name two enormous ones), or directly by the city (the New York Water Supply Commission is the largest single public utility in the world), or by the federal government, whose Navy Yard fronts the East River. An admirable system of publicly owned recreational beaches is administered by agencies of the State of New York. If tomorrow the railroads which serve the city were taken over by the federal government, the chief emotion inspired would be hope that the governmental operation would do a better job than private operation had been doing.

Inexperienced commentators sometimes insist that governments continuously increase their function as matter of aggrandizement. Empires do appear to do this, and so do power-monopolizing dictatorships. Democratic states, as a rule, are reluctant to tackle new economic functions. For the politician, it is risky business. If performance is unsatisfactory, the political consequences to those who entered upon and those who administered the enterprise are apt to be unhappy and can be disastrous. If successful, the rewards are not great.

2. "Created Capital"—Bank Credit

TO THE POOL of annual savings (including depreciation allowances), another capital item must be added. This is the amount of bank credit made available through commercial banks for capital purposes. This additional capital resource presents both opportunities and dangers, and shifts the power factors. For one thing, it is artificial.

Under the American system, when a project is undertaken, its capital, or at least a substantial portion of it, takes the form of money. To people who supply the labor, the materials, the technical skill, or the facility to get on with the job, one dollar looks like another. They do not ask where the dollars they are paid came from. Dollars from any source serve their purposes equally well. Whether true savings or dollars derived from a bank loan, it is all the same. They can push right ahead.

Nevertheless, there is a difference, though not to them. At least, not directly.

The difference, of course, lies in the fact that dollars derived from bank loans, that is, from bank credit, are artificially created by the bank itself. (More accurately, about five sixths of them are.) When a corporation goes to a bank and negotiates a ten-year term loan to be spent on capital improvements, the bank writes up a deposit credit and adds it to the corporation's account. The corporation can draw its checks on that account to pay for its materials, its workmen, its supplies, and other expenses of the project. The result is an expansion of the amount of currency and credit in circulation. But this is no affair of the corporation. It is the affair of the Federal Reserve authorities of the United States, acting under authority of the Congress.

Commercial banks have authority to make capital loans, within certain limits. These limits may be left for discussion elsewhere. They are indefinite, and somewhat controversial. It is enough to say here that a substantial addition to capital funds is available for immediate use at any given time from commercial banks. Not always; when the amount of loans of this kind begins to be dangerously large, the Federal Reserve authorities may step in, may restrict further use of bank credit and "make money tight," in the businessman's phrase. Conversely, under some circumstances the Federal Reserve authorities may intervene to "make money easy," and to make it possible and profitable for banks to extend loans of all kinds, including capital loans—up to a point.

In statistical fact, in each year corporations engaged in productive enterprise—that is, manufacturing, mining, transportation, public utilities, commercial distribution—draw about 60% of their capital funds from their accumulated earnings and depreciation allowances, about 20% from bank loans and bank credit, and about 20% from personal savings made available to them chiefly through savings institutions and insurance companies. Occasionally they get a little through direct personal investment. The bank-credit method of creating and supplying capital funds is thus substantial—the capital thus created is comparable in amount to the capital accumulated by tapping personal savings.

Classicists justifiably raise questions about capital created by banks. It introduces a new element into the proceedings. If a corporation (or perhaps a village or town constructing a capital development like a new water system, or, for that matter, the government of the United States constructing or assisting in the building of a transcontinental highway) draws on real "savings," that is one thing. Somewhere the economic system as a whole produced more than it consumed. The unconsumed balance of production is being used to construct the new plant, the new water main, the new highway. This means, among other things, that the floating supply of money or bank credit is not being expanded. This is considered "sound." Money and bank credit, the dollars in one's wallet or the bank account on which one can draw a check, ought to be kept in rough balance with the volume of goods and services presently available to be bought or hired. Otherwise, we may encounter a phenomenon of "inflation"—an ill-defined word, but one which certainly includes a situation in which dollars in currency or bank credit have increased too rapidly, so that too much money is chasing too few goods.

Obviously where true savings are used for capital, this does not happen. Goods and services have first been produced; the savings dollars pursue the unconsumed margin of these goods and services and mobilize them for capital purposes.

Classically, therefore, when a corporation approaches a bank and asks for a loan, it must explain why it wants the loan. If it wishes to buy a cargo of sugar to be transported to a refinery, turned into consumer-sized packages of white sugar, and promptly resold, the loan will be granted. "Commercial" merchandise will have been made. The amount of the loan is governed by its supposed market value. It is moving toward purchasers who presumably will pay for the sugar. The corporation will then pay the bank. Then the bank dollars created by the loan will be extinguished as the loan is paid. As the merchandise is consumed and goes out of existence, the loan is paid and the created dollars disappear.

It is quite otherwise with a loan made for capital purposes. The same corporation seeking to borrow from the same bank money on a mortgage upon its real estate for the purpose of building a plant ought, in classical theory, be told that this is no business of commercial banks. They ought not to "create" money for the purpose of putting up a building or buying machinery, neither of which will promptly move toward consumption. Nor, as a rule, will the loan for that purpose be paid off in sixty, ninety, or one hundred and twenty days. (The corporation certainly does not intend to resell the plant. It wants as many years as possible to pay off the loan.) So (in classical theory) the would-be borrower is told to apply to an institution which derives its funds from true savings—typically, now, to an insurance company or a savings bank. More recently pension trusts have entered the field. They also collect and must invest true savings.

This is the clear theoretical line. There were sound bases for the theory. Capacity to create money, either by printing it or through the device of bank credit, is a gift of the political state. Abused, it can lead to pathetic results.

Not a few new independent governments have set up banking systems. Discovering that they could create currency by this route, they have embarked upon and financed great capital enterprises by merely bringing into existence bank money and paying it out for construction of the projects. Presently, the amount of money increases; increases so fast that it outruns the supply of floating merchandise, goods, and services. Then inflation sets in. In vain does the government, or the banking system, as the case may be, responsible for all this explain that the project is entirely sound. The power plant is absolutely needed. Consumers of the power will be in quite adequate position to pay their bills. At the end of ten, fifteen, or twenty years the money borrowed will be repaid.

All true; but the timing is wrong. The power plant, after two or three years of construction time, will be serving customers. The money they pay to it for the service will enable it, slowly, to pay off its bank loan and the bank to reduce the amount of bank credit or bank money it has brought into existence. But, during the time needed to pay off the loan, the money created is out and circulating. It went out for the wages of labor, to sellers of materials, for salaries of engineers. These in turn have bought everything they wished with all of it, from shoes for the baby to a holiday at the beach.

Bank-created money (like any other kind of money) is an immediate claim on the present. The power plant will produce services of great value, but only in the future. Meanwhile, the fistful of money in hand, or the working personal checking account at the bank, can be, and commonly is, used to buy or to hire something or someone at once. Men with money in hand or in the bank as a rule want to spend it. On theoretical balance, the classicists are right.

But not wholly. Modern conditions have introduced some new considerations into the picture, and the dimensions of these seem to be growing. Taken together they do justify the artificial creation of dollars through bank credit, within carefully controlled limits, for capital purposes.

The first and perhaps the simplest factor changing the picture is the predictability, in America, that substantial savings will be made by persons and by corporations through profit withholding and depreciation and depletion allowances. Perhaps these facts were always predictable—one cannot tell. But the statistical system of the United States is now very good. We know, therefore, that in each year there will be personal savings of about the percentage of gross national product quoted above. We know, too, that corporations will save a part of their profits and will from current income accumulate their depreciation and depletion allowances. We know, month by month, about what our gross national product is. It thus becomes possible to create additional bank money through extension of bank loans in, let us say, the year 1963, and to allow these dollars to go to construction for capital purposes, knowing that in the year 1963 savings and depreciation will be more than enough to cover these dollars. The bank loan anticipates the process—just as a man buying an automobile and borrowing money for it anticipates that from his next eighteen months' wages he will save enough to pay off his installments. If not overdone, bank loans for capital construction are financially sound. Of course, this is borrowing from the future. But the future is reasonably predictable.

A second element is less calculable. It is the product of technique. Modern engineering and technical methods make it possible for certain kinds of capital assets to be brought into existence rapidly and, when in existence, to start producing goods in great volume. Some plants, for example, can produce goods whose value (after paying for raw material and labor) will in a single year equal the entire cost of construction of the plant itself. (This is an extreme case, but it will serve for illustration.) The corporation applying for a loan to construct such a plant would show its records, experience, and engineering estimates. The bank has before it an estimate that in a relatively short period of time, say, eighteen months or two years, the plant will have brought into existence merchandise whose value (over and above the wages and raw-material costs) will be equal to the loan.

Here the bank could grant the loan anticipating prompt creation of consumer products equal to it. From the sale of those products, presumably, the loan will be paid, and the created dollars will be cancelled. Bank-created dollars can be sound enough if there are plenty of goods and services in existence at present, and if future products giving value to these dollars come into existence fairly soon.

Yet consider: The bank—or banker—has used a power granted him by the state. He has decided to allow a particular capital-allocation job to go forward by making the loan. He has done so by creating some new money—not his, or yours, or mine, but by using a fragment of politically created power.

In doing so, the banker ceases to be a private citizen. He becomes, in tiny degree, a state planner. He is no capitalist at all; he is a hired manager of an infinitesimal part of an economic system.

3. Administration of "Incorporeal Capital"

IT IS FAIRLY EASY to identify the groups of men having power over that part of capital which is, or by spending money is to become, tangible things. The managements of corporations are identifiable. The administrators of the institutions pooling personal savings—insurance companies, savings banks, and their equivalent—are known. The funds gathered by the national and local governments are applied by their budget-makers and senior officials. The commercial bankers creating capital through bank credit are under steady public scrutiny. But now there is a new and growing margin, "incorporeal capital." Decisions to increase and apply it follow none of the accustomed rules.

In itself, incorporeal capital comprises the vast stratum from a mathematical formula in the mind of a university scientist to the engineers' calculation that an artificial satellite in space may transmit messages more cheaply than a transoceanic cable. It includes abstract ideas with infinite but undemonstrated possibility of use in practical matters. It is not individualized. The research scientist or the applying engineer work in and with a worldwide atmosphere of transmitted knowledge and information. The past two decades have demonstrated infinite possibility for practical result. But location of power over any single process or group of processes cannot be predicted until the last phase of the long struggle to reduce abstraction to tangible use.

Even the assumed line between public (or statist) ownership and use for private ends or profit here breaks down. Scientifically trained men alone have insight into possible use. Until the last phase, financial results are unpredictable. It sounds strange to think of a scientific institute of scholars as primary decision-makers in capital allocation (their members are rarely, if ever, "capitalists" in any identifiable sense). But in the end their insights, perceptions, and intuitions are the chief controlling influence.

Two thirds of all research, as noted, is paid for by the federal government. Much of it, probably most of it, is carried on by contract arrangements with universities, scientific institutions, and occasional nonprofit corporations. The results "belong" to the federal government or agency which contracts for it, notably the Department of Defense. More accurately, the results "belong" to the scientific and technical groups which did the work and understand the results; they can communicate this to the government agency, but of course it remains in their heads and in their libraries and oftener than not in libraries or files widely available to their fellow students. The next phase—sorting out promising lines of further endeavor, experimental work, and, ultimately, application—may be undertaken by anyone controlling "savings" and wishing to devote them to this end. In practice, the two great channels of application lie in government departments and in the research-and-development departments of the few most powerful corporations, because these are the only groups controlling accumulated funds adequate to tackle the job. Yet neither the government agency nor the great corporation can undertake this without the concurrence and probably the wholehearted support of the scientists and technicians engaged in the project.

I suggest that this aspect of decision-making as to incorporeal capital more nearly resembles the action of princes than of proprietors. It is too soon to make analysis. Yet it is clear that a new layer of decision-making is here appearing, living above the capital-making decisions to which we are accustomed. To take a crude analogy, there is in the making an "upper house" of capital control. Ultimately, the development, the working out, the application, and the ultimate use of the aggregate of work and knowledge we have called "incorporeal capital" can influence, if not actually direct, the operations of the largest private corporation or the most powerful state agency.

The conclusion must be that the location of decision-making in the economic world has shifted. Ownership ceases to play much decision-making part in from two thirds to three fourths (and perhaps more) of the American economic republic. Instead, that power lies in corporation managements, in administrators of savings-gathering institutions and pension trusts, in the offices of the larger commercial banks, in government agencies, and in an inchoate emerging group which may be called the "scientific community."

CHAPTER 4 THE "FREE MARKET"—
FRIEND OR MENACE?

1. The Profit Motive: The Declining Gods of the Market

NINETEENTH-CENTURY THEORY assumed that capitalist economy was driven by a single motive. That motive was gain. It is commonly called the "profit motive." It has sometimes been called the deification of greed.

Excited by hope of gain, businessmen sought profit. By supplying a human want, for a price, they both satisfied the want (a useful thing in itself) and made money. Presumptively, if there were no one able to pay the price, there was not want which really needed filling. In any event, where there was effective demand—that is, a want plus capacity to pay for the thing or service wanted—the function of supplying it was useful and necessary.

There were, of course, limits. Some wants are best restrained —by the police if need be—but as a rule the fact that the goods or the services were wanted established their usefulness. Buying them was also useful.

There was no conflict between the selfish motive of desiring profit and the ethics of carrying out the function. Most, if not all, men, classicists argue, wished, and had a right to wish, to be more affluent. The laborer wished to sell his services in the best market he could find. Manufacturers and merchants wished to sell their goods and to make profit doing so. The buyer knew what he wanted to pay, and what he could pay. In any case, in a reasonably free market, other sellers competed for the buyer's patronage. The buyer, in turn, paid a price determined by supply and demand.

If, by reason of scarcity, price was extortionately high, and the profit obtained by the merchant or supplier was unduly great, other suppliers would promptly rush to compete. Presently, the mere fact of an unduly high market or an extortionate price would cause the flow of manufacturers or suppliers whose desire for profit would lead them to enter that market. Competition would then bring the price down to something like a reasonable level. The existence of an unfilled want, anywhere, would lead some entrepreneur—possibly a capitalist—to offer fulfillment of that want for a price. Thus, as human wants developed, the capitalist system would lead to their satisfaction.

This is a thumbnail sketch only of the theory. It rested on a number of assumed motivations, usually stated as economic laws. For example, businessmen would always "buy in the cheapest market, and sell in the dearest." Regulation of this economic or business process was inherently unsound. It would prevent the free development of wants, and the free flow of capitalist enterprise toward filling those wants. Interference with prices, either by holding them below the level which the free market afforded or by raising them above that level, upset the automatic balance. A free market, free competition, absence of monopoly, untrammeled opportunity for enterprise to enter, or to withdraw from, or be driven by competition out of, any market activity accurately adjusted both present supply to present demand, and increase or reduction of allocation of capital and effort to any given function.

It was a splendid theory. The optimum distribution of goods and the optimum allocation of capitalistic effort were achieved by the regulating power of the free market.

As in the case of most sanctified theories, there was a good deal of truth inherent in its propositions. Business enterprises, individual or corporate, do seek profits. They do like to make as much money as they can. They do not go into projects which offer only prospect of loss. They withdraw from losing ventures as soon as they reasonably can. In any line of activity, they take those steps and do those things which tend to maximize their profit. Without that motive, a political economic system which relies on a privately owned and privately operated mechanism for production and distribution would probably break down. By the law of its being, private enterprise must at least break even to continue in operation at all. It must have at least a modest profit in order to expand as the population and its market expand, to pioneer new fields, either geographically (as the great oil companies do in exploration) or technically (as electronics companies do in distant research). There profits must be more than modest. They must be substantial—substantial enough, in fact, to accumulate the capital discussed in the previous chapter.

Dangers were nevertheless implicit in the theory. Accepting, as we must, its force in large measure, violent qualifications must be made on its effectiveness.

Incompleteness is the first criticism. Assumption was made that the process of production would generate enough distribution to provide a market for all the goods to be produced. The pay of the workers, the salaries of the executives, the goods produced by agriculture and required to feed and supply industry, the price paid by industry for such supplies, placed purchasing power in the hands of the public sufficient to buy the goods and services provided. This was Say's Law (named for the brilliant Frenchman who worked out the theory). Unhappily, at least under twentieth-century conditions, this was not true, if it ever had been.

With modern techniques, agriculture and manufactures demonstrated their capacity to produce more than the effective demand could pay for. Price-smashing surpluses piled up. These were the primary causes for recurrent depressions. There was, it appeared, at most times—perhaps at all times—an overcapacity in the field of production and an oversupply of labor.

"Wants" were by no means the same as purchasing power to satisfy those wants. Too many people were poor and could not pay. Others, impressed with the need for security, insisted on saving instead of spending. Their savings were not always directly invested in new plant. This was the phenomenon John Maynard Keynes christened "oversaving," though it might also have been described as unwillingness by those who handle enterprise to put these savings immediately to work through investment. Or it might be that there was imbalance between the compensation paid to labor and to producers, so that they had not gains enough to buy the product of the manufacturing and productive enterprises.

In twentieth-century technique, there is at most times a margin of capacity to produce over the capacity or willingness to consume, or ability to pay for wanted consumption, as the case may be. But that fact came much later than the development of theories of nineteenth-century capitalism. Further, as a system becomes increasingly affluent—that is, as production increasingly can be set at any level the managers of enterprise wish to make it—the assumed automatic balance ceases to be evident.

At all events, it ceased to be continuous enough to permit the running of a modern state. Too often great numbers of men were unemployed—the free market did not absorb their labor. Too often there was overproduction—the free market did not absorb the goods.

Now it was all very well for theorists to say that these situations would "correct themselves." So indeed they would. If enough laborers starved to death, this would unquestionably reduce the supply of labor. If enough businesses went bankrupt, unquestionably the supply would be reduced to correspond to effective demand. Unhappily, the human costs involved in these automatic balances were so great that they ceased to commend themselves to well-meaning men.

[It may be accurate to say, courteously but authoritatively, to the laborer whose services are not desired that he can best serve humanity and restore a market balance by starving to death in sweet reason. Obstinate man that he is, he refuses to accept this conclusion. [Even the businessman does not wholly accept the logic of the theories he himself espouses. If he, for example, is in the business of constructing houses, and he knows there is a shortage of houses, but for some strange reason there are not readily available men who want houses and who are also able to pay for them, he will at once undertake to upset the magic balance. He will (he does) go to the government to request that the government subsidize the building of dwellings at a lower price. Or, perhaps, he will endeavor to assist credit schemes making it possible for a buyer who has not presently the price to purchase on long credit terms. In brief, the human victim of the balancing operation will at once go into politics and insist that he be taken care of in some fashion. Patient explanation of market theory merely infuriates him and his friends. This reaction in a democracy is automatic and predictable, and the results make one conclusion inescapable. Automatic balances achieved at a high price in human misery are not acceptable in the modern state. No amount of grand economic reasoning will make them so.

Dramatic instance may be found in the fall of the Weimar Republic. In 1931, the well-intentioned men who were running the German Republic at the time were faced with a state of growing unemployment. They received the best classic advice available. The doctrine of Dr. Wilhelm Röpke, who acted as economic adviser to the then German Chancellor, Heinrich Brüning, parallels, in greater classic theory, the policy of the administration of Herbert Hoover when depression struck the United States in 1929. "Be firm, be courageous, have confidence. The balance will right itself. Do not indulge in artificial stimuli or schemes of relief. Let prices go where they will and bankruptcies fall as they must. In the end, the system will be back on a sound basis; there is no other way." In the case of Germany, this paved the way for the Nazi Reich of Adolf Hitler, just as in the United States it paved the way for the smashing defeat of the Republican party and the entrance of Franklin D. Roosevelt and the New Deal on the American political scene.

The underlying premises are plain. An economic system is not an end in itself. It exists to serve men. When it ceases to do that, it ceases to be acceptable—or, at all events, has demonstrated effects which require curing. Briefly, no twentieth-century state, having adequate productive resource and adequate means of securing all necessary material for production, can tolerate the creation of balance when the chief balancing item is a long continuation of human misery. Nor, as a rational matter, should any state or any society accept such a condition. There ought to be quite adequate ingenuity in modern society to see that where there is want on one side of the picture and adequate supply readily available on the other, the two are connected. If the motive of profit-seeking cannot connect them, well, some other means must be found which will.

Observation of the behavior of economic systems, and a reading of history, makes it reasonably clear, I think, that the profit motive, by itself, never did consistently drive an economic machine as fast as it could go. It never did arrange quite enough purchasing power to assure the expansion of productivity at satisfactory rates. It never did distribute quite enough to supply all the human wants which an economic system must satisfy. A margin over, outside the area in which private profit and hope of gain operate, has always to be found.

2. "Market Competition"—Acceptable and Unacceptable

THE AMERICAN ECONOMIC republic has maintained and built upon the classic conception of the "market" and its companion concept of competition. But it has drastically limited the area within which the "market" has final sway, and has intervened— and stands ready to intervene—when the market results are not acceptable.

In carrying forward the market doctrine, the United States was, of course, carrying forward a fiercely held but inexact and partly fictitious academic conception of the late eighteenth and nineteenth centuries. Classic capitalism assumed that all economy was balanced in and continuously adjusted to "the market." It postulated that in every human activity there was a sort of auction or exchange, a mart where bids and offers were made, trades were consummated, and prices determined. Many sellers offered their work, their product, their property, their technique, or their money capital, for sale, for wages, or for hire at interest. Many buyers bought or hired at the lowest price offered. Sellers delivered for the highest price they could get. In the process, sellers competed with each other, as did buyers. The market struck the price. Theoretically, the market governed the price of everything: from the wage of a day laborer peddling his muscle and his craft to the manufacturer vending his copper or his cloth. It set the salary of a university professor offering his capacity to teach and write. It fixed the terms reached by a mill agent buying raw material from a supplier and the rate of interest charged by a banker offering to lend money.

There was considerable validity—and also a wide element of fiction—in this theory. "Markets" in that sense did exist. They still do in certain areas of business. The stock market, for example, is a highly competitive forum where security prices are settled by the meeting of bids and offers. Similar markets for most staple agricultural products are found in America. In many areas of business, slower but similar process of bidding for and selling many kinds of services and goods does go on.

Yet at all times there were great areas where this process proceeded slowly and erratically, others where it occurred rarely, and many where it did not go on at all. The nineteenth-century American grocery store, often the only one in town, both bought and sold; but it had no nearby competitors and its "market" was rather different from the classic picture. When Adam Smith wrote, corporations had been outlawed for half a century; they became familiar in the latter nineteenth century. Monopoly was possible (indeed was not outlawed in the United States until 1890). At best, the actual world of classical economics was a series of disparate "markets." In many important areas competitive markets did not exist, or limped if they did.

Nevertheless, the "market" was a useful concept. Real or fictitious, commercial operations did set prices at which goods and services normally could be had and at which they normally could be sold. Actual competition, or the possibility of it, could and usually did restrain prices from becoming high out of reason —if only because a nonexistent competitor would be tempted to go into the business. But the "open market" was not at all effective in preventing the rise or fall of prices of goods from becoming periodically catastrophic. It was not designed to be. In the case of labor, competition for work led to depressed wage rates and fluctuations of employment whose results were literally inhuman. In the case of commodities, or money offered for loan, a "seller's market" could become sheer extortion. A "buyer's market," wrecking price and wage levels, could, and often did, become intolerably cruel.

The emerging economic republic introduced a new element. Possibly it was merely development and extension of an older unobserved fact. It is called the "administered price." This is a price set by the principal provider, supplier, or manufacturer of the goods or services in question, thereupon accepted and followed, by practically all competitors, and maintained over substantial periods of time, to be changed only by a new decision of the leading elements in the trade. (We owe the phrase "administered price" to my former colleague Dr. Gardiner C. Means, who coined it about 1936. The behavior of "administered prices" is described in his volume *Pricing Power and the Public Interest,* published in 1962.) Exercise of the power to administer prices is limited. The excitement over a price increase in steel proposed by the principal steel manufacturers in April 1962 resulted from attempted exercise of the power to set an "administered price" at a moment when the government of the United States considered that this particular price decision collided with a national interest to prevent inflation.

Price administration is an economic power proceeding from concentration of production in large corporations. The law of the American economic republic did not and does not allow monopolies in most areas of commerce. It did and does allow bigness, and, with it, what is called "oligopoly." The word means merely that two, three, four, or possibly five large concerns carry on most of the production and sale in any given industry—as, for example, General Motors and Ford at present carry on roughly 80% of the production and sale of all American motorcars. Where oligopoly exists, administered prices are the rule rather than the exception. The competitive element is relatively weak, or at all events operates slowly and within limits. Certainly it does not have the full force or effect ascribed to it in nineteenth-century economics.

"Administered prices" were not, and on the whole are not, in the writer's opinion, disliked in the emerging twentieth-century system. Violently fluctuating and especially unduly low prices in markets where fierce competition prevails yield human consequences which almost no one wants. Even competitors do not cheer when a business concern goes bankrupt. Fluctuation of employment produces intolerable hardship. As American economic life became more humane, indeed, communities had to pick up the cost of preventing direct or indirect victims of the competitive struggle from starving in the streets. Cities felt the bite; they took the loss whenever a plant closed its doors and its laborers, now unemployed, ceased to buy and to consume, being unable to pay. Competition might, and did, provide lower prices to some—but often at costs paid by others. The "administered price," on the other hand, did introduce an element of stability. Industries which could administer prices liked it. Communities depending on such industries to pay taxes, to employ their inhabitants, and on these employees to buy from local shops to maintain an uninterrupted flow of economic life were as vitally interested as the corporations themselves.

The "free market," if not tamed, was at least tempered, and the twentieth century preferred it so. As will appear later, it has been artificially maintained in the American economic republic —but primarily as a means to an end. Competition in a free market can be used as a flexible control to prevent excessive prices, even where prices are administered. It offers motivation, and method, for meeting new wants, for introducing innovations, or for providing goods and services in areas not adequately supplied. It enables capable individuals to seek their own level through self-employment outside the bureaucracies of state agencies or large corporate organizations. It provides a means of meeting wants in those areas where the consumers' desires must be paramount. Standard products like electricity or steel might perhaps be supplied through statist or monopoly operation, since taste plays little part in demand for these products. But it is unlikely that either oligopoly or public bureaucracy would adequately supply women's dresses, or music, or painting.

The "free market" has not lost its usefulness as an instrument. But it is, now, an instrument. It has been completely displaced as an infallible god, has been substantially displaced as universal economic master, and increasingly ceases to be, or to be thought of as, the only acceptable way of economic life.

CHAPTER 5 THE DEMOCRATIC

PROCESS: POLITICS AS MEANS

OF REDRESS

ECONOMIC ORGANIZATIONAL and social facts, as we have seen, were, and still are, reducing many nineteenth-century concepts to fragments. New conditions were, and still are, arising with breath-taking speed as historical development goes. Problems had been, and continue to be, steadily emerging, and apparently they could not be resolved to the satisfaction of reasonable Americans by automatic market processes.

Until a generation ago, most professional economists did not soil their hands with the grimy business of economic engineering, even in business, let alone government. Had they wished to do so, they probably did not have adequate tools. Professor Wesley Mitchell, of Columbia University, only gave the American republic its splendid system of statistics and measurement after 1920. Alvin Johnson's monumental *Cyclopedia of the Social Sciences* did not appear in print until 1934. Intellectuals were, in any event, not particularly welcome either in business board rooms or in governmental offices. Too often they had not much to say for themselves when they were. Until the great change, "practical" men were at a premium; theorists were discounted. And probably theory had not caught up with developing economic fact.

The American public, in times of economic stress, continued to follow its habit of turning to its politicians, small and great, from ward heeler to President. When conditions were bad, individuals had always sought assistance from a Tammany district leader, a county chairman, or a congressman. These were expected to pull wires, arrange jobs, get government contracts, meet the situation somehow. They did so. True, they pulled with as much vigor for great interests buying privilege as for poverty-stricken constituents seeking jobs. When their constituents' traffic reflected widespread distress in their constituencies, they concerted shotgun methods for curing specific sores.

In large matters of country-wide interest, the combination of local distresses tossed great movements into the political arena—movements which recked little and usually cared less about orthodox nineteenth-century theory. The Granger movement talked of public ownership of great public services such as rail-roads, assaulting the entrenched finance capitalism of New York. Populists advocated a series of measures foggily derived from European Socialist thinking. William Jennings Bryan was twice nominated for President in the nineteenth century (and once in the twentieth); he wanted to liberalize the money-and-credit system by modifying the gold standard and issuing money against free silver. One can go straight through the history of the United States, at least since the advent of Andrew Jackson, and find that its politics have been periodically preoccupied with redressing the unhappy results of the *laissez-faire* system.

For one thing, as industry developed under the corporate system, the *laissez-faire* free market left to itself was self-destroying. Thence came the monopolies leading to the Sherman Antitrust law. For another, it was (in mid-twentieth-century retrospect) financially lunatic. A system contemplating business "cycles," leading every seven or eight years to a crash in the banking system, made no sense save to callous and astute speculators. America has continuously and obstinately believed that an economic system is made by men to serve men—not men to serve the system.

And Americans had votes. Their governments, state and national, belonged to them—not they to their governments. Perhaps because of this, they were also aware of limitations on government capacity. Professors Colm and Geiger were entirely right (when writing *The Economy of the American People*) in insisting on the crucial role of the government in the economic process owing to the continuing causative force of American political democracy:

> On the one hand, Americans have widely held the conviction that justice demands an equal chance for personal fulfillment; that it is both possible and proper to improve the individual's situation and the conditions of society as a whole; and that the government has a responsibility to foster and assist the people's efforts to improve themselves. On the other hand, there has been the deeply rooted American concern for individual freedom; the belief that the government is the helpmate and not the master of the people; and the conviction that improvements must result primarily from the will and effort of the people themselves (p. 81).

The political process, with congressional elections every two years and presidential elections every four, provided the mechanism by which these convictions could be registered, grievances presented, and reasonably acceptable solutions worked out.[18]

At this game everyone could play—and can. Americans do. The least acceptable can form some sort of opinion and follow the politicians who make most sense to him under his conditions. Local political organizations are available in almost all corners of the country. If one does not wish to accept a political-party designation, a committee can be formed. Local newspapers will carry communications. Self-interested or altruistic pressure groups can be organized. Preachers and professors can be enlisted. Politicians, especially elected officials, have always been and are automatically conditioned to detect hoofbeats in the distance as they keep one ear to their political ground. Giving form and finding solutions to questions raised by movements of this kind is almost a specialty of American life.

Nor has the American two-party system presented obstacles. Factually, both the Republican and the Democratic parties in the United States are made up of many different, more or less organized, segments of thought. Every four years each party within itself pounds out the basis of continued coalition for all its various elements, much as in the old days a French prime minister pounded out a coalition of several parties to gain his parliamentary majority. Representing a common denominator of party opinion is essential to being nominated for the presidency, and the party platforms record the essentials of that denominator. Persuading the public that the resulting program is able to alleviate or cure recognized ills is the major objective in national and in most state campaigns. Elected, a new administration promptly begins, not to suppress the opposition, but to handle affairs so that its major complaints shall be allayed, if not removed. Politicians call this "eliminating the issue."

Volumes of print have been expended on the American democratic process, from Lord Bryce's monumental *American Commonwealth* to more modern work, like Charles and Mary Beard's *America in Mid-Passage*. The politician has been the perennial butt of critics, columnists, and cartoonists. Every charge is in some measure true. Yet, as in the case of the Protestant ethic, they must be judged by the outturn result. One fact cannot be laughed or jeered away. The democratic process has steadily worked—sometimes slowly, sometimes inadequately, sometimes crankily, but always moving toward, rather than away from, acceptable human solutions.

In different context, it has strengthened—or weakened—different ideas. The McKinley period undoubtedly favored great wealth, quite sincerely considering it a constructive force and quite wholeheartedly ignoring the increasingly devastating results of a plain plutocracy. Assaulting it, Woodrow Wilson in his time offered a formula: "The New Freedom"—progressive taxation of incomes, the re-creation of a free market under federal policing, and reform of the currency-credit system through a Federal Reserve system. He was opposed on one flank by President William Howard Taft, widely reckoned a *status quo* conservative, and on the other by Theodore Roosevelt, by 1912 a thoroughgoing radical. Roosevelt proposed government intervention in all kinds of ways, even advocating recall of judicial decisions to overcome the conservatives of the United States Supreme Court. The Harding-Coolidge-Hoover era did not plump for plutocracy, but it admired and fostered "big" business, considering big business as the real creative and dynamic force in the American economy, despite its lack of concern for sound distribution of economic benefit.

Political history is not the province of this study. An excellent review may be found in Arthur M. Schlesinger, Jr.'s *The Crisis of the Old Order,* fully documenting the political effects of growing inadequacies (not to mention cruelties) in the period following World War I.

We know, now, a great deal more about the root conditions of that time than was known forty years ago. We know that many economic troubles were capable of remedy—as was proved by later experience. Readers of the preceding chapters of this volume understand the quantity, scope, and relationship of economic forces far better, perhaps, than anyone could have understood them in (let us say) 1925. Yet even then almost anyone could understand that the old economic and social explanations did not describe, let alone fit, the emerging economic and social facts. At all events, situations were arising which increasingly insulted common sense as well as common humanity.

Probably, though this defies clear-cut economic analysis, a watershed was crossed some time in the decade 1920-1930. This was the phenomenon of productivity, or at least of capacity to produce, substantially beyond the "effective demand"—that is, beyond the purchasing power of industrious human beings who needed or wanted more food, shelter, housing, and other goods than they could buy. The spectacle of masses of underfed and underprivileged Americans on one side of a plate-glass window, on the other side of which was visible unexhausted (if not unlimited) capacity to satisfy those wants—sometimes, indeed, goods in warehouses and certainly readily available—seemed increasingly irrational. Malthus, John Stuart Mill, and Marshall all rolled together could not make sense out of that. But then, they never had tried. They, of course, had assumed Malthus's premise that human wants beyond a bare minimum of poverty-stricken subsistence could never be met by production. There was increasing consciousness that the state was part creator of the situation. It could, therefore, take an increasing hand in modifying it.

Corporations, meanwhile, were creations of the state, given nationwide scope by the decisions of the Supreme Court. They were—or could be made—amenable to state guidance. The banking-and-currency system, made more flexible by Woodrow Wilson's Federal Reserve Act, was increasingly recognized as a system created by the state, rather than a mystical order of things dependent on possession of, or capacity to get, gold, or to organize a bank. Markets, protected by the Sherman law, and now policed under the Clayton Antitrust law and the Federal Trade Commission Act, were seen to be the potentially self-destroying forces that they are—useful for some purposes, intolerable for others. Awareness grew that the state—if it would—could somehow break the plate-glass window between want and supply in a good many ways. In case of need, the democratic process of the United States could put into power a state that would do so. That same vote could prevent the state from becoming master.

These dim and ill-expressed feelings of distressed minorities —and of equally distressed individuals not themselves in want but offended by the human facts—were, as they always are, muted in years of great prosperity. They became briefly vocal in the economic republic during the brief depression following World War I (1920-1921). They were allayed by growing prosperity following the year 1927. They were almost drowned out by the brassy crescendo of speculative furor in the New York Stock Exchange from 1926 to 1929. It looked rich, if not good. No one had then pointed out that stock-exchange operations, spectacular or modest, were contributing increasingly less to formation of capital or to production, and certainly were not distributing wealth on any rational basis. Not religion, but a ticket in the stock-market lottery was for a brief period the opiate of the masses. Even then, plenty of minority groups and, notably, the growing labor organizations felt somehow that the economic room had no floor to it. They looked to the state to bridge the gap between theory and reality. It would have been hard to find American economists whose solutions would have met their problems.

In their thinking, Americans had never excluded the state as an influence on the economic process. Only classical economists had attempted to do that.

The stage was thus set for a classic operation in democracy. The 1929 crash, the slow recovery of 1930, and the ensuing spiral descent into an abyss of unemployment, bank failures, and commercial paralysis was not corrected by market processes. The contemporary business captains, working desperately (as they did) to meet the situation, failed completely. Following established precepts of the American political process, the public—and the American voters—increasingly asked that the political state propose a program and act.

Necessarily, this meant considerable reorganization of private business. It might, and did, as the event proved, require substantial reorganization of the national government as well. Out of the crisis was born the American economic republic as we know it today.

PART TWO

Organization and Structure

CHAPTER 6   ASSUMPTION OF RESPON-
SIBILITY BY THE POLITICAL STATE

THE FIRST PART of this volume examined some of the changes occurring in the basic concepts and institutions of American economic life. This second part outlines the salient features of the current (1962) organization of the American economic republic.[19]

The economic republic began to assume its present form as a result of the crisis of 1933. Under stress of the Great Depression, culminating in collapse of the banking system, the federal government assumed responsibility for the functioning of the economic system. The political act was the work of President Franklin D. Roosevelt. Similar assumption probably would have been forced on any President holding office at that time. Most of the conceptions, elements, forces, and institutions used and regrouped in the new order were already in existence prior to 1933. (Use of old institutions for new purposes often occurs when major political changes take place.) They, with new focus and new institutions, were reoriented, extended, combined, and developed to set up the structure we now have.

This assumption of responsibility, in the political context of the United States of 1933, was an innovation of the first order. Before then, the economic system, motivated and limited by the free market, was supposed to work automatically. Capital sought profits; its owners therefore invested and managed capital so as to produce the goods and services needed by the country. Men and women needed wages to pay their living expenses, and to save for old age and misfortune; they therefore sought jobs and supplied labor. The profit motive, or fear of want, drove the machine and all parts of it. Competition and the open market were supposed to allocate resources and prevent inefficiency and abuse. The total of these private activities, guided by the market, was supposed to produce adequately. Wages and profits were supposed sufficiently to distribute purchasing power, enabling the recipients to buy the product. When government intervened (usually by state, and not federal, legislation), the reason was usually to exercise a police power—for example, to limit employment of women in dangerous occupations, or require safety appliances to prevent accident, or perhaps to limit child labor, though there were occasional exceptions. The economic machine itself was supposed to work adequately under its own steam without impetus from the political state. The primary role of the government was to carry on foreign relations, provide for national defense and public order, assure freedom of commerce (that is, a common market between the several states), deal with tariffs and foreign trade, and assure an adequate and dependable system of money. In combination with the state governments, the federal government protected property and enforced contracts—the underlying conditions needed to provide a private mercantile society.

Exceptions to this "night watchman" principle had nevertheless been recognized. Enlarging the principle of regulating interstate commerce, the federal government had declared for regulation of railroads in 1887, and had actually commenced rate regulation in 1906. Monopolies had been prohibited with passage of the Sherman Antitrust Act in 1890, and since 1900 the government actively enforced the prohibition in a number of major cases. The political state had intervened to secure better prices for agricultural products by passing the McNary-Haugen Act in 1928. Through tariff policies, it had always taken an active hand in controlling currents of foreign trade. In other, less important, ways, the government had sometimes moved in to alter or affect the balance of employment or commerce. But these were efforts to deal with specific, limited situations. Only when the entire economic system had almost ground to a halt did the national government itself assume responsibility for its adequate functioning.

On March 3, 1933, the closing of practically all banks in the country paralyzed the supply of currency, and with it a large part of the production and distribution of the United States. Continuance of that condition inevitably would have increased the breakdown. The newly elected government was inaugurated on March 4. The record of emergency actions taken runs as follows:

1. Commercial banking was almost wholly controlled, and investment and finance at least partly so. This was accomplished by the Emergency Banking Act (March 9); abandonment of the gold standard (April 19); powers of monetary expansion in the Agricultural Adjustment Act (May 12); an emergency farm-mortgage act refinancing farm mortgages (also on May 12); the "truth in securities" act setting up what is today the Securities and Exchange Commission (May 27); abrogation of the gold clause in public and private contracts (June 5); the Home Owners Loan Act, providing for refinancing of home mortgages (June 13); the Glass-Steagall Banking Act, splitting commercial banking from investment banking, and guaranteeing bank deposits (June 16); and the Farm Credit Act, providing for reorganization of agricultural credit activities (also June 16). This, with the expansion of power of the Reconstruction Finance Corporation to handle investment-banking operations not otherwise covered, placed virtually all commercial banking and finance within the control of the federal government.

2. The agricultural market was taken under government control. The Agricultural Adjustment Act of May 12 was the forerunner of the present system controlling agricultural prices and production.

3. Nonstatist industry prices and wages ceased to be matter of private decision. For practical purposes, the free-market conception of market-determined prices was abandoned under the sweeping provisions of the National Industrial Recovery Act (June 16). This provided machinery by which, under govern-

ment regulation and supervision, prices and trade practice could be fixed by trade associations representing the various industries, and the decisions could be enforced. In its way, it was the greatest single departure from the old system, and was destined to be short-lived. For the moment, however, prices, wages, and conditions in industry were no longer to be fixed by the market, but by government-supervised agreements.

4. Direct distribution of national income; the Federal Emergency Relief Act (May 12, 1933) set up a direct program of distribution to the unemployed. A prior and similar arrangement for direct provision for unemployed youth had been made through passage of the Civilian Conservation Corps Act on March 31, 1933.

A multibillion-dollar public-works program designed to give the government direct spending power to stimulate production and employment was adopted on June 16, 1933, along with the National Industrial Recovery Act.

These were emergency measures. In aggregate, the federal government emerged with almost complete control over commercial banking, over investment and finance, over agricultural production and marketing, over industrial production and marketing, and, within limited scope, acquired some power over direct distribution of national income. This was done not as matter of doctrine, but of temporary necessity.

It was not a revolution, though sometimes described as one. (I was present, and a small part of the operation, and here hazard a few observations.) Never as far as I could see was great change less revolutionary. The American public did not want to overthrow its government; it wanted its government to go to work. It did not want to upset its financial institutions and corporations; it wanted a great many of their managers fired. It did not want a new economic system; it wanted the system mauled to a workable whole. It did not want dictatorship; it wanted leadership.

One result has been the almost total inability of Europeans to understand what happened as the system emerged. To Europeans, social change on this scale then implied revolution. Moves toward such revolution had become almost as stylized as a minuet. The American method was to them inconceivable. There was no particular reaction against property. (Paraphrasing W. S. Gilbert's Earl in *Iolanthe,* Americans had a great respect for property; they merely wished they had some of it themselves.) There was no direct institutional or doctrinal change. "Capitalism," which in Europe would have been made the intellectual villain of the piece, was hardly discussed. Yet at the close of the Congress of the Hundred Days, the interdependence of the political state and the economic system had been fully established, with ultimate responsibility residing in the state; this remains the case today.

The history of the political phase has been fully recorded, notably by Professor Arthur Schlesinger, Jr., in *The Coming of the New Deal.* Of particular interest is the fact that the population, in economic agony, rather consciously sought not to invoke the wastes (and worse) involved in revolution or class war.

From the emergency base wrought in 1933, the current system emerged. It modified older institutions of the United States while retaining as much as possible of their nominal form. It maintained the institution of private property and wealth. It maintained, though in limited measure, the institution of the "market economy." The economic lines of organization in ensuing years became stabilized in their present form, though they are still evolving. There appears no present likelihood that a new basis will be sought in the foreseeable future. There is every likelihood that, whenever difficulty appears, the political-economic system will move toward achieving results more satisfactory to its people.

CHAPTER 7 GOVERNMENTAL STRUCTURE OF THE AMERICAN ECONOMIC REPUBLIC

THE BASIC LAW setting up the structure of the American economic republic rests on a small group of constitutional rules and federal statutes which have attained a measure of constitutional stature. These are amplified and carried out by law, partly statutory, partly administrative, and partly unwritten. They determine or control the functions of the chief governmental and private (that is, nonstatist) institutions through which the economic life of the country is carried on.

Only an outline is here offered. No study of less than encyclopedic size could describe all the governmental and private institutions, and all the rules performing or influencing the vast operations of the American economy.

Changes in point of view, changes in structure itself, are steadily taking place. The economic republic is young. Had one attempted to draw a design of the American political state thirty years after its Constitution had come into force—say in the year 1820—the sketch would differ vastly from any outline of the structure of the United States government we know today. The economic republic has one surpassing virtue—its capacity for continuous evolution.

1. Direct Government Power: The Basic Rules

THE CONSTITUTION—POWERS

The Congress shall have power . . .

To regulate commerce with foreign nations, and among the several States. . . . [Art. 1, Section 8, paragraph 3]

To borrow money on the credit of the United States. [Art. I, Section 8, paragraph 2]

To coin money [and] regulate the value thereof. [Art. I, Section 8, paragraph 5]

To lay and collect taxes, duties, imposts, and excises to pay the debts and provide for the common defense and general welfare of the United States. . . . [Art. I, Section 8, paragraph 1]

To establish post-offices and post-roads. [Art. I, Section 8, paragraph 7]

To lay and collect taxes on incomes, from whatever sources derived. . . . [Amendment XVI]

THE CONSTITUTION—LIMITATIONS

No person shall be . . . deprived of life, liberty, or property, without due process of law; nor shall private property be taken for public use without just compensation. [Amendment V]

No State shall . . . deprive any person of life, liberty, or property without due process of law, nor deny to any person within its jurisdiction the equal protection of the laws. [Amendment XIV]

A . . . corporation . . . is a person within the meaning of the Fourteenth Amendment declaring that no State shall deprive any person of property without due process of law, nor deny any person within its jurisdiction the equal protection of the laws. [United States Supreme Court, by Justice Harlan, in *Smyth* v. *Ames,* 1897]

The quoted provisions have given the American political state power to construct a national economic system. It has done so. The system must observe, and in fact is based upon, private rights, including property rights. "Private" does not mean merely "individual." Corporations, however large, are held to be "persons" (though jurists like Justices William O. Douglas and Hugo Black have objected that this should never have happened).

THE MARKET

Every contract, combination in the form of trust or otherwise, or conspiracy in restraint of trade or commerce among the several states or with foreign nations is declared to be illegal. [Sherman Antitrust law, 15 USCA 1]

Every person who shall monopolize or attempt to monopolize or conspire with any other person or persons to monopolize any part of the trade or commerce among the several states or with foreign nations, shall be deemed guilty of a misdemeanor. [Sherman Antitrust law, 15 USCA 2]

The Sherman Antitrust Act, adopted in 1890, about a century after the formation of the American political state, has been described as having quasi-constitutional standing. No equivalent legislation then existed in any other major capitalist state. British common-law courts maintained (in form at least) a somewhat similar doctrine, though its scope was quite different. The Sherman law is said by American courts to codify previous common-law doctrine, but in application its results are not the same. The political state has the task of enforcement. This legislation, with companion acts of application (the Clayton Antitrust Act and the Robinson-Patman Act), is, in theory, the chief legal bulwark of the competitive, open market—that is, of classic nineteenth-century economic theory. Having been accorded a dignity approaching that of constitutional law, it is subject to continuous reinterpretation in the light of current conditions.

When enacted, the Sherman Antitrust law was intended as an assault on concentrated economic power. Concentrations in some industries had become "monopolies," and threatened to produce monopolies in many more. (Communist attacks on the American system today continuously use the phrase "monopoly capitalism.") Politically, courts construed the rule as protecting "equality of opportunity" in American economic life. By that was meant the capacity of any individual or enterprise to enter any market, to trade in it, to succeed or fail. The future of corporations and their size, scope, and market power was perhaps not then fully apparent. In theory, a basic open-market ground rule was laid down for the American economic republic.

It is still a basic conception. Great areas nevertheless have been removed from the operation of the classic competitive-market institution. Price-fixing by private parties was made and now is per se illegal. Prices may be fixed only by the political state. Division of territory between private commercial concerns is prohibited. Yet the political state may, and does, fix prices or require divisions of territory, or both, in the case of enterprises carrying on great sectors of the national economy, notably communications, land and air transport, broadcasting, and supplying public utilities like electric light and power. Monopoly is prohibited; great size is not. Factually, a majority of the industry of the country is now carried on under a system of oligopoly—several large corporations carrying on most of the production and distribution in their respective industries. The state of the American economy now bears little resemblance to the nineteenth-century small-unit production and market exchange the framers of the Sherman Act probably intended to perpetuate.

Nor, indeed, was there—or is there now—any clearly identifiable limit to the doctrine of "restraint of trade." Decade by decade that conception has been reinterpreted. Successive political administrations have used the Antitrust law to attack and break up selected private formations of economic power, reinterpreting the rule as they did so. Oscillation has occurred. At times the growth of large units with great power has seemed acceptable, and the courts have been tolerant of it. The "rule of reason" did not protect the Standard Oil Company from dissolution in 1911. But it was applied to leave the United States Steel Company undisturbed in 1921. Antitrust procedures were invoked in the decade of the thirties against the Aluminum Company of America. No dissolution of a major enterprise has since been decreed. The breadth and indefiniteness of the statute made it possible for the political state to intervene in any situation where economic power had become highly concentrated and the public, or some sector of it, believed the power was abused or unacceptable.

The results of the Sherman Act, after seven decades, can be summed up as follows. It has prevented private monopoly, save in fields of commerce regulated by the state. It has not prevented, and probably was not intended to prevent, oligopoly. It has prevented iron-clad private price-fixing, but has not prevented and probably will not prevent the "administered price." It has maintained a substantial degree of competition—sufficient to limit the power of any single enterprise to set prices, terms, and costs completely at will. But competition thus maintained is less immediate, less direct, and less rapidly operating than that contemplated by classical economists. This is necessarily so; for competition carried to its logical end means that the strongest or cheapest producer could eventually bankrupt all competition, emerging as "monopoly" proscribed in economic theory and by the Sherman law. Then, of course, the state would have to intervene, either to administer the enterprise itself or to break it up and start the process all over.

POLICY, GOALS, AND RISE OF POWER

After the economic crisis of 1933, and federal assumption of economic responsibility, the economic health of the country was, and now is, the major domestic preoccupation of the political state. Under unwritten practice, uses of governmental power in the economic field grew up. By the Employment Act of 1946 they were embodied in explicit statutory law. The Congress of the United States then declared it to be "the policy and responsibility" of the federal government to use all practical means

to coordinate and utilize all its plans, functions and resources for the purpose of creating and maintaining, in a manner calculated to foster and promote free competitive enterprise and the general welfare, conditions under which there will be offered useful employment opportunities, including self-employment, for those able, willing and seeking to work and to promote maximum employment, production and purchasing power. [15 USCA 1021]

This declaration of policy has become a basic provision in the constitutional law of the American economic republic.

2. The Political-Economic Organization

THE PRESIDENT of the United States is the head of the economic administration of the country because he is the chief executive of the political state.

In that capacity, he is required to administer and enforce the laws of the United States applicable to its economic affairs.

Since 1946 he has also been specifically required to observe economic conditions, and to use all discretionary powers he has and all federal "plans, functions and resources" to assure that they are healthy or at least satisfactory to the public, meaning thereby "maximum employment, production and purchasing power." He is directed to recommend new measures, general or specific, as may be needed.

The Employment Act of 1946 directs the President, not later than January 20 in each year, to send to the Congress an economic statement, reporting existing levels—and foreseeable trends—of employment, production, and purchasing power, and presenting those levels "needed to carry out the policy" described above, and a program to meet them. His report must review the economic program of the federal government, and conditions affecting employment, production, and purchasing power.

This is a wide and inclusive responsibility. A parenthetical note of contemporary application may be in order. When a President interests himself in the price of steel, or in the levels of wages sought by a labor union, as President John F. Kennedy did in 1962, he is *not* obtruding himself without warrant into affairs set apart from presidential or governmental power. He is obeying a mandate and carrying out a policy of the Congress.

Utilizing all the "plans, functions and resources" of the United States government to foster free competitive enterprise and the general welfare, and to promote maximum employment and production and purchasing power, is a sweeping grant of power to the President. It imposes a heavy burden.

Paradox is evident in the two major rules on which the American economic republic is constructed. A competitive economy, without monopoly, is posed by the Sherman law. An economy of full employment, wide distribution of purchasing power, and high production is contemplated by the Full Employment Act of 1946. Assumption is made that the goals of the latter will not conflict with the economic method imposed by the former. Yet it is evident there may be conflict at any time.

When this occurs, the application of the Sherman law is usually modified.

Sporadic unemployment is one result of competition. The more active the competition, the greater the threat of unemployment in any industry, at any time. Full employment calls for continuous production on a steadily rising scale and steady sale of the product in a volume and at a price adequate to pay good wages, replenish capital, and yield a profit. Active competition by hypothesis involves an attempt by each competitor to interrupt the flow of business toward his fellows and direct it to himself. In doing so, he may very well interrupt the stability of employment and the flow of wages in their enterprises.

One cannot escape the conclusion that the economic republic really wants to have it both ways—and has gone a long way toward achieving just this. It has accepted a substantial modification of the principle of free competition by accepting large-scale enterprise and oligopoly without permitting it to reach the stage of monopoly. It has maintained competition as a means of preventing the large-scale enterprise from accumulating too much power, from abusing its capacity to administer prices, and from having a position so well fortified that it did not need to improve its technique or its product. Competition increasingly becomes a potential limitation, rather than the direct, immediate influence it was supposed to be in nineteenth-century market economy; a means to an economic end, rather than a way of economic life.

3. The Council of Economic Advisers

THE PRESIDENT'S privy council in economic matters is the Council of Economic Advisers.

Informally, every President in American history has relied on a group of individuals in his confidence to observe, report, and advise on the economic problems of the country. Not infrequently, these men or some of them were also in the Cabinet of the United States. As a rule, one of them was the Secretary of the Treasury.

The present statutory structure is somewhat different. The Council of Economic Advisers is set up by the Employment Act in the Executive Office of the President. It is composed of three members chosen by the President, "by and with the advice and consent of the Senate." They are either professional economists or men of economic experience, qualified to interpret economic developments, to appraise programs and activities in the light of the policy declared, and to formulate and recommend national economic measures in accordance with that policy. They hold office at pleasure of the President, who names one of them chairman. They have such staff as they may need. One direction given them in law is of interest: they are authorized to issue a monthly publication entitled *Economic Indicators,* and to supply a copy of it to all members of the Congress.

Under current practice, the three economic advisers are drawn from the top rank of professional economists in the United States. Familiarly, they are men from academic life—university professors or heads of economic-research institutions. As a rule, they are not widely known popular figures, despite their position of enormous influence. This may change as political attention becomes increasingly fixed on business and economic affairs. Not infrequently they regard service with the Council as an interlude in their professional lives, returning after a tour of duty in Washington to their universities, though they usually can, if they wish, command high positions in private finance.

Though not so stated in terms, they are expected to, and do, draft the President's economic report. They are directed to watch all trends and to determine whether developments or trends are or are not interfering with achievement of maximum possible employment, production, and purchasing power. They are required to keep in touch with and appraise all the "programs and activities" of the federal government and determine whether they contribute—or do not contribute—to the goals of this policy. Among their duties is that of developing and recommending to the President national economic policies for these ends, and also "to avoid economic fluctuations or to diminish the effects thereof."

They may constitute advisory committees, may consult with

such representatives of industry, agriculture, labor, consumers, and state and local governments as they believe advisable.

Since they are in the White House and part of the President's staff, they have actual power aside from and beyond that directly given by statute. They can make suggestions to the heads of the executive departments (for example, the Departments of the Treasury, of Labor, of Commerce, and of Agriculture) and also to the independent agencies (for example, the Federal Reserve). Between the executive departments and the independent agencies there is a difference. The Secretary of the Treasury is a member of the administration of the President. He carries out the President's policies—else he is likely to lose his job. Presumptively, policies recommended by the economic advisers are the same as those favored by the President. Executive departments presumably pay close attention when they suggest. On the other hand, members of the Federal Reserve Board and other independent agencies, though appointed by the President, are not arms of "his" policy. They do not necessarily have to follow the President's directives. They are responsible to the Congress— a point for later consideration.

4. The Congress: Joint Committee
on the Economic Report

THE CONGRESS participates in making policy for, but does not have executive power in, the economic republic.

In the American political state, the Congress holds the power paramount. The President and the executive departments are, in most matters (though not all), ultimately subject to it. Following this theory (though without similar power results), the President's Council of Economic Advisers is paralleled by a statutory committee of Congress. By the legislation of 1946, there was established (15 USCA 1024) the "Joint Committee on the Economic Report."

It consists of seven members of the Senate and seven members of the House of Representatives appointed by the President of the Senate and the Speaker of the House and includes representatives of the political parties, majority and minority. This committee must study the matters brought up in the President's economic report. It must study means of co-ordinating programs to carry out the "maximum employment, production and purchasing power policy." It may (and invariably does) hold hearings on that report, and must file a report before March 1 in each year containing its findings and its recommendations on the main proposals made by the President (these are, in fact, the proposals worked out with and for him by the Economic Council). The Joint Committee report is supposed to be a "guide to the several committees of the Congress dealing with legislation relating to the economic report."

Under current congressional practice, no committee of the Congress is bound to pay any attention to this central economic committee. Whereas the President's Council of Economic Advisers can powerfully influence action by the executive departments, its opposite number, the Joint Committee on the Economic Report, can be cheerfully disregarded by its congressional colleagues. On the legislative side, the institutional factor has not yet attained itself. Fifteen years after its creation, the Council of Economic Advisers, sitting in the White House, is a recognized force in Washington and in the economic republic generally. Top echelons both in government and in private business and financial affairs know this, and pay attention to it. The equivalent congressional committee only slowly moves toward the degree of influence its position should confer.

In the economic republic, as in the political state, institutions take time to attain themselves. Eventually, the recommendations of the Joint Committee on the Economic Report, especially where they coincide with the recommendations of the Council of Economic Advisers, will be important, if not determinative, in fixing the policy of new legislation.

5. The Bureau of the Budget

THE SECOND great instrument in the President's office giving power and influence over the functioning of the economic system is the Bureau of the Budget. Its position in this hierarchy depends in large measure on unwritten law.

So far as written law goes, the Bureau of the Budget, headed by its director, is responsible for preparing the budget for the United States proposed by the President to the Congress. It receives from the various departments and agencies their requests for appropriations, and it receives from the Treasury estimates of revenue. Then, under the President's orders, it makes up the budget and submits it to the Congress for enactment.

Obviously, the budget itself has a powerful influence on the economy of the country; more so now than ever, since the United States under its budget directly collects and spends over 15% of the entire national income. Where this goes, by whom it is spent, and what for, and who receives the money as pay, or as compensation for contract work, military or civilian, or as subsidies, as in the case of farm prices, or as gratuity, as in the case of payments to veterans, goes far toward determining the shape of economic affairs.

A secondary budget effect is believed to be no less powerful. If the budget calls for collecting more revenue than expenditure —that is, provides a surplus—the result tends to depress the level of economic activity. If it calls for more expenditures than revenue—that is, produces a deficit—the federal government will be required to borrow. In doing so, it is likely to add to the amount of outstanding currency or credit. The result of this tends to stimulate business and economic activity, but if carried too far can be inflationary.[20] Over all, therefore, handling of the federal budget in and of itself exerts a powerful economic influence.

But the Budget Office by unwritten custom and executive practice has accumulated other functions of growing significance. These functions have crystallized. They are at present part of the unwritten legal structure of the American economic republic.

Its major accretion of power came as Presidents used the Bureau of the Budget to "co-ordinate" the work of the executive departments. In 1934, President Franklin D. Roosevelt directed that all executive departments, all independent agencies, and all emergency agencies should file their organization charts with the Bureau. In 1939, it was transferred to the executive office of the President, and there it remains. In 1950, by statute, the Director of the Budget, in consultation with the heads of the departments and executive agencies, was charged with the task of achieving consistency in accounting, and of "supporting" expenditures by giving "information on performance and program costs." In practice, the power is rather greater. Most plans or programs which involve spending money are finally worked out through or with this office. They usually begin in the departments or independent agencies, but the Bureau of the Budget has the last look. Few departments or their heads, however powerful, care to quarrel with it.

At this point, an unwritten but obviously essential relation begins between the Bureau of the Budget (in the President's office) and the Treasury Department. The Treasury has to estimate how much the government will collect by way of taxes; and what kind of taxes will be imposed. The Budget Bureau, on behalf of the President, recommends to the Congress how much money is to be spent, and for what. Decision has to be made whether the budget is to be "balanced"—that is, whether money coming in from tax collections is to be equal to the money spent—or whether the government will run at a deficit. This is a presidential decision, but the Economic Advisers, the Budget Bureau, and the Treasury all join in the determination. If deficit is decided on—or likely—the Treasury must go out and borrow the money. It may issue long-term government bonds—seeking to absorb savings. Or it can issue term obligations—sold chiefly to banks, increasing the volume of money and credit. Deficit financing may have an "inflationary" effect. This may be desirable if there is a recession. It may be dangerous if there is a boom.

Whether a budget surplus or a balance or a deficit is desirable or not in keeping the economy of the republic in satisfactory shape at any given time is a decision of grave importance. The Council of Economic Advisers, along with the Budget Bureau and the Treasury, has to have this in mind. Authority to make the decision is one of the really serious economic power factors in the republic.

Adding the power factors in the political state, the executive headship of the economic republic unquestionably has now been located in the presidency of the United States. The Council of Economic Advisers is responsible for formulating and recommending to the President economic policy on all matters likely to settle whether the republic is to achieve maximum employment and development of competitive private enterprise and purchasing power. These add up to the prosperity of the country.

The taxing and spending power of the United States is perhaps the largest single factor in the economic complex. Formally under control of the Congress of the United States, the spending function in actual fact is really controlled in most matters by the requirements of the executive departments working under the President. The Bureau of the Budget is there to determine these requirements. In combination, they go beyond meeting the financial needs of running the political government. They determine the direction and impact of distribution of a substantial part of the national income. They affect the largest single factor (surplus or deficit) in determining the supply of money and credit available to the public through the banking system.

Beyond existing power, the President can always ask the Congress to adopt additional programs, financial or otherwise, affecting federal expenditures, or the structure of taxation, prices, wages, or interest rates. He may ask the political state to intervene further in the operations and results of nonstatist business. The Congress may or may not agree with him. In that case an issue affecting the economic republic is presented and fought out in the political forum. The decision, when taken, adds another stone to the political-economic structure of the American economic republic.

6. Direct Government Buying Power and Control of Tax Levels

AN APPRECIABLE POWER of the political state lies in its capacity (subject to congressional limitation) to channel its own buying.[21]

Volume of this buying power is large. In one capacity or another the federal government buys goods and services (over and above the pay of its regular salaried employees) at a cost of between $30 billion and $40 billion per year. In general it buys in the open market at the best prices offered, like any businessman seeking raw materials or any consumer seeking needed goods. But much of its purchases, especially for defense purposes, are in areas in which the government is the only buyer, and free-market conditions scarcely exist. The largest part of these purchases supply the defense establishment, the Army, Navy, and Air Force. By placing the business in one or another area of the country, the government can increase (or, if need be, decrease) employment activity and flow of income in that area by executive order. For example, in 1952, the federal government undertook to channel part of its government contracts into what were called "labor surplus areas" (Defense Manpower Policy No. 4, 17 Federal Register 1195, February 7, 1952). On May 1, 1961, policy was codified in the Area Redevelopment Act (42 USCA 2501). This directs the Secretary of Commerce to designate areas of chronic unemployment or underemployment as "Redevelopment Areas," under rather careful definition. Direct loans may be made to establish new or expand old plants in these areas, expenditures for public facilities and subsistence to unemployed workmen in course of retraining may be made, and public expenditure, where practical, may be channeled into these areas.

The President recently requested discretionary authority to spend substantial amounts of federal money on public works, both in the interest of maintaining a high level of national economic activity and to deal with specific areas of growing unemployment. Such authority had not yet been given by the Congress in 1962. Passage of such legislation is not unlikely in event of an economic recession. Opposition to it comes not merely from economic classicists who fear "public spending," but also from those who fear undue growth of the power of the political state.

With the political state's direct power to buy or spend should be associated another power, never yet granted to the President but now sought by him at the instance and with the approval of powerful business, labor, and intellectual groups in the American economy. This is the power, to repose in the President, in emergency to raise or lower the rate of the income tax—and to restore the legislatively fixed rate when the emergency has passed. It was recommended by the Commission on Money and Credit, a bipartisan commission of economists, financiers, and business-men, to enable the President to meet his responsibility through prompt and decisive action under the Employment Act of 1946. (*Report of the Commission on Money and Credit,* New York, 1961, p. 136.)[22]

The theory here is that lowering the income tax at once gives the American consumer greater spending power. The evidence indicates he will promptly use it. Increase of consuming power increases demand for goods, and consequently increases employment and business activity generally. The Commission on Money and Credit accordingly proposed that the President should have discretionary power to issue a statement that economic conditions are running counter to the objectives set forth in the Employment Act of 1946—and, having done so, should be empowered to raise, or to lower, the income tax rate by five percentage points (in effect, 25% up or down) as circumstance might indicate. At the same time, recommendation was made that both the 1946 Employment Act and the Federal Reserve Act be amended to state as national goals a "low level of unemployment, an adequate rate of economic growth, and reasonable price stability." The Federal Reserve Board, without statutory mandate, has accepted and is working toward these goals now, as matter of unwritten law. So is the President, under the explicit language of the Employment Act of 1946, quoted above, though "growth" and "stability" do not appear in the statute.

The proposal is for a new tool toward bringing about stability, namely, presidential authority, without waiting for the Congress, to move the income tax up or down. This would increase or decrease the direct spending power of the American consuming public—that is to say, of practically all the population. Presumably the effect would be to add to or diminish private spending. The plan has encountered opposition and will not be adopted at once. In some quarters it has been vigorously attacked. I hazard the guess that if recession really threatens, the proposal will be accepted by the Congress.

Capacity for direct public spending is itself a substantial power of the political state to enter the life of the nonstatist economic republic. Capacity to increase or decrease the spending power of the American public (within limits) is perhaps a greater power, though it leaves to the American consumer the decision as to how the money shall be spent. The American economic republic is extremely cautious about attempting to guide individual consumption. Power of control over a man's consumption comes perilously close to being power over his manner of living, or, indeed, his life.

7. Guidance of Nonstatist (Business) Economic Decisions

THE POLITICAL STATE has also established itself as the ultimately determining factor in the private, nonstatist enterprise, though it does not, and is not allowed to, control most of the decisions made by such enterprises.

A previous section noted the chief constitutional and legal declarations of policy and goals of the political state with respect to economic conditions. We observed location of executive power in the President, and the growing institutions by which his power is organized. We noted certain direct economic actions the President, as head of the political state, can take under the accepted power of that state.

Yet the American economic republic is not a statist system. It contemplates that most of the economic work of the country shall be done through nonstatist enterprise, commonly called "private." The word "private" is open to question. An individually owned retail shop or farm or small plant is undoubtedly "private." But can the same be said of the 500 or 600 giant corporations carrying on two thirds or more of the industry of the country and influencing conditions in much more of it? I doubt it. Some of these enterprises have stockholder lists running into millions; all run into many thousands. The customers they ultimately serve comprise many millions more—in fact, most of the American population. The individuals employed by them are a substantial segment of the American people. A better description is that they are nonstatist institutions of public account and responsibility.

At all events, in the American economic republic, nonstatist business operations, big and little, account for most of the production, most of the sales, and a long percentage of the payment of wages, interest, and profits. In aggregate they must not only produce, but must distribute—not only goods, but purchasing power as well. Not only must they distribute purchasing power through wages, salaries, interest, and dividend payment, but also, within limits, they must, and do, accumulate, for capital purposes, a preponderant portion of the savings of the United States. They must apply these savings, as capital, to innovation and investment in new enterprise, or to enlargement of old. The political state intervenes, nevertheless, directly, to control, and indirectly, to influence decisions made by nonstatist or private enterprise in various areas of their activity. It cannot under current practice leave its population at the mercy of blind open-market results.

CHAPTER 8 MONEY, CREDIT, AND CAPITAL

1. The Federal Reserve Board and the Treasury

CLOSE TO THE TOP in the political-economic power structure come the agencies entrusted with power over supply of money and credit, and influencing the flow of capital. Though the powers exercised are governmental, their impact is on the decision-making power of individuals and nonstatist, or private, institutions and enterprises not directly subject to the will of the political state.

The most important instrument is, unquestionably, the Federal Reserve Board of the United States. It works through twelve regional Federal Reserve banks, controlled by it. The Board, whose responsibility is directly to the Congress, is an "independent" agency, not subject to the orders of the President. For practical purposes, this means that it is uncontrolled by anyone most of the time. If its actions or policies were to occasion general revolt, the Congress could abolish it, change its powers, or otherwise deal with it. Occasions of this kind rarely happen. The Federal Reserve Board is rapidly reaching unwritten constitutional status as a co-ordinate power, like the Supreme Court.

Its greatest responsibilities are not contained in written law. They are responsibilities long since assumed by the Board, with general consent, and completely accepted by the American public.

Technically, the Board is charged with maintaining a "sound" national banking system. By remote implication, the responsibility was slightly enlarged in the legislation of 1933 creating

117

the "Federal Open Market Committee" (which is merely the Board of Governors of the Federal Reserve plus five representatives of the regional banks). That committee governs the action of the Federal Reserve System in buying government securities in the market (which may include supporting the price of government bonds), or selling them. The result of these operations is to expand or to contract the available supply of credit and currency, making money available and cheap to borrow, or scarce and expensive to borrow. In carrying them out, the Board must act "with a view to accommodating commerce and business and with regard to their bearing upon the general credit situation of the country" (Federal Reserve Act, paragraph 263). This is as far as the written law goes.[23]

Yet, in fact, by unwritten law the Federal Reserve Board justifiably considers itself mandated to work (so far as credit and money management can do so) for two general purposes. One is to prevent, or at least minimize, inflation. The other is to avoid the ups and downs of the business cycle, or at least to mitigate their effects. Probably it also considers itself under a duty to aid in increasing production. No economist, least of all the Federal Reserve Board, would claim that management of money and credit alone can achieve these results. "Inflation," defined most simply, means a rise in general price level, which for individuals means a rise in the cost of living. This can also be stated as a fall in the purchasing power of the dollar. The Federal Reserve, by expanding the supply of money, under some circumstances can contribute to inflation. By contracting it, the Board can reduce the possibility. Business "booms" may be the result of an unduly large supply of credit or of its misuse—for instance, the use of bank loans to finance stock-market or commodity speculation. Equally, too rapid contraction in the supply of credit can force liquidation of stocks and commodities or raise interest rates, making it unduly expensive for business to manufacture and distribute goods. Such contraction, forced by the banking laws before their revision in 1933, unquestionably contributed powerfully to the financial catastrophe of that year.

In 1914, the Federal Reserve System was constituted primarily to assure that banks should not fail, should have funds to finance crop and other commodity movements, and should be assured of a means of getting cash to pay their depositors. So far as the provisions of the written statute go, this is still its function. In 1933, it was clear that the Federal Reserve Board powers were too limited even for those purposes. Consequently, their capacity to create currency or its equivalent in bank credit and to guide its use was greatly increased. The public certainly desired solvent banks: many had gone under in 1933, causing great distress. But it also wished that the tool of credit expansion and contraction should be used to prevent "booms and busts." At the end of the 1950-1960 decade, most Americans also wished the tool used to avoid inflation and to maintain a stable dollar. The Federal Reserve Board accepted the first responsibility as matter of course. It was ahead of the general public in accepting the second: it undertook to curb credit inflation during the Truman administration. It finds itself now (next to the President and his advisers) close to the top of the management structure of the economic republic.

Here is an interesting point in the unwritten constitution of the republic. The political state is a democracy. Presidents, senators, and congressmen are elected. They may, under pressure to get votes or to be popular, advocate measures and policies immediately attractive to voters but likely to have dangerous economic consequences. One political storm area is that of inflation. It is usually popular to spend money, and almost always unpopular to lay and collect taxes. The political state is thus often under temptation to spend more money than it takes in. There are times, indeed, when this ought to be done—for example, when there is substantial unemployment, when inventories lie unsold in warehouses, when factories and plants are idle. There are also times when overspending is extremely dangerous —for example, when a boom is at its highest, when prices are rising, when everyone is, or thinks he is, making money through speculation. An elected officer finds it extremely unpopular to call a halt early enough to prevent the boom from ending in a speculative debauch, with ensuing disaster.

The Federal Reserve Board—not being responsible to the President—considers itself entitled to assert policies independent of, or occasionally even in opposition to, those advocated by the head of the political state or his Secretary of the Treasury. By expanding credit, the Federal Reserve can make it easy for the United States government to borrow money to cover deficits. By contracting, it can make such borrowing difficult. In consequence, when the Treasury and the Budget Bureau decide that a budget deficit is desirable, they must take into account the attitude of the Federal Reserve Board. During World War II, the Board considered that it must follow the executive policy. Credit was needed for war purposes—and winning the war came first. The writer had considerable contact with the Federal Reserve Board as it adopted this policy in September 1939, when the war broke out, and later, when, after Pearl Harbor, the war financing was worked out. The Board followed executive policy during most of the administration of President Truman. Finally it came to the conclusion that inflation (a certain amount of which is inevitable in any case in wartime) would be enhanced if after the war's end the policy were not changed. The specific question was whether the Federal Reserve Board would continue to support the price of government bonds (then yielding about 2½% interest) by continuing to cause the Federal Reserve banks to buy long-term government bonds in the open market, thus "pegging" their price. The Board thought it should not. If the federal government and its Treasury wished to incur a deficit, all very well; the Board had nothing to say about it. But in that case they must borrow to cover the deficit by offering bonds paying a rate of interest which would attract savings, instead of selling them, at lower interest rates, to the banks, with the Federal Reserve buying to support these prices. A struggle took place between the White House and the Treasury, on the one side, and the Board, headed by William McChesney Martin, on the other. It was resolved pretty much on the terms of the Board; and the Federal Reserve has maintained its "independence" of the White House ever since.

This is not to suggest lack of co-operation. Relations between the Treasury and the Federal Reserve are usually of the closest. Policies as to currency and credit are worked out in a running conference between the two, and in the light of the views of the

Council of Economic Advisers. As a rule they are in agreement. But the President cannot dictate to the Federal Reserve Board, while the Federal Reserve Board can only rarely assert its "independence" to thwart a settled and reasonable economic policy proposed by the President.

Behind this obviously lies a very deep question. The American economic system is not an end in itself. It is a means to an end, namely, a satisfactory life for the American people. Men were not made merely to serve a sound currency system. The soundness of the currency system must rest on the fact that it satisfactorily serves the needs of the population. This is the precise difference between the modern central banking system and the age of the Rothschilds in Europe, or of the Morgan and Kuhn, Loeb groups seventy years ago, when (gold then being the ultimate form of currency) private individuals, groups, or banks could, and actually did, deal with and manipulate the money supply for their private profit.

2. Banks and Banking: Credit and the Interest Rate

BELOW THE Federal Reserve Board and its twelve regional banks are some 15,000 privately owned and privately operated banks by which credit and currency of the American economic republic is handled. These are nonstatist. Nominally, they are "private business." They function independently and they, not the Federal Reserve, make the decisions whether loans shall be made, and to whom, and on what terms. From time to time the Federal Reserve has received power (and used it) to limit the uses for which money may be borrowed. The Federal Reserve can now limit the amount of money that may be borrowed to purchase stocks; this is done by setting (under statutory authority) the "margin" required in stock-market transactions. (Currently the rate of margin is 50%—which is to say, a buyer of stocks must pay at least 50% of the price in cash and may borrow only 50%.) At one time, the Federal Reserve Board was empowered to control the amount of credit available to consumers. Twice since World War II, the Federal Reserve, by regulation, has set the terms of "consumer credit"—that is, has set the kind of paper a consumer must sign when he buys an automobile or furniture or anything else on installment credit, and thus limited its use. This was not popular. In 1947, the Congress of the United States inserted in the Federal Reserve Act a section (paragraph 249) specifically forbidding the Federal Reserve Board to "exercise consumer credit controls"—except in time of war or national emergency declared by the President. The Federal Reserve Board resumed power to deal with consumer credit at the time of the Korean War, but the power lapsed in 1953 and has not been renewed.

Here we touch one of the controversial frontiers of the American economic republic. Power to say who shall and shall not have credit can be pervasive. It can powerfully control not only the conduct of business, but also the lives of individuals. The political state has been cautious in entering that field, either where credit—that is, borrowed money—is used for business purposes or where it is used for consumption.

Yet, under stress of circumstances, it has occasionally done both in peacetime. In wartime, the rules, of course, are different: credit is provided as matter of course to finance war industries, and is controlled for most other purposes. From 1933 on, the federal government provided credit for business through the Reconstruction Finance Corporation. It then empowered the Federal Reserve banks to make direct loans for small business and industry. (A power, by the way, the Federal Reserve banks still have, but do not exercise and do not intend to.) The circumstances providing the stress were that capital markets were then closed for most practical purposes, while short-term credit was very seriously restricted. Accordingly, the political state stepped in and carried on the function—but not willingly. A single federal capital-lending agency could, at that time, have dictated a large area of American activity by giving or withholding long-term loans. The Reconstruction Finance Corporation Act itself, nevertheless, provided that its capital-lending facilities should be available only where loans were not available on reasonable terms through the private markets. It carried most of the capital-lending task until private lenders and investors were once more able and willing to do the work.

In controlling loans for personal consumption, the political state has been even more cautious. This is ground for controversy—another internal frontier of the American economic republic. The Commission on Money and Credit, a private inquiry, though instituted at the request of the federal government in 1958, split about evenly as to the desirability of giving stand-by authority to the Federal Reserve Board to control "consumer credit." There was realization that the use of credit to finance consumption—automobiles, furniture, and whatnot—diverted loan funds into consumption which at times might better be used to finance commercial needs or investment, and that it could add to the violence of ups and downs. The contrary view was forcibly put by Fred Lazarus, Jr., head of Federated Department Stores, and no stranger to consumer credit. He insisted that the American public showed a remarkable power of self-discipline, not going more into debt than was prudent. He therefore opposed giving the Federal Reserve "selective credit controls" (the technical name for this kind of intervention) except in grave emergency.

Yet it is clear that the federal power to regulate the use of credit selectively could be enormously important in planning and maintaining orderly economic growth. In the year 1955, for example, the three major automobile companies estimated that they could sell about eight million cars. The economic department of the First National City Bank estimated (correctly, as it proved) that there was a sound market for about six million. The companies did, indeed, manufacture and sell eight million cars in that year, 90% of which were sold on consumer credit financed mainly by bank loans to finance companies who lent the money to the buyers. The customer signed an obligation to pay the finance company, and the finance company, on the security of that paper, borrowed money from the banks, with which it paid the automobile companies.

But the following year the automobile companies, having oversold the market, sold only four million cars. This was a substantial, if not the major, cause of the "recession" of 1956.

By limiting credit for this sort of consumption in 1955, it would not have been too difficult to keep the automobile business on a steady and entirely profitable level, without hardship to the consumers, and without reducing business activity and increasing unemployment in the following year.

Sovereign control of money and credit, in brief, carries with it sovereign capacity to intervene in allocating the country's resources. Using the money-credit tool, the government may allocate by diminishing consumption and increasing capital. Within limits, it could allocate as between one or another of the major fields of consumption. At present, the doctrine of the republic has been that the political state ought not to use this tool in resource allocation save to prevent stock-market speculation and in time of war. A powerful minority believes that intervention through use of the money-credit tool is justified to achieve accepted goals otherwise not readily attained.

3. The Function of Privately Owned Commercial Banks

COMMERCIAL BANKING is not carried on by the political state. It is handled by about 15,000 banks, a majority (though not all) of which are members of the Federal Reserve System. The member banks account for 95% or more of all the assets held and operations conducted by banks in the United States.

Nominally, a bank is a private corporation, chartered either as a national bank by the federal government (acting through the Treasury) or as a state bank by the government of the state of its location. It accepts deposits and makes loans. There is no direct control over any lending operation if, under standards laid down by bank examiners, repayment is believed certain and credit risks are sufficiently distributed. A bank may decline to accept the deposit of anyone it really dislikes. It can refuse to lend money to any applicant, giving no reason. Subject only to the easily evaded or (more often) nonapplicable prohibition of usury laws (they do not protect borrower corporations), it can charge any interest rate it chooses. No one has a legal right to banking service.

Despite this freedom, most banks in each community know that they must serve all comers conforming to accepted standards of credit worthiness. No one has yet attempted a hard-and-fast definition of "credit-worthy." Yet disagreement is usually rare among banks and merchants. It used to be the boast of the Rothschild Bank in England that it accepted deposits only from its "friends"—and, presumably, followed the same policy in making loans. A somewhat similar practice is said to have prevailed among the big banking houses in New York in the nineteenth century and the first two decades of this century. Partly because of this, the policy of the political state was (and still is) to foster competition and to assure that there would always be more than one or two banking houses available in any community or area. The combination of a more or less competitive system and of public dislike of discrimination by banks on the whole has produced an adequate result.

If in any area there were substantial monopoly, or if discriminatory practice became generally known, one can forecast almost with certainty that the political state would step in. Probably its intervention would take the form of requiring banks (as is required of railroads and other transportation agencies) to establish "reasonable and adequate service and facilities," to establish, observe, and enforce "just and reasonable rates and charges," and of prohibiting giving "unreasonable preference or advantage" to any person, or subjecting any particular person to undue or unreasonable prejudice or disadvantage. This, with some variation in words, is the classic formula of intervention by the political state. Responsible banks and bankers know this. Few would care to force the issue. So far as the record goes, banks, subject to minimum standards, have the absolute responsibility and uncontrolled authority to determine credit worthiness. But if they violate the unwritten yet now accepted standard that banking is a variety of public service, they are perfectly aware that the political state would probably intervene.

Somewhat the same immanent rule prevails in respect of interest rates. What is known as the "prime rate"—the interest charged on the notes signed by borrowers who have first-rate credit—is published in the major banking centers. Determined by a consensus of the banking community, it is nevertheless closely related to the rediscount rate—the rate charged by the Federal Reserve banks for loans made by the Reserve banks to the commercial banks. In general, the higher the rediscount rate, the higher the prime rate. The rate is fixed by supply of money and demand for it in the market place—but the Federal Reserve Board, by using its powers, or some of them, can increase or diminish the supply. For practical purposes, the prime interest rate is uniform and is thus controlled, though not fixed, by the Federal Reserve.

Why this dependence on private or nonstatist institutions for an absolutely essential economic function? I was present at the debate on the question while the banks were closed during the "Holiday," March 4-12, 1933. Why not nationalize the banks and be done with it—treating them as we treat the post office? It was already clear that the commercial banks from then on would be virtually substations of the Federal Reserve System. The reason for continued dependence on private banks was that there was less danger of tyranny, discrimination, mistake, or abuse if the system remained nonstatist, and maintained a reasonable degree of competition. The system would operate more rapidly, more efficiently, more flexibly. Equally, there could be no doubt from that time on that banks were performing a public function. Failure to perform it could only lead to direct political intervention—intervention the political state did not wish to exercise, nor the banks to undergo, nor the public to experiment with.

The late E. A. Goldenweiser, for many years economist for the Federal Reserve Board, a silently great servant of the United States, stated the case to me succinctly. "Banks," he observed, "exist to assure that money gets into and stays in the right hands. That is what banks are for." By "money," he meant, not savings, but money created by the Federal Reserve and by the banks themselves, and loaned by the banks. By "right hands," he meant the hands of men who borrow and use it for the purpose of production and carrying on the legitimate economic tasks of the country—men who will not steal it or gamble with it. "Credit worthiness" includes a judgment that proper use will be made of the loan by men and enterprises able and willing to make that use—and no other. Making these judgments is the prime responsibility of banks and bankers. The American economic republic has consistently preferred, where possible, to leave this task to nonstatist, rather than to political, institutions. It assures a measure of open-market competition to protect against tyrannical use—and it controls the supply of money and credit, so that proper demands may be met.

There are advantages and dangers in any system. Surveying the results, this writer believes the American economic republic has reached a wise solution. Statist banking in a totalitarian system like Communism or fascism becomes at once a direct instrument of tyranny. In a nontotalitarian system, it dangerously tempts to favoritism and corruption. It must be noted, however, that banks may be nonstatist though not privately owned. The economic republic has maintained private ownership as a device for assuring independence of banking judgment and bank management. There are cases in which such ownership has shrunk to ritualistic significance only. I believe this is almost true in the case of the largest banks in the United States now. The Bank of England—corresponding roughly to our Federal Reserve System—is still "privately" owned. But ownership of its stock is, rightly, considered rather as a sentimental or ritual privilege than as a commercial profit-making investment. For practical purposes, Bank of England stock yields a minimal return—and affords holders no power of any kind.

4. Capital: Its Accumulation and Investment

CAPITAL, we noted, is a necessity in any system, including Communist systems. As a general principle, in the economic republic, capital is accumulated ("saved") privately, and privately invested. Once more exception must be taken to the word "private." More than half the capital of the country is "saved" not by private individuals, but by the great, publicly held collectives and corporations. Aside from this, most of the balance (individual savings) is lodged in the hands of great insurance, fiduciary,

and thrift institutions and funds. Investments by the corporations, the institutions, and (in limited measure) by individuals
allocate capital to various activities. Some is artificially manufactured by commercial banks, and great, unreported amounts
are handled by them through their trust departments.

In only a few fields has the American economic republic
called on the political state to guide the flow of capital investment—though these fields are not small.

Capital, its accumulation and investment, is essential both for
the maintenance and for the growth of any economic system.
For smooth operation, the flow must be adequate, even, and
uninterrupted. Without steady and continuous flow of savings
into construction and enlargement of plant, facilities, housing,
and permanent improvement, a good part of the American industrial plant would lie idle over great periods of time. A substantial number of American workmen would periodically or
continuously be unemployed. The public here has a double
interest. It needs the additional housing, roads, electric facilities,
and other construction to supply its wants. It also needs the jobs
and wages this construction generates all along the line.

If the open market for capital worked perfectly, state intervention would perhaps be unnecessary. Unhappily, classic capital markets never did work that way. Investors from time to time
fear to invest, and hoard money. (This is one of the most direct
ways of bringing about a depression.) Or they may choose to
speculate, or seek investments whose return is high, leaving
unserved some major need—for example, low-rent and middle-
income housing. Or those having power over capital allocation
may abuse that power. In distress, or anticipation of it, some
sector of the public is sure to appeal to the political state. In the
economic republic, the state intervenes.

The amount of capital required at any time may vary. An
economy may need capital development—and ought to cut down
on consumption—using its increased savings to build plant and
facilities. This is commonly true in "underdeveloped" countries,
if their level of production is great enough to allow accumulation. Or it may be overdeveloped in production, able to meet all
demands, with capacity and labor lying idle. Then, the need is

for greater consumption and less saving. (Wholly planned economies like those of the Communist states control this, chiefly by rationing. They limit consumption, and channel the balance of their production to capital use. Presumably by ending these limitations, their consumption will rise, while savings, capital formation, and investment will diminish.) The American economic republic has no reliable device for raising or diminishing savings, either by individuals or by corporations.

In classic theory, savings will increase if the interest rate is increased, and diminish when interest rates fall. It is assumed that individuals will save more if they can get 6% on their savings than if they can get 3% or 4%. Alas for the theory; there is no evidence that raising or lowering the interest rate has any appreciable effect on the volume of individual savings. The volume of corporate savings does not depend at all on the interest rate, but on the volume of the corporation's sales and the amount of its profits. Factually, the volume of savings in the United States varies somewhat from year to year. It appears to depend more on the level of business activity than on anything else. The savings volume has proved adequate. Yet a time might come in peace (as it did in World Wars I and II) when means might be needed to increase the rate of savings, and assure its investment in capital construction. The writer believes this need may arise in the not too distant future. One can forecast that the political state will then be asked for assistance.

A cautionary observation must be made. In American folklore, purchase of stock, directly through the stock exchange or indirectly through mutual funds, is called "investment." So it is —for the individual. His "investment," though, is in the stock-market quotation, not in the corporation. Money used to purchase stocks or shares in mutual-investment funds does *not* finance the corporations whose stock is bought—save in rare instances. It merely buys out the shares of a previous holder. There is no evidence that money spent for purchase of outstanding stock ever goes to finance building of new housing, plants, or facilities.

Exception occurs when some corporation gets out an issue of

new stock and sells it to obtain additional capital for use in the business. This happens from time to time. The volume of "new issues" of stock which result in investment of new capital in corporations is tiny compared to the total volume of stock bought and sold on the exchanges.

Stock exchanges do not allocate capital. They shift wealth from one hand to another. They distribute ownership of existing claims (stock, bonds) between wealth holders. Arbitrarily and unpredictably, they add to the wealth of some when stocks increase in price, and diminish that wealth when stocks go down. Properly analyzed, stock markets have only a distant relation to real investment—that is, to actual application of savings as capital to new public or business construction and operations.

This is not to contend that the stock exchanges have no usefulness, or that purchase of stock accomplishes nothing. Neither would be true. It is to point out that stock markets have relatively little direct connection with the business of accumulating savings and applying them to the capital needs of the country. The economic system probably could get along quite adequately without them. There is indirectly a psychological connection. Individuals, corporations, and institutions are more likely to invest and construct when the stock market is booming than when it is slumping. Sellers of stock may invest some of their gains in bonds or other securities representing actual investment —though such use must be relatively small.

In the economic republic, nevertheless, a classic, competitive market predominantly does determine investment allocation of savings—up to a point. This market exists primarily with respect to flotation of bonds, most of which do in fact represent new capital application. But the bond market has been powerfully modified by certain essential facts in the structure of business enterprise. In certain areas, the political state has been called in to provide capital directly, or to influence the flow of capital into activities not adequately served by the competitive market.

The largest single block of "savings," that is, of accumulated money available for investment, is accumulated by business corporations—especially the 500 or 600 largest. The Federal Trade Commission reported that manufacturing corporations alone (these do not include transportation, electrical, public utilities, or retail-trades concerns) saved more than $18 billion in the year 1961. This was after paying taxes and dividends. Rather more is being saved in the year 1962.

These savings result from charges made by these corporations for depreciation and depletion, as an item of cost, of goods or services sold, together with about half the profits—after taxes—of these corporations. These items are included in the price of the goods or services sold. The consumer thus provides the largest part of the capital accumulated in the economic republic. He is not asked whether he wishes to do so. If he wants or needs the goods, he pays the price—part of which becomes capital. Corporations thus accumulating actually do invest the capital their operations thus internally generate. In doing so they intend, as matter of course, to maximize their profits. They look within the framework of their own business for the use they can make of this capital likely to yield them the greatest return. So far, they follow classical economic theory.

But not completely. Their first motive is, invariably, the safety of their organization and the improvement or expansion of their primary operations. They will, therefore, apply capital to expand or make more efficient production of those goods or services they are expected to provide—even though such application may be less profitable than investment in some new or alien field. After providing for this, they will seek investment in lines closely allied to or growing out of their chief lines of business. They will usually stick to investment in the kind of operation they understand, in preference to operations promising more profit but outside their field of experience. Only when these two fields are exhausted will they seek green fields and pastures new—a process called "diversification." Experience and capacity in new business is usually acquired at considerable cost, and businessmen know it. A corporation is not a capitalist roving the market, seeking the greatest return.

More classic are the motivations and actions governing investment operations of the great institutions whose business is accumulating and investing individual savings. Chief among these are the insurance companies (of which the life insurance companies are far and away the largest), the pension trust funds, savings banks and savings departments in commercial banks, and the unknown, unreported, but huge accumulations of personal trust funds concentrated in trust companies affiliated with or joined to great commercial banks. These institutions do seek investments, predominantly in bonds and in mortgages. They do choose those investments bearing the highest interest rate. Competition here is keen. Any of these funds will buy bonds of the government, of the states, or of private corporations, depending on their yield. But they shift to real-estate mortgages if the mortgage interest is enough higher than the bond interest to compensate for the greater difficulty of selling the mortgage for cash in case of necessity. The markets for bonds and for mortgages do in fact "allocate" capital. There, enterprises do bid for capital.

The American economic republic relatively rarely invokes the aid of the political state in guiding the flow of capital. On principle, it rather dislikes the idea. But it does do so in certain areas. It does this because public demand arises for certain kinds of facilities which apparently do not command adequate capital in the competitive market but which a substantial sector of the public wants. Then, in one form or another, the political state steps in to make it more attractive for capital to enter and finance the activity desired. In extreme cases, the political state itself raises the money by borrowing or taxation, and directly provides capital.

Without doubt the greatest field in which capital guidance has been exercised is that of investment in publicly owned operations —those carried on directly by municipalities and towns, state governments, or less directly through "authorities" (toll bridges, toll roads, other public facilities) maintained by them. Bonds, notes, and obligations of these agencies and of local government yield interest not subject to federal income tax. Financially, therefore, they are far more attractive than other investments, especially (as one might expect) to investors whose income is large and whose income-tax bracket is high. In 1962, for example, the thirty-year bonds of private enterprises having absolutely top credit paid an interest rate of about 4½%. Similar bonds of a state enjoying good credit—for example, New York—paid an interest rate of about 3¼%. To an individual whose income-tax bracket is 50%, it is more advantageous to buy a 3¼% tax-exempt bond than a bond paying 4½% yield of which he will have to pay one half to the federal government, leaving him 2¼% net return.

Although the reason for tax-exempt bonds is historical, continued maintenance of the system is unquestionably intentional. States, cities, and local governments desire it. So also do their citizens, because it substantially reduces the interest cost of schools, roads, port facilities, toll bridges, and other facilities they must provide. These facilities do not cease to be part of economic life because they are publicly owned: the business community would be paralyzed if they were not provided. By exempting the interest on these bonds from taxation, the federal government in effect gives a form of tax subsidy. This influences the flow of private capital toward investment in these activities. In this particular case, the source of capital is really "private"; individuals of wealth are predominantly holders of this form of investment. Tax-exempt bonds may not last forever; but the institution is at present well entrenched.

The second substantial field into which capital has been guided by the political state is that of middle- and low-priced housing. A number of devices have been used to make investment in mortgages, whose proceeds are used for housing construction, attractive to investors. The Federal Housing Authority, an agency of the federal government, insures—that is, guarantees—payment of certain types of mortgage loans. By 1960, according to the Commission on Money and Credit (*Report*, p. 190), the Housing Authority had guaranteed about $63 billions of such mortgages. Because of their guarantee, insurance companies, savings banks, and other lending institutions have been willing to lend to individuals money to buy houses at far lower down payments and substantially lower interest rates than home buyers or builders could have obtained without the guarantee.

Savings and loan associations under federal encouragement (including guarantee of deposits) have likewise attracted savings from depositors amounting to more than $20 billion and have loaned these out on mortgages. Through the Federal Housing Authority, the government has organized a corporation, the Federal National Mortgage Association, which buys and sells mortgages to give them a degree of liquidity they otherwise would not have. (This enterprise, incidentally, introduces an interesting novelty. It is a state-operated enterprise—but privately owned. Stock in the corporation is publicly bought, sold, and quoted.) Additional credit facilities are provided to private credit institutions through the Home Owners Loan Corporation, whose capital comes from bonds guaranteed by the United States. The Federal Public Housing Administration places the guarantee of the United States on bonds issued by local housing authorities for construction of publicly owned apartment dwellings. These, being obligations of state or municipal agencies, are tax exempt.

In less spectacular fields, the political state has been asked to channel capital toward specific investment areas. Agriculture is one of them. Federally sponsored credit agencies channel private funds into the Federal Land Banks, the Federal Intermediate Credit Banks, and production-credit associations; about $4 billion at present (chiefly private savings) have been loaned for agricultural purposes. Rural electrification became possible because the federal government borrowed money on its own credit, and directly relent it to co-operatives to build transmission lines connecting rural areas with electrical supply. Most American ocean-going ships are built on loans guaranteed or provided by the federal government, motivated by considerations of national prestige or national defense.

At close of 1960, private loans, partly or wholly guaranteed or insured by federal agencies, stood at about $67 billion, while direct federal loans to various specific activities amounted to about $23 billion more. These are chiefly the accumulated results of the years following the close of World War II. They evidence substantial interventions by the political state, intended to direct long-term loan funds to particular types of investment. The intention in each case was to assure greater flow of investment than would be provided by the uninfluenced open market. In so doing, they allocate capital resources—with the effect of building or providing housing and other facilities which otherwise would not have been provided (certainly not to the same extent) merely by the classic capital market. Currently, about 40% of all residential (nonfarm) housing, for example, is thus financed every year. Far fewer houses would have been built without this intervention.

Availability of money and credit and availability of capital—and the price paid for either by way of interest—exercise an overriding effect on private decisions. They determine whether or not transactions can be made, or plants built, though they play little part in determining the detail of any transaction or the kind of plant. If credit is easy, the merchants and manufacturers can enlarge their operations; if not, their volume of business is held down, their capital expansion limited. When it comes to consumption, a man (prudently or imprudently) will buy a new house or a new car if only a small down payment is required and he can pay the rest of the price over a long period of time. If required to pay a third of the price in cash, he will wait. The total of all these decisions determines whether the whole economic machine moves slowly or rapidly; whether, if rapidly, it moves faster than the year before.

On this rate of activity depend other consequences, not easily measurable. Although we reckon in dollar amounts the "value" of the assets possessed by enterprises engaged in production—and by all of us as consumers—we know very well that these figures are illusion rather than reality. When the economic machine is turning over rapidly, the resale value of this plant or that house is reckoned high. When the great machine slows, values are rated lower. When, as in 1933, it almost came to a stop, these values proved small indeed. Power to speed or retard, exercised in part through the monetary system and the flow of capital, is thus crucial, affecting nearly every cranny of life.

The nineteenth century endeavored to operate its market system on the principle that (coinage aside) money and banking should be left primarily to private enterprises. (Historical vestige of that principle, without significance, remains in the fact that the stock of the Federal Reserve banks is still owned by private commercial banks.) Great private operations intended to expand or to contract credit, whether to achieve speculative profits or as a result of combined private imprudence, were tolerated. Individual groups thus could—and did—tamper with this force for their profit, or, by their folly, affect it with disastrous consequence for everyone.

In retrospect, the wonder is not that the American economic republic now has a controlled system, but, rather, that it tolerated a virtually uncontrolled system until 1913, and inadequate control until 1933.

CHAPTER 9 THE CONTROLLED MARKETS

1. Transportation, Communications, and Public Utilities

DIRECT DETAILED price-fixing has long been settled practice in certain great areas of the economy. Its origin is historical, with roots in past centuries. Modern expansion has expanded impact of this sector. It comprises transportation, communications, and public utilities.

A decisive political battle was fought out in 1906. At that time President Theodore Roosevelt obtained an addition to the early (and not too effective) Interstate Commerce Act of 1887, giving the Interstate Commerce Commission the power to fix maximum railroad rates. This directly transferred power over the price of railroad service from the private companies to the federal government—and the railroads were then the most powerful and entrenched interests in the country. The now standard "just and reasonable" formula for price- or rate-fixing then emerged in federal legislation. Now far away and long ago, the classic struggle for passage by the Congress of the "rate bills" is almost forgotten. Its outcome paved the way for structures of price-fixing found in defined areas of the present economy. The process moved slowly, nevertheless. Not until 1920 did the Congress grant the Interstate Commerce Commission power to fix *minimum* as well as maximum rates—in other words, to set the definitive price of railroad services.

Thereafter the political state, through one or another agency, increasingly came to set prices for all manner of transport, public-utility, and communication industries. A list of the major examples (it is not exhaustive) suggests the scope. Rates are set for motor carriers, including trucks and buses; for air transport and civil aviation; for barge and barge traffic and inland waterways; for pipelines transporting oil and natural gas; for telephone and telegraph lines; for radio and wireless communications. The governments of the fifty states set prices for the intrastate operations of these enterprises.

Each item covers a great industry, and often a whole congeries of allied industries. The reason why the political state could thus invade the theory of the free market was historical. Under classic Anglo-Saxon law, public utilities such as ferries and toll bridges could be constructed or carried on only by grant from the Crown. Such grants sometimes included requirement that the grantees should serve all comers at a reasonable price. Even without such requirement, the English common-law courts held them to that duty. As these and like functions were extended by modern technology into vast enterprises, the historic practice of the Anglo-Saxon political state to fix prices in (originally) small enterprises grew to cover a correspondingly vast economic territory.

But they did not grow unrestrainedly. The American political state believed in, and its Constitution guaranteed the rights of, "private property." The Fifth and the Fourteenth Amendments to the Constitution had settled that, and the courts enforce it. They did not give private property immunity from state price-fixing in enterprises "affected with a public interest." But they did prevent the political state from fixing prices which would be "confiscatory." Private enterprises carrying on such activity were held to be—and are—entitled to a "reasonable" return on their property, though that word has been variously defined and struggled over. By and large, the results have been satisfactory to private investment, especially since they were made reasonably secure through the "natural monopoly" status of the enterprises. Profits of the public-utilities industries sufficiently demonstrate this fact, although the problem is a source of steady controversy. Private enterprise usually insists that it needs high prices, or that its property investment is greater than the state is willing to grant, or that it is entitled to a fair return, not on what was prudently invested, but on the current value of the property (irrespective of its cost), and so forth.

Small libraries evidence the complexity of the theory and practice of rate-making. Yet the system jogs on, in general, satisfactorily—until the day comes when a transport or utility enterprise finds it difficult to make expenses or pay its bills. (Some parts of the railroad system are in that condition at the present time.) Not infrequently, examination develops that the difficulty lies less with rates than with the condition of the industry. Competition from other facilities and technical development changing demand for service cause losses in private operation far more often than unduly low rates. When this occurs, the stage is set for the next step. Profitable or not, the job has to be done; the public needs the service. Then, either a reorganization or a technical change in the industry has to take place—or the state may have to intervene, and either subsidize or take over and provide the service itself.

Acidly one observes that the economic republic opposes direct take-over by the political state, and its direct entry into production whenever production can be carried on at a profit. Where the operation appears to be nonprofitable, opposition ceases. The public-utilities industry carried on—and still carries on—a running campaign of agitation against operation by the United States of the Tennessee Valley Authority, which produces and sells electricity in large volume. (Profits can be made by producing and selling electricity, even at state-set rates.) Nobody opposed the take-over by the City of New York of its rapid-transit system when that system had ceased to become profitable under private enterprise.

Take-over by the political state of the transportation industry (by land, sea, and air), or of communications by wire and wireless, or of the transmission of electrical energy, and probably transport of other energy-producing material (such as oil, gas, and, in future, perhaps coal) is relatively unlikely—so long as these industries are profitable. The public distrusts the power of private enterprises performing these functions enough that it expects the political state to regulate the prices and the terms on which they operate—particularly because, by their nature, these enterprises are natural monopolies. On the other hand, in general it distrusts at least equally the concentration of power which could occur were these functions wholly performed by the political state. Yet because they are essential in a modern industrial country, and certainly to assure the American standard of living, there is little question that the political state would directly enter in and perform the task should private operation for any reason fail to do so.

Meeting the public demand for services deemed essential is one of the unwritten laws of the economic republic.

2. Agriculture and Farm Products

THE ECONOMIC REPUBLIC has caused the political state to fix the prices at which most raw and some manufactured agricultural products are sold. At the base of all economic life is production of food, and food is derived chiefly from land tilled by men. This may not continue forever. Chemists may well discover methods of providing food not based on agriculture. This has not yet happened. Until it does, tilled land and the men who work it are a necessity.

Until the twentieth century, farms, farmers, and farm workers were the greatest single population element in the United States. Their relative proportion has been rapidly decreasing since the turn of the century. In 1920, 27% of American families were engaged in and supported by agriculture. They produced 14% of the national product. Now only 8.6% of the population live on and derive their living from farms. Though their product has absolutely increased, proportionately it is less, amounting only to 3.8% of the present national product. Actual production of farm products increased both absolutely and per man, as chemistry, mechanization, and technical research steadily multiplied the amount of wheat, corn, cotton, oats, and other products capable of being produced on each tilled acre. To feed itself—and more—the American economic republic needs far fewer men and much less land than it needed in 1920.[24]

This may be contrasted with the Soviet Union. In that country, about 65% of the entire population works on farms. Productivity is low. The Soviet Union reportedly has about the same amount of food per capita as did the Russian empire in the closing days of the tsars. Production of food in the United States, on the other hand, now greatly outruns the consumption needs of the country. Evidently the economic republic is now quite able to cut down its agricultural manpower and still have all the supplies needed to feed its people all they wish to eat, and this not because the country is too poor to afford the amount and kind of food it wishes. Few sectors of the American population do not eat and drink about as much as they care to.

Growth of agricultural production beyond the limits of the available market for the product yielded a situation unacceptable to the United States. While the classic open market in agricultural products prevailed, the classic law of supply and demand resulted in price levels so low that farmers and farm enterprises considered they could not live. This led the farm communities to appeal to the political state, and the political state to intervene. A series of attacks was made on specific problems. General intervention came in 1933 with the passing of the so-called Agricultural Adjustment Act. With many changes and amendments, this is the basis of agricultural action today. The effect has been to end the classic market system in the major areas of agriculture, and to put in force a regulated price system, maintained by purchase by the political state, with money raised by taxation.

The method is of interest. The Congress declared that the "disruption of the orderly exchange of commodities in interstate commerce impairs the purchasing power of farmers and disturbs the volume of agricultural assets which support the national credit structure" and that these conditions affect transactions in agricultural commodities "and the national public interest" (7 USCA 601). It undertook to maintain "orderly" marketing conditions so as to establish, as the price paid to farmers for their products, "parity prices." These prices are intended to assure "a gross income from agriculture which will provide the farm operator and his family with a standard of living equivalent to those afforded persons dependent upon other gainful operation"—that is, to assure that farm operators shall make as much income from their work as do laborers in industry. Elaborate calculations to determine "parity" have to be made by the Secretary of Agriculture, and are provided for in the statute.

Not one, but two results were sought. It was considered that a greater amount of the national income ought to be directed toward and put in the hands of farmers, because they needed it, and also because, by putting purchasing power in their hands, the market for manufactured products would be maintained and expanded (7 USCA 1301). The chief purpose, as a number of courts ruled, was to "regain for farmers the favorable financial conditions which they had previously enjoyed" and to "raise farm prices and thus restore to the farmers loss of purchasing power."

On this base, price structures were calculated and built up. These were applied in respect of wheat, corn, cotton, tobacco, rice, potatoes, wool, milk, dairy products, and soybeans, not to mention a number of less important products—for example, tung nuts and honey. Prices are supported for these commodities at not less than a stated per cent of the "parity" price. In practice, the farm producer may deliver to a government-organized, -owned, and -subsidized corporation, the Commodity Credit Corporation, the product in question, which at once "lends" to him the "support price" fixed by the Secretary of Agriculture. If the product cannot be sold by the farmer at a price sufficient to pay out the loan, he leaves it. The Commodity Credit Corporation then takes over the product in payment of the loan— the producer is not liable for any deficiency (7 USCA 1425). The so-called "loan" to the producer is, in effect, a purchase from him at the supported price. If by chance the price goes higher, the producer can pay his loan, take back his product, and sell in the open market. Since production in most commodities outruns the demand, this means that the support price is never less than the market price, and the Commodity Credit Corporation takes over an unsold surplus.

There are many subsidiary devices within this general frame. "Market agreements" are used to make possible combinations of the sale of, for example, milk, and these combinations are exempted from the provisions of the Antitrust law. The President has authority to limit imports—or increase duties—if products are, or are likely to be, imported which would interfere with the price-support program. Quotas may be proposed limiting the amount of production on land in production or of land on which particular commodities may be grown; the proposed quotas are then submitted to a referendum and may be adopted if two thirds of the producers so vote. In that case, an allotment is made of the acreage which may be used, or other method of limitation, and excess production may be penalized. The scheme carries down into great detail. The important point here is the direct and almost complete discarding of the "open-competitive-market" principle. From 1933 on (the tendency had begun before that), the United States simply ceased to rely on the classic economic-market process in dealing with most of its agriculture.

The results were satisfactory to most farmers. From being poverty-stricken, all save marginal farmers became moderately comfortable, and many became affluent. Larger producers made fortunes. The American economic republic, of course, paid the bills, and, in doing so, acquired huge and now unmanageable excess supplies of most staple products. Various plans for more drastic limiting of production either were rejected by the Congress or, when adopted, proved insufficient to match the rapidly growing productivity of any reasonably good land cultivated with increasingly effective modern technique. It is clear that the American economic system can now produce, and can increase production of, almost any given food or agricultural product. True, it is in somewhat the position of the sorcerer's apprentice who learned the magic charm for bringing in the water—but had not learned the charm which would shut off the supply.

One of the frontier questions has been how to adjust supply more nearly to demand and reduce the annual expense, which, being on the order of five billion dollars, is substantial. On the other hand, a country does not starve from oversupply, and the burden has thus far been tolerable. The economic republic has had to choose between an unnecessarily large but prosperous farming community with a concomitant oversupply and a tax burden or reverting to the old nineteenth-century market economy, where oversupply reduced the price enormously—and the producer to poverty. It has thus far chosen the former.

And, clearly, it will not revert to the old system in the foreseeable future, even though it considers the present solution a poor one. It will seek, and eventually find, a way of cutting down agricultural production; but it will not leave producers to the hazards of an uncontrolled, supply-and-demand price. No one, it seems, wants the unregulated free market in agricultural products again.

CHAPTER **10**   THE FREE-MARKET SEC-
TOR: INDUSTRY AND ITS CONCENTRATION

1. Realities of the Free Market

THE LARGEST, the driving, and the most dynamic business
sectors of the American economic republic are coldly classified
as "industry" and "the service trades." The service trades cater
to consumption and therefore are, perhaps, of somewhat lesser
importance. For example, food processing, a manufacture, has
more potential impact on prices and conditions than do retail
grocery stores—classified in the service trades.[25]

These sectors are supposed to operate under the rules of the
free market. So, in large measure, they do. Yet the free market
is in fact a statist device to encourage production and,
through competition, to encourage distribution and also to keep
prices within acceptable bounds. It is a method of fostering
individual and nonstatist initiative and of permitting free entry
by any who wish to build new enterprises or expand old ones.
We have already noted that the free market is a delicate plant.
Whatever businessmen may say or economists may hope, its
existence depends upon the Sherman and Clayton Antitrust acts,
the policing of the Federal Trade Commission, the provisions
included in numerous statutes, and somewhat more than one
new antitrust prosecution by the Department of Justice in every
week of the year. These operations do not merely "police" the
free market. They maintain it. Without them, most of the free
market would rapidly freeze into monopolies or cartels.

However, the free-market device is not applied to certain
great areas.

From the whole area of production and distribution, as previous chapters have shown, three large sectors have already been withdrawn from the assumed processes of the nineteenth-century open market. Currency, credit, and banking aside, the political state has taken to itself a substantial sector in which it directly carries on the processes of production and distribution. In a second sector, it has intervened to control rates, prices, and entry into the market, or has combined these controls. In this sector are the transport and public-utility enterprises. Management of the enterprise, be it railroad, airline, pipeline, or light-and-power company, is not the chief decision-maker. It is less shopkeeper than steward; less merchant than manager. The third controlled sector comprises practically all agriculture.

There is no state control, at least in theory, in the sectors of mining and manufacturing industry, merchandising (commerce), and the service trades. Where they are concerned, the chief impact of the political state is, in theory, conventional. It enforces police regulations. It collects taxes. It influences the supply of money and credit. Enterprises in this sector naturally are affected by these. But each enterprise is expected to make the four chief decisions in commercial life: what goods or services it will supply, what capital investment it will make, what quantity of goods or services it will offer, what prices it will charge.

As will later appear, in some industries the political state exercises more influence or control than is commonly thought to be the case. In them the market, for most enterprises, is not as free and uncontrolled as classic or business folklore likes to assume. Perhaps, indeed, the greatest intervention of the political state lies in its persistent activity to maintain the so-called free market.

2. Industry and Its Concentration

PRACTICALLY all manufacturing industry is carried on by corporations.

Corporations here can be divided into two groups: public and private, though the dividing line is hazy. For practical purposes, the line can be drawn when a corporation (or, more often, its former owners) "goes public," that is, has distributed securities and, particularly, shares of its stock to the investing public through the open financial markets. When this takes place, the management of the corporation automatically changes both position and point of view. No longer is it managing the private investment of an entrepreneur or small group for whom it is, in effect, an employed agent. Increasingly, also, it becomes an independently responsible professional manager of other people's property and a professional supplier for profit of goods or services needed or wanted by the consuming public.

About a million corporations are in existence; about 300,000 carry on all the manufacturing industry of the United States. The exact figure for 1958 was 288,182. This figure tends to increase slowly. Its range includes tiny one-man corporations, with perhaps a single clerk or assistant, to huge concerns, themselves complexes of many corporations, whose stockholders and employees run into the hundreds of thousands. These companies employed about 15,400,000 employees and distributed annually $74 billion in wages and salaries. Of interest is the fact that, of the employees, only 11,500,000 considered themselves "laborers." The rest were white-collar and executive staff—including the presidents. No count has been taken of their consumers. Directly or indirectly, they add up to the entire population of the United States.

Figures perhaps suggest the fallacy in the usual assumption that the American economic republic is by necessity politically wedded to the free market as an institution, though it certainly desires many of its results. Stretching every figure, the chance of an adult American outside of agriculture becoming a proprietor of any kind of substantial enterprise cannot, at best, be greater than one in thirty or forty. Many of these proprietorships (especially in the service trades), indeed, might be found to command a profit less than the pay received by most laborers in skilled trades.

Market mentality obviously extends beyond proprietors, or heads of enterprise. Family, friends, hopeful employees, and members of the younger generation identify themselves, perhaps, with proprietorship or enterprise managers. Yet, at best, one might find a possible 15% or (as an outside figure) 20% of the adult population whose economic interest or aspiration lies with the "market." When politicians refer to "business," this is the group referred to.

One factor gives greater political appeal to the open-market idea than these numbers would imply. It is psychological. Anyone in America may dream of becoming an enterprise head, if not an entrepreneur. The brakeman in the railroad yard can aspire (however distant the chance) to become president of the road. (Quite often the actual president was once a brakeman.) The employee in the big steel company can hope to reach a top rung in the ladder, though in fact steel companies now more often draw for their executives on highly educated men entering from the professional services they retain or employ. Yet the employee can, if he wants it badly enough, attain that training and education. The upward route, however arduous, theoretically is never closed. Class societies like those existing in Europe in the nineteenth century and caste societies definitely and effectively closed the ranks for all but a tiny upper group. Men can in the United States aspire to be President of the United States, or of General Motors. If the road is impossible for them, they can hope that their sons may achieve comparable success. It happens often enough to underline the possibility.

The transcendental margin of the United States (hereafter discussed) early provided free elementary and (somewhat later) secondary education, and now provides a great measure of higher education. This is increasingly available to everyone really desiring it. Absence of a social class system has removed the chief artificial barrier to hope. However forbidding the statistical probability, employment or individual entry in open-market industries offered—and still offers—a direct path to individual progress and possible superlative position. This was, and still is, the political appeal of the free market. Opportunity to enter as a proprietor, opportunity for the small proprietor to grow, opportunity for the local boy to make good, opportunity for the professional student to attain a powerful position, opportunity for a man to be his own master, holding a position not dependent on an employer's opinion of him—this is the bid made by the open market for a political constituency which will defend it in the arena of the political state. It is an appealing platform.

Realities, as matters work out, considerably contract the dream.

In 1958 the fifty largest manufacturing corporations carried on 23% of all the industry of the United States; they carried on 17% in 1947. The largest 200 manufacturing companies in 1958 carried on 38%; they carried on 30% in 1947. Since they have been slowly increasing their share, a fair estimate would be that the 200 largest carried on 40% of all manufacture in 1962, based on their actual sales and shipments of goods. Add 400 or 500 more, and these would account for between 60% and 70% of all manufacturing in the country, if not more. Their proportion of direct ownership of plant, property, capital, and assets probably was somewhat greater. Since World War II, they appear, gradually and implacably, to be increasing their share.

Figures here understate the case. A great part of the "small-proprietorship" group takes its life from the large corporations. An aspiring entrepreneur cannot set up a gasoline station (a "small business") without making a contract with a large oil company to supply him with gasoline; that company, not he, makes the chief economic decisions. Many small proprietors in service trades, from automobile dealers to drugstores, depend on similar contract, agency, or franchise relations with powerful suppliers. Even in direct manufacture, substantial numbers of small fabricators, nominally "independent businessmen," survive because some large automobile or electronics manufacturer buys their product. Without this buyer, they would cease to exist. Most of the 200 large corporations thus group around them a great many small businesses living in the penumbra of the great neighbor. Their "market freedom" is to please their chief customer. It differs little from the opportunity of the laborer or the employee to please his chief and gain promotion thereby. The "market" here is not "free" in the classical sense —if, indeed, the classical free market ever did exist. It is controlled or guided by sheer weight of the large productive enterprise.

All industries do not exert the same power in affecting conditions within the economic republic.

Steel, oil, and chemicals, for example, being basic, exert or can exert enormous influence. All industry, as well as much direct individual consumption, must rely upon and eventually come to these industries for essential material or supply. Concentration within these and similar industries, therefore, impinges on the supposed free market far more than concentration in less essential matters. Two, three, or four companies might, for example, monopolize or dominate the business of making tobacco pipes (in fact, four companies do manufacture 80% of them) or house slippers (where there is no concentration) without great consequences. Concentration in any of the primary metal industries is a different story. It happens that concentration runs high in the most important industries. "Concentration" is here defined "arbitrarily" as control of half or more of an industry by four or fewer corporations. The definition is not wholly satisfactory. There are industries in which the over-all rate of concentration is low although in any given region one or two companies have an overpowering position. Aluminum is almost entirely produced by four companies, as is 80% of tin cans and tinware.

The Bureau of the Census has defined the "largest" corporations as those shipping out a billion dollars' worth of products or more—this includes shipment of all kinds of products. Corporations of this size handle many lines. The four largest companies accounted for 75% of the motorcar business, for 53% of steel products, for about 60% of all aircraft, for 78% of synthetic fiber (rayon, nylon, and the like), for 69% of tractors. Four companies shipped 80% of all primary copper, and about half of electrical appliances, tubes, and control apparatus. The same four electrical manufacturing companies sold 92% of all electric bulbs. Running over the whole long and diverse list, we find that the largest corporations in industry pretty steadily emerge as having half or more of the market in most of the primary manufacturing lines, and that such corporations also manufacture more than half of many of the lines directly consumed, for instance, cigarettes, sugar (taking cane and beet sugar separately), and photographic supplies.

Concentration in large corporations thus is a phenomenon if all manufactures are aggregated. It is markedly a phenomenon in the production of most of the essential raw materials.

It is a logical phenomenon. If competition means anything, it means that the strongest eventually prevail over the weakest. Classical economics made the implicit assumption that the "strongest" were presumably the most efficient—a justified assumption if "efficiency" means more than producing the best quality or at the lowest price. Brute financial size enables a large corporation, unless restrained from doing so by law, to quote a lower, or inordinately low, price to a large customer in order to drive a competitor out of business; or to quote a lower price than it charges elsewhere to bring a customer into its fold and away from a rival. Or such size can enable the corporation, as purchaser, to exact a price from a supplier dependent on it so low that others stay out of that business, or to survive bad times or falling prices which put weaker enterprises out of business. An enterprise with great laboratories, thus likely to be a step ahead in technical developments, can make itself master of a field and of those able to work in it; International Business Machines has gone far toward doing this in its own province. Efficiency therefore means more than producing a better product at a lower price. It may mean organizing such a volley of advertising and publicity that the customer buys the brand rather than the product, while the corporation satisfies a custom-made public habit even more than a particular need or taste. Cigarette advertising is a case in point.

Forces, financial and psychological, are here involved. In most of the great lines of consumption, indeed it is never quite clear whether the consumer buys tobacco or a motorcar or whether he buys the most seductive publicity picture on a poster. Efficiency may mean neither good quality nor reasonable price; it may mean, as the head of a great cosmetic concern once observed, creating and satisfying an emotion, or (as some drug and toothpaste manufacturers have discovered) creating and allaying a fear.

This is the arena in which market forces are freest, freest in the sense that the profit motive and the desire to make money find fullest scope. There is no room for doubt that production and distribution have been stimulated. One may question the concentration, yet in the context of the American economic republic it has proved able to supply the market at least as rapidly as the market was prepared to take the goods. It has called into existence a variety of new products which the public apparently wanted—or was made to want sufficiently to buy them.

3. Problems of Antitrust Policy—Artificial Competition

DOES the American economic republic wish concentration or fear it? Maneuvers in the political state reflect a steady and unresolved conflict. One group of forces desires as "free" a market as possible. Concentration is considered a danger; therefore the political state should be used to limit or prevent it. Less vocal forces consider that the free market yields a large by-product of waste, confusion, erratic conditions, higher ultimate cost, and greater unemployment. The problem was under study by a Senate committee in 1962 (the Special Committee on Antitrust and Monopoly), constituted by the Senate Judiciary Committee and headed by Senator Estes Kefauver, when the free-unconcentrated-market advocates appeared to have the law on their side.

The Clayton Act, implementing the Sherman Antitrust law in many respects, was a principal product of President Woodrow Wilson's "New Freedom" and of his crusade against concentrated wealth and business. Cobbled up by later amendments, it now requires the Federal Trade Commission to pass, in advance, on the merger of one corporation with another, and on the purchase of assets of one corporation by another. Merger is one of the familiar methods by which a corporation grows (the other principal method is to compete with such strength that its competitors lose their business to it, go bankrupt, or leave the field). Mergers substantially tending to "lessen competition" may be forbidden.

The Supreme Court of the United States in 1962 had to deal with the problem of concentration of economic power *without* any element of monopoly. The third largest manufacturer of shoes (Brown) proposed to merge with a chain store controlling more than 1,200 outlets (Kinney). The government sued, asking an injunction against the consummation. The court found that the four largest shoe manufacturers, including Brown, produced 23% of the nation's shoes, and Brown was third largest, and also that there was a "trend toward concentration." Brown and Kinney together would control 7% of retail shoe stores, and 2.3% of all retail shoe outlets of all kinds. Monopoly was thus not even remotely involved. But, said the Supreme Court (*Brown Shoe Company* v. *United States,* June 25, 1962), the dominant theme pervading the Clayton Act (with amendments) was "fear of what was considered to be a rising tide of concentration in the American economy," and of "the threat to other values a trend toward concentration was thought to pose" (pp. 20, 21), and "Congress saw the process of concentration in American business as a dynamic force; it sought to assure the Federal Trade Commission and the courts the power to break this force at its outset and before it gathered momentum" (p. 22). Its desire was not to protect "competitors," but, rather, the "institution of competition." The court noted a remark of Judge Learned Hand's in his famous decision ordering dissolution of the Aluminum Company:

Throughout the history of these [antitrust] statutes it has been consistently assumed that one of their purposes was to *perpetuate and preserve, for its own sake, and in spite of possible cost, an organization of industry in small units which can effectively compete with each other.* (Italics mine)

Considering that the antitrust laws required that "tendencies towards concentration in industry are to be curbed in their incipiency," the court forbade the merger of Brown with Kinney. Consequently, the law of the political state has been successfully invoked to prevent, not only monopoly, but concentration, at least if brought about by merger, though the result may be greater cost to consumer and community.

To this writer it is clear, despite all this, first, that the American economic republic has not yet closed the question, and, second, that small-unit competition will not become the norm in most manufacturing. In most lines in the current phase, small-unit technique belongs to the past, increasingly so as automation (too expensive for small units) enters the field. The values threatened by concentration (referred to by the Supreme Court) need further examination. They have never been carefully stated. Men who had lived with them, like the late Fiorello La Guardia, considered small-unit competition a menace to decent life and standards of living. Statesmen of the labor movement, for example, Walter Reuther, of the United Automobile Workers Union, consider that a system of this sort without controls makes for bad allocation of resources in both production and distribution. I think it likely that political insistence on an artificially maintained free market (itself a contradiction in terms) will presently be accompanied by equally artificial limits on its results. The republic's justified refusal to accept monopoly did not necessarily imply acceptance of sweatshops, instability of employment, or a good many other by-products of free-market small-unit competition. There is no great danger, of course, that an undue rash of small-unit competition will be the result, irrespective of the line of thinking held to be the intention of Congress by the Supreme Court of the United States. Corporations will continue to expand. They will do so by stiff competition. Large corporations are in existence; not many will shrink. Modern conditions being what they are, the largest will tend to prevail in the competitive market. Competitors not of comparable size will be eliminated, not through merger, but through commercial conquest. Meanwhile, the small units will clamor to the political state for help or protection, or both. The result is likely to be not nineteenth-century competition, but twentieth-century oligopoly. Atomization as a remedy will not do. I doubt if we can bring back the England of the late eighteenth or early nineteenth centuries, or that we would tolerate it if it returned.

Other students do not agree. See, for instance, a powerful argument against concentration by Professors Walter Adams and Horace M. Gray, *Monopoly in America,* published in 1955. "Monopoly" as they defined it means substantial economic power held by a small group of enterprises.

However the dispute is resolved, the constructive side of concentration needs to be studied. It is substantial. The large corporation can generate most of its own capital, freeing it from "finance capitalists." It can plan and construct ahead, assuring that future needs for production will be met. It can devote adequate assets to research and technical development, maintaining continuous growth in efficiency, innovation, and development of new products. It can keep up investment of capital when small enterprises must hoard assets, giving a measure of stability in cyclical recessions. It can pay adequate wages, and within limits maintain continuity of economic operation, minimizing unemployment. Values thus realized may prove as persuasive as the values fostered by preserving through unlimited small-unit competition the individual's chance (not more than one in thirty or forty) of becoming proprietor, irrespective of the cost to the community. The great debate has, I believe, yet to reach its outcome.

At this point we must turn to a portion of the supposedly unregulated market where the debate has taken place and has been resolved. As in the case of agriculture, in a number of industries, and notably two, small-unit competition did reach a climax, occasioned distress, and the political state was called in to change the system.

4. The Semicontrolled Businesses

WITHIN THE AREA of nominally uncontrolled enterprise there are a number of great industries operating under systems of planning. In them, price is not regulated or fixed, but measures are taken by the political state to adjust supply to demand. Their effect is, naturally, to prevent undue supply from depressing the price, and, conversely, to prevent shortage of supply from unduly raising it. These plans usually involve control of supply by one or another device, while competition is maintained between a number of private enterprises in production and distribution. This is a limited use of the "market" principle. Were there monopoly, the principle would not apply; the monopolist would fix the price as it chose. On the other hand, if there were not large-scale production and relatively high concentration in a few corporations within the industry, the devices used for equating supply to demand probably would not work. The two principal illustrations are the petroleum industry and the sugar industry. Attempt has been made to apply the principle to bituminous coal (an unconcentrated, highly competitive industry), but with indifferent success. Sporadically, using the power of the political state to buy stockpiles of strategic materials, temporary measures have been taken in the nonferrous-metals industries—copper, zinc, lead. The driving motive in all of these cases seems to have been an oversupply of the product, threatening or causing violent fall in its price.

Contrary to nineteenth-century doctrine, the economic republic has come to consider an unduly low price as dangerous (if not as immoral) as an extortionately high price. Someone loses property values, if not life values, when the price paid does not cover reasonable cost of labor and other production costs at levels yielding the producers, employer, or employee, as the case might be, an acceptable minimum remuneration.

There would perhaps have been no plan for oil had it not been for the discovery in the late twenties of a number of new and immensely productive oil fields, notably in Oklahoma and in Texas, which flooded the market with crude oil. Supply then rapidly outstripped demand. The day arrived when oil was selling on the coast of the Gulf of Mexico at a price less than the cost of pumping it to the wellhead. No one, it seemed, thought this condition should continue. Various abortive attempts at control plans were attempted—some impractical, some prohibited by the antitrust acts. In 1933, under the National Recovery Act, a plan was worked out by which the supply of oil taken from the wells was prorated and limited. Consumption of gasoline and other petroleum products was estimated, and production allowed in about that amount. When the National Recovery Act was held to be unconstitutional in 1935, a separate statutory system was promptly enacted carrying forward the essential elements of the plan. By the Interstate Oil Compact (a treaty among the oil-producing states, approved by Congress), these states agreed to regulate the amount of production from their wells. The federal government agreed to supply estimates of consumption through the Bureau of Mines in the Department of the Interior. The Congress made transportation of "hot" oil —oil produced in violation of the prescribed limits—a federal offense. The companies refining oil established the practice of accepting for purchase none but lawfully extracted crude oil.

Within this limit, crude oil was produced, bought, and sold, and the refined product (chiefly gasoline) was marketed under competitive conditions by the oil companies whose refineries supply the product. The oil industry is less concentrated than some others; but eight large enterprises refine more than half the output. The result, as might have been expected, and presumably as desired by all hands, was an "administered" price— a level set by one or two large corporations, followed by the others, modified from time to time. Since a measure of competition exists, the administered price cannot be too high, else competitors would undercut. Yet everyone's interest is to get as good a price as he can, so a reasonable price results. At all events, a price level acceptable to producers, refiners, and the public has been reached since the plan came into operation thirty years ago.

A somewhat similar plan governs the supply of sugar. Two elements are involved. One is the beet-sugar industry. A large part of the American sugar supply, especially in the central part of the country, is manufactured from American-grown beets. The other element is sugar refined in this country from raw cane sugar grown in tropical countries outside the United States. The price of cane sugar if uncontrolled would be low enough to drive American beet sugar out of the American market. This could be prevented merely by maintaining an import duty high enough to prevent imported cane sugar from entering the market here. But in that case the result might well be an unacceptably high price for beet sugar. The swing element was obviously the amount of sugar allowed to be imported from the cane-producing countries. Accordingly, under the Sugar Act of 1934 and the various subsequent revisions of it, the political state, acting through the Secretary of Agriculture, annually determines the probable consumption of sugar in the United States. He then assigns about 60% of this consumption to the beet-sugar industry, and permits the import of raw cane sugar at relatively low duty, to be refined in the United States, up to the amount needed to match estimated consumption. Quotas for import are assigned to the various producing countries. Naturally they are avidly sought—producers in these countries sell their quota sugar for a higher price in the American market than they can obtain elsewhere. These low-duty quotas are fixed, but may be varied, so that the sugar supply, beet and cane combined, shall approximately balance demand. Again we find use of the control of supply to assure that the price shall not be unduly low, and use of competition between domestic sugar companies—again, within limits—to assure that the price shall not be unduly high.

The two plans serve as illustration. Both use the market. Both affect the market by assuring reasonable balance of supply and of demand. Though no one admits the fact, the administered price has a great deal to do with making the plans work acceptably—as they have for more than a quarter-century.

The writer surmises that the future may see more, rather than fewer, of these plans. The fact appears to be that the American economic republic, while in form insisting on it, in fact does not accept unlimited application of the free-market principle. The costs are too great, though not necessarily in terms of price —from time to time free-market prices may be very low. But the free market can also exact a terrible toll from producers, investors, workers, and the community. Its logical result—the survival of a few strong enterprises, rich enough to survive losses bankrupting their competitors—is oligopoly. And the American economic republic, if the Brown case is the whole story, does not accept that either.

The two plans given are perhaps the most highly developed. Less-institutionalized forms of them appear in a number of other major industries—notably the nonferrous metals. They usually take the form of permitting the President from time to time to limit importations, thereby maintaining the position of the domestic supplier.

Still another form, yet unevaluated, relates to the so-called "defense industries." Here the government is for all practical purposes the sole buyer. Single-buyer situations have been christened by economists (may Euripides forgive the bastard Greek!) "monopsony." Whatever this system is, it lacks one major element of a free market—competitive buying as well as competitive selling. In practice, the government develops close working relations with a number of large corporations having known capacity to produce, and achieves a relation more nearly approximating partnership, than adversary, position. In any case, the government has, within limits, capacity to force the seller to meet its terms or stay out of business. The proportion of this market to the total has never been adequately calculated. A fair guess might be that its direct or indirect effects dominate more than 10% of American industrial activity.

The unrealized fact is that competition, carried to its logical end under current interpretation, does not maintain a continuous free market. Logically, it makes for alternations between an intolerable degree of competition and a surviving monopoly—whereupon the political state is expected to intervene, break up the monopoly or perhaps atomize the oligopoly, and start the process all over again, or, perhaps, industry by industry, to change the system.

5. Stability under Competition—the "Administered Price"

CONCENTRATION—a trend toward oligopoly or its fact—is the outstanding phenomenon of the supposedly uncontrolled sector of industry and commerce in the American republic. Stabilization arrangements, formal (as in the case of oil and sugar) or informal (as in the case of sporadic use of government buying for stockpiling or defense), are almost equally conspicuous.

Both are carried on against an obbligato of insistence on the "values" of free competition, small-unit competition, and small proprietorship and business generally. Clearly the head wants one thing, the heart something else.

Two lines of evolution are possible, and both have manifested themselves. One is an industry-by-industry attempt to avoid the social waste and cruelty of the small-unit competitive system. The oil and sugar plans reflecting older solutions have been made in various other industries—notably the bituminous-coal situation, though there elaborate legislation failed to change the situation very much. Powerful labor unions, like the International Ladies' Garment Workers' Union, endeavor to stabilize prices and competitive conditions for the benefit of a certain industry as well as themselves. Use can be made, and often is made, of the semimonopoly power of a highly organized labor union to stabilize, just as use can be made of concentrated corporate ownership.

Probably, as industry after industry reaches a point of impact on community welfare, such stabilization plans will be worked out. The impact may be because the industry approaches monopoly and the community becomes alarmed, or because, being highly competitive, it imposes too great cost and suffering on its labor and its entrepreneurs alike. A third impact may take place—as it did in the steel industry in 1947 and as it has steadily in the field of low-cost housing—when there is failure to provide supply to meet an obviously unsatisfied demand. My belief is that impacts of this kind will continue, industry by industry, and that industry-by-industry plans are likely to be made to resolve the problems. Since private plans are outlawed by the antitrust acts, the political state will be called in—either by labor or by unsatisfied consumers or by the corporate proprietors, as the case may be.

The other line is frank acceptance of size, oligopoly, and of the phenomenon of the "administered price." Dr. Gardiner C. Means, in his trail-breaking *Pricing Power and the Public Interest,* proposes to classify corporations as "collective enterprises" when they reach a certain size ($100 millions of assets). Above that arbitrary line, corporations should be "audited" as to their economic performance. Higher earnings and lower taxes thereon should be permitted to those corporations found to have performed well. Good performance would be judged by adequacy of supply, by lowered price, by cost of its capital. Means would try to shift the thrust of incentive, making economic performance, rather than mere profit, the major motive. It is an idea that requires much more development and more study. Other solutions propose arbitrarily placing oligopolist enterprise in the class of public utility and transport enterprises. Pursuit of either line is possible, but presents difficulty in determining standards and organizing adequate administration. An "Economic Performance Board," auditing the performance in one industry, would be presented with an enormous task. It would have to develop conceptions of "good performance" and objective tests. Equally, subjecting large corporations in industry to the not-too-satisfactory techniques of public-utility commissions probably would retard operations and might or might not produce a more satisfactory result for labor and for the consuming public.

The fact appears to be that all parties want a good deal of market freedom, but do not want certain of the free market's logical results. A degree of concentration and of oligopoly and of administered price, responsibly handled, seems to have provided a more or less acceptable balance. When it does not, industry-wide plans seem the most practical solution.

It must never be forgotten that industry in the American economic republic has proved more productive than any other organization of industry in the world. (Communist industrial organization, as yet, cannot compare with it.) Atomization into small units would be a plain and impractical attempt to tread the road to yesterday. Unwritten standards of the republic insist that the market power achieved shall not reach the point of exploitation. But they also insist that demand shall be supplied, and that technical progress shall be maintained. When any of these standards are violated, the political state is expected to intervene—and in fact regularly does so.

A variety of discipline thus controls concentration. Where necessary, the political state may help as well as forbid. It, too, needs satisfaction of the needs of the three groups of citizen-subjects of the economic republic: consumers, labor, and producers. When all is said and done, the lot of many millions of Americans is ultimately at stake. Their welfare is the ultimate test of the system, and of the success or failure of the economic republic.

CHAPTER 11 LABOR: ITS POWER AND PRICE

1. The Problem of Organized Labor

ORGANIZATION OF LABOR and the means by which wages reached levels acceptable to employees and the community were absolute necessities as the nineteenth century came to a close. Every charge of exploitation of labor then made was fully justified. As production rose in the first two decades of the twentieth century, little justification could be found for that exploitation on any ground. The unorganized laborer could only take what the employer was willing to pay, under conditions the employer set. He held his job at the pleasure of the employer or his agents. Few who remember conditions prevailing in the factories and plants of that era would endure them now.

The struggle for labor's right to organize is classic in American history. In the latter nineteenth century and the early twentieth century only two methods of redressing an intolerable wages-and-hours-of-work situation presented themselves. One was massive intervention by the state, either the federal government or (as thinking then went) the state governments. The other was building up the bargaining power of labor by organization sufficient to give it the power to strike.

For practical purposes, organization with capacity to strike began to be general in the third decade of the twentieth century, though many industries were still unorganized. Beginning was made in 1914 when the political state, through the Congress, enacted that the "labor of a human being is not a commodity or article of commerce," and that labor organizations were not to be held "conspiracies in restraint of trade" under the antitrust laws. In 1932 came the Norris–La Guardia Act, virtually preventing federal courts from issuing injunctions in labor disputes—with narrow exceptions—and exempting labor unions from antitrust laws. The sweeping nature of this statute has recently been reaffirmed. In 1935 the National Labor Relations Act (sometimes called the Wagner Labor Act) directly declared the right of employees to form, join, and assist labor organizations, and to bargain collectively through representatives of their choosing and through labor unions. Their management, internal administration, rules of admission, and discipline are unregulated. With modifications, the Taft-Hartley Act of 1947 carries the recognition forward. During this period an elaborate structure of labor unions grew up, capable of meeting employers, including the greatest corporations or combinations of them, on more or less even terms. Many labor organizations now are wealthy in their own right.

The defined position of labor and its organized units achieved in 1935, and the increase of the power of labor that followed,[26] was a conscious choice of the American economic republic. A key section of the Wagner Labor Act has in fact become a part of the effective constitution of the economic republic. It reads:

Employees shall have the right to self-organization, to form, join, or assist labor organizations, to bargain collectively through representatives of their own choosing, and to engage in other concerted activities for the purpose of collective bargaining or other mutual aid or protection. (29 USCA, paragraph 157)

The purpose was to remove a source of industrial strife by encouraging methods of friendly adjustment of industrial disputes. The hope was to restore equality of bargaining power between employers and employees. The policy of the United States was stated to be

the elimination of obstructions to free flow of commerce by encouraging collective bargaining

and by

protecting the exercise by workers of full freedom of association, self-organization and designation of representatives of their own choosing for the purpose of engaging the terms and conditions of their employment or other mutual aid or protection. (29 USCA, paragraph 151)

The political state claimed (and the United States Supreme Court recognized) its power to enter this field of economic organization as an exercise of its right to regulate interstate commerce. Manifestly enough, this visibly extended the area of federal power.

The National Labor Relations Act recognized the collective associations known as labor unions, but did not undertake to settle how they should be run. It legitimatized them as bargaining agents for groups of workers and provided a method (election) by which workers could indicate that choice. It did not undertake to instruct either employers or labor unions as to bargains they could or could not make. It did insist that where workers organized, or were organized and so chose, agreements as to wages, plans, and benefits must be negotiated with the group and not with each individual. Implicitly, rather than explicitly, it recognized the right of a labor union to strike, just as it implicitly accepted the power of an employer to go out of business. Therewith it left the respective economic groups to work out their problems, and it set up the National Labor Relations Board to prevent specified unfair labor practice both by employers and by labor organizations. No attempt whatever was made to limit or regulate the terms of any collective bargain. Balance of bargaining strength and the limits determined by business possibility were supposed to be adequate in causing both sides to reach satisfactory accord. Restrained though the act was, it changed the face of things.

As in the case of most political changes, the National Labor Relations Act recognized forces already in being. Labor unions were moderately powerful before 1933; their total membership amounted to about 2,900,000 members. In 1962 the membership was about 16,000,000. Most of these were, and still are, loosely affiliated as autonomous units in a central organization (then the American Federation of Labor; today the American Federation of Labor–Congress of Industrial Organizations) comprising in all about 13,000,000 members. A number of unions (some of them, like James Hoffa's Teamsters' union, of great aggressiveness and strength) remain unaffiliated with this central body. Should they act in concert to do so, the combined power of organized labor could completely paralyze the operations of the country. It virtually could immobilize all individuals in the large urban communities and could cripple much of the life of rural areas. In fact, this has never happened; labor unions are many and they have no monolithic organization. The United States has yet to experience a "general strike," and there is no present likelihood that it will.

The effect of current labor legislation is to legitimate negotiation and, if need be, strikes in respect of particular disputes over wages, hours, and benefits, in particular plants and with particular employers, and in some cases with particular industries.

But labor unions are not supposed to use their capacity to bargain and to strike outside the framework of purely economic disputes over pay and conditions. Only rarely has attempt been made by labor unions to bring their power to bear on unrelated political matters.

Herein labor in the American economic republic differs sharply from labor organizations in most other parts of the world. Outside the United States, labor organizations frankly and overtly use their power to strike for political purposes. They may strike in protest against government policy (as French unions did in connection with some aspects of the policy of the French government toward Algeria) or to prevent an unwanted government from assuming power. Just prior to World War II, political use was made of the French labor unions to prevent the then French government from manufacturing airplanes for its defense. American labor unions possibly have the physical power to do this. But use of the power to strike for such purposes has not been legitimated by the political state. It is contrary to the overwhelming consensus of American opinion, and probably contrary to the overwhelming consensus of the members of organized labor unions themselves. In labor power-centers (as also in management power-centers), there is strong bias against using economic power to obtain political ends.

This is partly reflected in the provision of the National Labor

Relations Act requiring every labor organization and the national or international organization with which it is affiliated to file annual affidavits that their officers are not members of the Communist party or affiliated with it, and that they do not support any organization teaching overthrow of the United States government by force or by unconstitutional methods (29 USCA 159 (h)). Communist doctrine, of course, contemplates making specific use of labor organization, not to obtain good pay and working conditions, but to break up and overthrow any government the party does not favor. Failure to comply with the provision requiring affidavits puts a labor union outside the pale of recognition.

In sum, labor unions are economically very powerful; politically, far less so. A labor union which does have the steady support of its members in wage and hour matters commonly finds itself quite unable to persuade its members to follow the union leader's desires in political elections.

2. Labor as Power

THE INSTITUTION of collective bargaining and the economic terms reached through it are, like administered prices, on the frontier where the economic republic is in full state of evolution. The power to strike can affect lives and comfort of vast numbers outside the area of a particular controversy. Such stoppages can collide with the policy and interest of the political state, just as administered prices can be pushed to a level of similar danger. There is question whether the supposed limits imposed by economics, market conditions, and equality of bargaining power sufficiently restrict collective-bargaining results to protect the public. A union in New York City felt justified in striking—thereby stopping all construction—to obtain a twenty-hour work week! This was obviously absurd; either it amounted to a demand for overtime pay far beyond twenty hours or it amounted to a demand that the men should receive extravagant pay for half the normal work week so that they could (and most of them would) hold other jobs as well.

An association of airline pilots whose pay ran from $12,000 to $17,500 annually tied up the Christmas traffic of the United States with a demand that pay should range up to $40,000 a year. A flight engineers' union tied up a substantial sector of civil aviation from June to September of 1962 over a trivial jurisdictional dispute. In a great many smaller but crucial industries or operations, work stoppage can paralyze a large fraction of the industrial and transportation processes of the country. Demands can be, and in some cases have been, made to obtain pay based less on performance of work than on threat to victimize great numbers of the public as well as employers if the demands are not met. Distinction between this and the power of gangsters to levy extortion here becomes hazy. Nor is it distinguishable from the power of a monopoly to levy an unconscionable price for an indispensable service.

Again we encounter the immanent power of the political state. Abuse of power causing appreciable distress inevitably causes a cry that the political state shall intervene. Where the situation created by use of economic power is intolerable, the political state almost invariably does intervene, albeit reluctantly. The fact that it can and will do so, indeed, is the ultimate restraining factor persuading holders of economic power in the republic to be moderate in their use of it.

Professor John Kenneth Galbraith (in *Countervailing Power*) has pointed out the danger in a situation where the corporations carrying on production can administer the price, and the labor unions can determine the rates of pay, fringe benefits, and hours of work. It is easy, he suggests, for the labor unions to claim about what they want, threatening a strike and economic paralysis if they do not get it. It is easy for the corporations carrying on industry to accede to the demand—and push up their administered price to cover the increased cost with a little additional profit. This, Galbraith suggests, is a plain invitation to cost and price inflation. His argument suggests that the political state may have to step in, setting limits to the process. In fact, a few years after he had written this analysis, the administration of President John F. Kennedy intervened to moderate demands of the steelworkers for higher wages, to modify the decision of the steel companies in setting their new prices, and to restrain a union of flight engineers from enforcing their demands by a work stoppage. In all cases, the political government acted through persuasion (not unaccompanied by intimation of the wrath to come) rather than by laying down specific solutions. But it was clear that the political state would find ways and means of imposing a solution if needs must, by expanding legislation and enforcing it.

In place of doing this, the federal government thus far has intimated that economic "guide lines" should be worked out, indicating how far either labor or management can safely go in asking wage increases or shortened hours, or in pushing up prices. This is a long way from setting up institutions (courts, tribunals, or commissions) to determine settlements. Plainly the debate will go a great deal farther, and the economic jurisprudence of the republic will be developed as it proceeds.

Economic power is secondary to political power. Sophisticated holders of it know this. Rather than push matters to a point where the political state must intervene, and set up institutions (this automatically entails loss of part of their power), they have a powerful motive toward maintaining moderation and restraint. But it is doubtful that this influence will indefinitely postpone institutionalization.

Organized labor in recent years has not greatly increased its membership. The figure has stood for some years at about 16,000,000, though the actual labor force of the country has steadily grown. In part this may have been due to diminishing confidence in the character and standards of some of the men who direct labor unions. Some have been tyrannical, some corrupt. Some have endeavored to establish unconscionable controls over the lives of their members. In recent years, a substantial sector of the labor force has endeavored to get the best wages and hours it could without subjecting itself to demands, dues, and in some cases unauthorized, but entirely real, interference with their personal conduct and choice of life. Organized labor is now in somewhat the same position as was industry before 1920. Then, owner-managers considered their prerogatives

absolute, ignoring a rising resentment against their administration of affairs. Eventually they found themselves shorn of a good
deal of their power when the political state moved in—though
the frame of organization was not changed. The same results
could happen to organized labor. The framework blocked out
by the National Labor Relations Act is probably permanent and
not likely to be drastically changed. But specific application of
it—for example, defining the limits of labor organization, regulation of the amount and collection of dues, and other control
devices—can be added, and some labor practices may be made
illegal, or otherwise altered. The power to strike is likely to be
controlled. One of the wisest labor leaders, David Dubinsky,
of the International Ladies' Garment Workers' Union, has observed that a stroke of the legislative pen could wipe out overnight much of the position of organized labor achieved through
the years.

In point of fact, labor organization, collective bargaining,
and the handling of wages and industrial rates probably have
been one of the largest (perhaps the largest) contributing causes
of adequate income distribution in the American economic
republic. Without them, wages conceivably might have been
kept at the subsistence level predicted by both Marx and Malthus. And in that case, as Marx had argued, mass markets
would be far smaller than they are now, and industry correspondingly smaller and less progressive. Power of labor unions
to demand and secure a greater share of income for workers
was recognizably one of the tools used for economic development. In aggregate, the result has been good: an increase in
"real" wages for American workers of about 3% annually. An
American workman can expect that ten years from now he will
have about 30% more actual purchasing power than he does
today.

The excesses and difficulties and dangers in the power position of labor, great as they are, nevertheless are capable of
solution. They will be resolved, as in considerable measure they
have been solved on the management side. In the case of
labor, as in the case of management, public accountability is
being insisted on and the curbing of excesses is being dealt with,

case by case. Accumulation of precedents, growth of law, and legislative evolution of institutional power—these are part of the development process of the economic republic.

3. The Price of Labor

THE POLITICAL STATE has fixed a minimum price for labor, organized or not, in most areas of employment since 1950. This is done under the Fair Labor Standards Act (29 USCA 206). It now provides that "every employer shall pay to each of his employees who is engaged in commerce or in the production of goods for commerce" wages of not less than $1.15 an hour. The rate rises to $1.25 per hour in September of 1963. A companion section prescribes that no employer shall require a work week of longer than forty hours, unless he pays his employees time and a half for the overtime. The provision does not apply to certain limited classes of workers, chiefly those working in local retail establishments; nor to farm labor, fishermen, foresters, and lumberjacks or workers in canneries and certain other trades.

Steady pressure exists to extend the provisions of the Fair Labor Standards Act to the uncovered trades. The theory is crude but direct. A business enterprise unable to pay wages at this level is thought to have no right to exist. An enterprise able but unwilling to pay this wage rate is considered a danger to the healthy economic life of the community.

These are minimum standards. The real fixing of the price of most labor is done by a contract embodying the result of a "collective bargain" between the employer and a labor union representing the employees. Many of these "bargains" are, in effect, industry-wide, or have that result. Elsewhere we noted acceptance by the political state of labor unions, not only as bargaining agents, but actually as a locus of economic power. The bargains struck have (as they should) pushed wages to far higher levels than the statutory minimum wage and standards.

Largely because of labor unions, wages have steadily risen in the United States. A gradually increasing share of product of business has accrued to labor. Hours of work required have diminished to an average level slightly under forty hours per week. Most American workers have merged from the "proletariat"; they now live as members of a middle class. For practical purposes, collective bargains struck by labor unions fix wage levels in most of American industry, although substantial areas, geographical and industrial, remain outside their direct influence.

The chief contribution of the political state to this sector of the American economic republic was the grant of the right of representation to labor unions, protection of their personnel and organization from counterattack by employers, and enforcement by the National Labor Relations Board and by the courts of the right of negotiation and of contracts made.

Capacity of labor unions to exact and, by agreement with employers, to fix the price of labor can, of course, result in a labor price dislocating the economic structure—particularly when a small group of laborers represented by a union has power to tie up a whole industry or community by depriving it of an essential supply. The wage level can lose all relation to the worth or productivity of the service. The shoe is then on the other foot: instead of exploitation of labor by an employer or producer, based on his economic power, the labor group may seek to exploit both the employer and the public.

Only recently (specifically, in 1962) has the political state seriously wrestled with this problem. The case presented was a strike (in the nature of a jurisdictional dispute; their real quarrel was with the airline pilots) by the flight engineers' union, paralyzing one of the larger airlines. President Kennedy, as he had intervened to prevent a rise in steel prices, intervened, to oppose the strike. In the end, the flight engineers lost, and the airline resumed operation without them. In the longer future, it is difficult not to foresee establishment of the principle of compulsory arbitration in industries whose continuous operation is of public interest—a principle not yet established in the American economic republic, which still operates on the fictitious theory that labor contracts embody the results of a free-market "bargain." Thus far, neither business nor industry nor organized labor has accepted compulsory arbitration. Yet the consuming public, increasingly irritated and slowly becoming alarmed at periodic disruption of their personal lives, seems almost ready to cut the Gordian knot. It will probably find the sentiment echoed among many union laborers (though not among labor-union leaders). Few workers like to have their jobs and pay interrupted because some quite extraneous labor union chooses to shut down essential industries without which nothing else can function, so that they are thrown out of work though they have no interest in the dispute. But few labor leaders enjoy the prospect of having their power modified by the political state—just as few businessmen (for example, the managements of the steel companies) welcome intervention in their price-making and other managerial powers.

Here again we are at one of the frontier areas of the evolving American economic republic.

Monopoly is forbidden to employers and owners. But the antitrust laws do not apply to the organization of labor. Where monopoly is permitted in industry (as, for instance, in transportation or public utilities), the political state has been required to intervene and regulate the price. Comparable development, though with quite different rules, is no less possible in the field of labor. Yet it must be remembered that labor is not a commodity, despite classical nineteenth-century market theory. It relates to the worker's life, and to social ideas as to the fair share of labor in price and profit, and to the ideas of the community as to labor's contribution to production. Over against almost any form of labor there now looms a shadow—the shadow of the automated machine. Exact rules for resolving the price of labor in any given situation will not easily be worked out. This is why labor and industry alike have thus far clung to the "collective bargain" and to the myth that it somehow reflects the "market," and why the political state is not anxious to enter that particular arena. As the "market" recedes into the background, as power elements become the greater factors, the developing unwritten law of the economic republic must push into new ground. Sheer economic power now is not, in the public consensus, adequate justification for the price of anything, either commodities or labor.

Discernible in the workings of the labor-management system, there is a tendency for labor unions to require, and for courts to recognize in growing measure, the "right" of a workman to a "job." This is most often accomplished by including in union contracts the right of a workman to "seniority." The man longest in a job cannot be discharged until all his juniors have been laid off. When rehiring is begun, he has the right to be rehired first. Another provision requires "separation pay"; in case of discharge, he is entitled to a stated amount of added compensation. These rights continue even though the employer may move his business from one state to another. Increasingly, the preoccupation of labor unions is not merely with the rate of pay, but with assurance that jobs will continue. They would really like guaranteed jobs for their members for life or for a term of years. As automation threatens to reduce the need for labor, there is increasing concern. A new variety of right—it is variously described as a "property" right, a "status" right, or a "contract" right—of a man to a job is gradually emerging, urged by and enforced through his union, for better or worse.

Nominally, all this is a "market operation," a "collective bargain" between equals. Actually, it is a balance struck between unions having power and employers having power, limited more or less by an impersonal economic factor—the capacity of the employer to raise his price or in some fashion to reduce costs elsewhere to compensate for the higher cost of labor. As long as the struggle is kept in balance, as long as the employer does not merely raise his price to cover demands of labor, as long as the public is willing to pay and the employer can collect the increased price, the balance will work out acceptably. But if the power of the union can demand a wage industry cannot pay, or if the industry is required to raise the price for its goods or its services to a level the consuming public cannot or will not accept, trouble must be expected.

Foreseeably, in that case, the political state will have to devise new methods. It will seek to avoid this as long as it can. Fixing wages by the political state or any agency of it involves it in all manner of problems. Yet the public will not—and should not —tolerate, and by consequence the political state cannot permit, a prolonged breakdown in the economy as a whole or indeed of any necessary operation in it. Should either occur, the political state must intervene. That fact in itself has thus far exercised a moderating influence on both power groups. How long the uncontrolled balance will continue depends on the good sense and good will of both sides.

CHAPTER 12 THE WELFARE STATE: THE SOCIALIZED SECTOR

IN EVERY ECONOMIC STATE there is a stratum of individuals temporarily or permanently unable to pay for their current needs with current work or previously accumulated wealth. Neither the economic republic nor Communist societies can avoid this.

Some individuals in this group are defeated. There are those who have refused or been unable to accept social obligations and social discipline, who prefer to be (or at any event act as) vagrants, criminals, or irresponsibles. A larger group may be defeated by addiction to alcohol, narcotics, or other habits rendering them unable to work and pull their weight in the social and economic boat. Still others are defeated by injury, physical ailment, or bad health, putting them out of the running. Some societies assume that all these men and women are products of the prevailing system. The economic republic prefers to believe that they are or may become masters of their own fate. In either case the situation has to be met. This group is comparatively small.

There is a second group defeated by age and the passing of years. Defeat by time comes inevitably to all who live beyond a certain span of years. In the nineteenth- and early twentieth-century free-market economies an enormous majority of the population in all countries proved unable to accumulate wealth sufficient to meet this period of life. Classical economists begged the question, and merely accepted the thesis that failure to acquire sufficient wealth for this period was presumptively a defect or fault of the individual. This, I think, was error. Under a fully competitive system, a workman could indeed acquire enough if (a) he went through life in good health, (b) was continuously employed, and (c) competently invested his savings. Included in "competence" was capacity to anticipate and hedge against inflation. Few men could, or even now can, expect a lifetime of perfect health, uninterrupted employment, and sure-fire skill in investment. Aside from a tiny class possessing comfortable wealth, the aged wound up living as state-supported paupers or, more often, on the charity of their relatives. The agricultural system of family farms made a kind of human adjustment to this. The industrial system did not.

And always there were children. Infants are wholly dependent. Growing children can contribute a trifle. Youth somewhat more. Full participation means being an adult. Meanwhile, they must be fed, educated, equipped with tools to work, and launched in adult life. Responsibility is placed on the family to take care of this. If the families cannot do this from their own resources, then help has to be provided.

Finally, there is unemployment, sporadic or permanent, not caused by irresponsibility, addiction, or bad health. The individual is willing to the extent of his capacity, but the opportunity is not there.

Obviously, the combined total of these individuals falls into two groups. Some are defeated primarily by the operations of the social-economic system itself. These include the wealthless, the aging, the unsupported children, and the unemployed. Some are defeated by themselves, or, more accurately, by the combination of their lack of moral or intellectual strength and a set of circumstances with which they are unable to cope.

The economic republic considers that it has three responsibilities. The first is to the victims of the system. There, the system can be made to provide. The second is to the irresponsibles, the addicts, and the sick. Responsibility here is scientific as well as personal. Not only do the individuals have to be kept alive, but the business of the state is to seek ways and means for prevention and cure. Disease can be prevented by research in health; possibly, though not certainly, addiction likewise.

Psychiatry, sociology, and criminal research may eventually reduce the incidence of all these. The task is one of relief, public-health measures, and social public health. For the third responsibility, the political state must arrange relief and assistance for those who (for these and any other reason) lie outside the areas in which wealth is distributed through salaries, wages, or otherwise by the economic system.

The American economic republic recognizes all these responsibilities. This combination has been christened "The Welfare State." There is no foreseeable likelihood of its discontinuance. Controversy there was, and will be, but it relates to the methods to be used, the extent of the responsibility, and the degree to which the conception shall be applied. The political state, represented by local agencies (towns and cities, counties; to some extent, state government), has traditionally dealt with some part of these problems for centuries. The transcendental margin (hereafter examined) in the United States added a great number of private agencies. Organizing the responsibility as an expression of national function by the federal government has been very recent.

Crisis conditions compelled the federal government to intervene in 1933. Before that year it had not done so. Factually, the American complex long before then had evolved into a national economy. In the breakdown of that national economy no state government (let alone local government units) could possibly cope with the cumulative tide of unemployment and resulting destitution. The 1933 intervention really picked up, in crisis conditions, an accumulation of nationally unfinished business. The issue had been present for some years; crisis then demanded that it should be met. A series of emergency measures, which will always be associated with the name of Harry Hopkins, evolved at length into the present organized instrumentalities.

These proceeded on two theories. Individuals displaced from time to time by the economic system, or defeated eventually by old age, needed wealth sufficient to meet their necessities when they no longer had wages or pay checks. Accordingly, the political state undertook the task of collecting from time to time from them, or from the system, enough wealth to be held for their account, and paid out in time of need. In effect, it forced savings by them in conjunction with their employers, and supplemented it by insurance arrangements, and paid these to unemployed or aged in their time of need. Second, the federal government could provide, or assist local governments in providing, direct relief in areas where wealth could not be accumulated by or on behalf of the individual himself. Many students, myself included, consider that old-age and unemployment insurance (and the same would be true of health insurance if it is eventually adopted) are really additions to wages and salaries, whose payment is deferred. In the areas of pure relief, of course, there is true "socialism"—taxes are directly levied to take care of individual need or misfortune.

By 1961, total federal expenditures for all these groups amounted to $37 billion. Of this amount, $22 billion represented, not taxation, but forced savings, collected through the Social Security system from employing enterprises and from workers as payment for social insurance. These were in effect deferred wages. In addition, and quite apart from the Social Security system, a comparatively small but rapidly rising amount was annually being collected and held for or applied to social-security benefits by nonstatist pension-trust funds. Many workers in old age collect pensions from these funds in addition to the payments they receive through the federally established Social Security system.

Slightly over $15 billion was collected by the federal government through taxation and applied directly for assistance or "relief," usually supplementing funds raised by local government. Taking all items together, between 7% and 9% of the gross national product of the United States is annually directed by way of forced saving or through taxation to the Welfare State for distribution.

It cannot be said that the economic republic has allowed its less fortunate stratum to go without food or shelter. Actually, an unemployed workman drawing insurance pay is better supplied with goods and services than a fully employed and paid workman in the Soviet Union or Czechoslovakia. The lowest "reliefer" is economically placed far above the level of the "proletarian" classes in most parts of the world. The republic is still not satisfied, nor will it be satisfied until its "lower stratum" has shrunk to its irreducible minimum of irresponsibles and incapables, and perhaps not then.

The Welfare State reached its present form of organization with the advent of the Department of Health, Education, and Welfare under President Dwight D. Eisenhower's administration in 1956. The new department, with the Treasury as administrative partner to handle social-insurance funds, inherited general jurisdiction over two great instruments. The best known is the Social Security Act of 1935, subsequently amended. This provides for forced savings—insurance premiums collected from employers and employees—to be accumulated and paid in pension form to individuals attaining retirement age (presently 65 for men) and, within limits, to wives, widows, and children, with particular privileges for parents caring for children. Payments from this fund should not accurately be included in "state" assistance. The funds have been collected by levy on employers and employees. They really amount to delayed payment of wages or salaries earned during the individual's working years and paid to him in his old age. About $12 billion was paid out under this scheme in 1961.

The other instrument is the so-called Unemployment Compensation Act, also passed in 1935, and now administered under the Social Security Act. The arrangement undertakes to pay to an involuntarily unemployed individual a stated portion of his average monthly wage for a period of six months of unemployment. In case of a major economic depression, the period probably would be extended. In addition, facilities (not too effective) are provided to help find the unemployed individual a new job. Not quite $4 billion was expended for these purposes in 1961. Obviously the amount of payments varies with the extent of unemployment.

In less defensible addition, nearly $5 billion was expended for pensions and compensation to veterans of past wars. Some of this is dubious as provision for "welfare." The writer, a veteran of World War I, is entitled to veterans' benefits, though his need is nil—certainly not enough to set up any claim on the economic republic. Some veterans, of course, are in the "defeated" class, and their defeat in some cases (especially where they were wounded in war) may be directly related to their war service.

More than $4 billion was paid for "public assistance," and this is real. In this field need does exist. There are uninsured aged, there are dependent children, there are mentally and physically disabled, and there are blind. Usually through grants to the several states, arrangements are made for this relief, and the several states themselves pick up an added part of the load.

The remaining expenditures (nearly $5 billion) deal chiefly with hospital and medical care, medical facilities, medical research, maternal and child-health services, and public health. There is a current proposal for a comprehensive medical care, forced-savings, and insurance program. It is at present under debate, exciting violent opposition—and no less forceful protagonists, including the President of the United States.

Classical economics included an assumption that every man will be as lazy as he dares be. Quite possibly this was a valid point. Especially in weaker and less-educated sectors of the population, there has always been a propensity to be supported in idleness if it can conveniently be arranged. President Franklin D. Roosevelt picked up the relief load from necessity in 1933, but did not like it. President Harry S Truman, who brought the system to its present form in 1950 (the so-called "Welfare State" as we know it now), had two views about it. He wanted involuntary defeat or misfortune taken care of, but he also wanted to be sure that individuals do not surrender the struggle merely to get insurance benefits or relief payments. When a man is out of a job, it is not always easy to determine whether it was his fault or desire, or his employer's fault, or the result of the ups and downs of the free market. When an individual is sick, it is not always certain that he is not malingering. Even when an individual is old, it is not certain at what point years take from him his capacity to contribute. (Being over sixty-two, this writer could call it a day instead of teaching, writing, practicing law, and in the course of it earning a living—but this would be mere surrender, not defeat.)

The welfare frontier of the economic republic will be in conflict as long as human nature maintains its present form. One current of public opinion, more nearly classic in its idea, asserts that the cost of the Welfare State is already too great, that the workers carry too much of a load to provide for too many drones, and that these burdens retard the country's work and production. Another, taking a more generous view of human nature, believes that alleviations of the free-market casualties by the welfare route should be carried much further—as evidenced by the support of the new and somewhat expensive program for medical care to be paid for by additional forced savings collected in the form of Social Security insurance.

An economic analyst, endeavoring to separate himself for the moment from the transcendental margin, introduces a different thought. Thirty-seven billion dollars taken annually from the prosperous of the country and spent among the less prosperous increases and tends to make continuous the market for goods and services. Capacity to produce these exists. The Welfare State puts purchasing power in the hands of individuals who otherwise would not have it. Consequently, the item is sometimes referred to by businessmen (who are always anxious to sell) as a "built-in stabilizer"—the maintenance of effective demand and therefore of a market sector which will continue more or less irrespective of those economic ups and downs euphemistically called "booms" and "recessions." About 8% of income paid to individuals has been "socialized" and applied to "welfare" needs. To that extent the erratic distribution of income by the free-market system has been, if not tamed, at least kept in some bounds of humanity. At all events, a large proportion of the former casualties has been better taken care of than by poorhouses or private giving, and one effect is to maintain a current of private consumption.

Moral arguments, of course, enter a different field. Does the economic republic become too soft, too flabby, too lazy if it fails to apply the ruthless law that those who do not or cannot work shall live in acute misery? Is a hardy race maintained in greater vigor by the severity of individual economic struggle, with attendant individual fear of the ghastly consequences of defeat? I do not know. The American conscience never considered acceptable the results of such struggles as one finds them described in Dickens' *Bleak House* or *Oliver Twist,* or in Upton Sinclair's *The Jungle* (which was not a great exaggeration of Chicago in 1900). Neither does it morally accept the right of a drone or parasite to exist. Probably, therefore, the conflict will go on, continuously endeavoring to separate the malingerer from the weak, and the drone from the unfortunate, dealing harshly with the first and generously with the second, and having some difficulty in making the distinction.

Quite aside from either relief or welfare, however, the economic republic has an unsolved problem on its hands. This is the problem of unemployment.

Current statistics (1962) indicate a total unemployment of slightly over 4,000,000. The figure should be looked at a bit critically. Under the definitions of "unemployed" applied in Western Europe, American unemployed would be counted more nearly at 2,500,000. Taking the larger figure, this would be a little over 2% of the population and in the neighborhood of 5% of the "working force"—that is, individuals who can be and normally are expected to be employed. At the smaller rate, it would be considerably less.

Economists commonly consider that of this number about 2,000,000 are not only unemployed, but unemployable—the irreducible minimum of people who are mentally, morally, or physically unable to contribute. The figure also includes a certain number of employables who are temporarily not working as they change jobs or readjust to some dislocation. The real problem, therefore, is with the other 2,000,000. These presumably can work and would work, given a "reasonable" chance. Theoretically, they are out of a job because the free-market system does not offer them a readily available opportunity to go to work.

To the extent that this is true, it is a blot on the scutcheon of the American economic republic. Under any theory of American life, anyone who can work and wishes to work should be able to work, to contribute, to participate. This is quadruply true in the case of young people. It is immaterial that these individuals are not in grave want, and that most of them are supported through Social Security, public assistance, or otherwise. This is not the point. The life of a dole-beneficiary, let alone a state-supported pauper, is too close to the life of a prisoner. The torture of being without occupation is a barbaric form of cruelty. Under it, disintegration of men, though not irremediable, is unlimited and dangerous. Means can be found —and must be found—by which virtually anywhere a man desiring work can go to work, not, perhaps, at the thing he would like to do, but at tasks enabling him to say at nightfall that he has contributed something to the day's work of his time.

Comparison here with the Soviet Union is inevitable. Communist states boast that they have no "unemployment." The state always employs all. This is perhaps Communism's finest affirmation. Unhappily, it does not stand up. In a Communist society also, men are separated from the system—and their jobs—because they are in conflict with, or defeated by, the system. Thereupon they are frequently called "delinquents," or even "criminals." The charge may be insubordination (meaning that they do not get on with their boss) or sabotage (meaning that they were lazy or worked badly enough to spoil the product) or perhaps that they are "disturbing factors" in the organization (meaning that they are critical of it), or any other reason why. As a result, there have always been more prisoners in Russian concentration camps than there have been unemployed in the United States. In Stalin's time, sheer police savagery resulted in putting at least 12,000,000 (6%) of the Russian population behind barbed wire; they were used as slave labor on state projects. Khrushchev, to his credit, has materially ameliorated the severity. There are, at a sophisticated guess (no figures are available), about 4,000,000 in concentration camps or forced residence now. These equate to the American figure of unemployed. If the American economic republic has not solved the problem, neither have Communist societies; and as between the lot of prisoners in Siberian compounds and the lot of an individual drawing unemployment or on relief, there is no comparison whatever. The Communist system did not eliminate unemployment, but merely gave it another name.

That, of course, does not excuse the American economic republic. Economically, it is quite able to support a large percentage of individuals in enforced idleness—its production is ample and capable of increasing. It ought to be able, in fact it is able, to give them work. The plea here is not to economics, but to social justice.

PART THREE

Value

CHAPTER 13   THE VALUE SYSTEM AND THE "TRANSCENDENTAL MARGIN"

IT IS FASHIONABLE (as Professor Walt Rostow has pointed out) for economists to pay their tribute to the Protestant ethic. The phrase is ascribed to a German philosopher, Max Weber. It is not unfair to note that some of the writers are not well acquainted with the Protestant ethic. Most merely emphasize two or three of its tenets which tended to encourage industry and thrift and liberate economics from earlier trammels. Actually, it embodied the driving value system of nineteenth-century America. The Protestant ethic has proved far more dynamic in the development of American economics than has perhaps been assumed. For that reason, it is well to try to state its chief principles.

1. The Protestant Ethic[2]

THE UNITED STATES, *par excellence,* is a child of the Reformation. Protestantism was in fact one of the substantial reasons why the United States was colonized in the first place, and why, during its early history, its civilization took the form we now know. The drive of the Protestant movement settled our West during the early nineteenth century; it was, perhaps, at its strongest at the very time that the mechanist theory first propounded by Adam Smith as an argument was adopted as a theory of the state by Great Britain. In the last half of the nineteenth century, its theories, and the practices induced by its principles, had a vast causative effect over great parts of the United States. This is not to suggest that the United States was chiefly animated by altruistic and religious motives. It is to assert, with some confidence, that the doctrines held, and their actual effective impact on human beings, modified in substantial degree the results of the classical economic theory. Further, the operative principles were only secondarily economic. Primarily, they were philosophical in the deepest sense.

To the Reformation Protestant, the function of man on earth was no mystery. Man's chief end was to glorify God, and serve and praise Him forever. This he could do with every human action, and in every phase of his life. He glorified God by worshiping in church, or by making a first-rate pair of shoes, or by performing services in such fashion that he made his employer and his associates and those around him happier. A sin was not necessarily the performance of an act bad in itself; it was the choice of a lower course (possibly itself good) when the choice of a higher way was available. Always in the presence of God, and without intercession by any earthly agency such as pope or priest, the responsibility was continuous and unlimited from childhood to grave.

> Work, for the night is coming
> When man works no more

ran the familiar hymn; and men believed it.

"Whom the Lord loveth, he cherisheth," was an essential part of the doctrine. To have served the Lord did mean, save under rare circumstances when martyrdom might be needed, that men were rewarded in this world, as well as in the next. That the honest servant should be well paid, and should move above the status of servant into that of a wealthy entrepreneur, was entirely in order. That the merchant should accumulate a fortune was entirely in accord with the theory that the laborer was worthy of his hire, and that the Lord would forward the fortunes of his faithful servants. The making of money did not, of course, necessarily mean that the maker had been a true servant of the Lord; the Devil also could give increase; but the inscrutable processes of Divine justice would take care of that in due time. Prima facie, prosperity resulting from economic activity was not a proof of guilt. Rather, it was proof that the Lord had destined the fortunate one for greater fields of work and wider service.

That, however, did not mean that the fortunate one, having received his reward, could do as he pleased. To the contrary: the greater the reward, the greater the obligation. Even as the reward of virtue was received, it was conscripted in the larger service of the great ideal—that is, in the service of the community according to the value system then prevailing. The Protestant ethic did not in the slightest socialize production. But it conscripted income and profits in a fashion rarely equaled in history. True, there was not direct conscription as to what must be done with the affluence resulting from high pay or great profit. The principle was general. "Thou shalt love thy neighbor as thyself"; and the law and the prophets hung on this corollary to the First Commandment. It was the business of the men who followed this system of ethics to seek where and how that impersonal and selfless love should be given effect.

It is amazingly easy to ridicule this simple, swift, and surprisingly dynamic faith. Writing in the latter part of the twentieth century, one is struck both by the fact that this faith is so simple as to be considered naïve, and by the fact that the major principles inculcated by it are still the major motivation of most Americans. At all events, the results are undeniable. They can even be measured quantitatively. Without question, few if any men lived up to the full measure of the obligation imposed by this ethic. Violators appeared on every side, and violations frequently were carried out with apparent impunity. All men did not live up to this majestic standard; no men lived up to all of it. But the premises were so widely accepted that they acted as pressure on men who may have had no use for the philosophy itself. Willingly or unwillingly, few men failed to pay some tribute to its appealing force. Long before the state began to be a major instrument in economics, the force of this branch of the Protestant ethic made itself evident through the construction and operation of private institutions from whose resources we derive much of our going power today.

Through coincidence of history, the controlling drive in America happens to be the Protestant ethic. The Catholic ethic and the impulsions of Judaism appearing much later reinforced, rather than derogated from, the earlier principles. Reinhold Niebuhr has pointed out that the Protestant ethic primarily emphasized the motivation of universal and selfless love—men were not justified merely by saving their own souls. The conception of justice remained more dynamic in the Catholic tradition. When Catholicism became strong in the United States, this added element gave greater form and perhaps greater application to the less-defined Protestant theory. Today the instinct for what is called "social justice" is powerful in the United States—powerful as a political principle as well as a principle of private ethics.

No less powerful is the instinct of more or less selfless love —the conception that men in some measure are their brothers' keepers. Anyone who has watched through the last decade the steady and regular appropriations for foreign aid pass the Congress of the United States knows very well that these appropriations were not passed primarily to give Washington an added tool of foreign policy. Unquestionably, that motive also was present—motives are usually mixed. But the driving motive has been the essential generosity of the American people—a generosity which is not merely the satisfaction of a temporary emotion, but the response to a duty laid on them by their conception of man's relation to the universe, and to a rational— or perhaps a personal—God, depending on his philosophical synthesis. The results are numerous; a few illustrations may be given.

Quite early in the history of the independent American republic, secondary schools were established as a result of this impulse. In the early days these were private, privately endowed, and privately established. One finds them in tiny New England towns, like Brigham Academy, in Bakersfield, Vermont, or Tilton Academy, at Tilton, New Hampshire. Greater and more famous ones, like Phillips Andover, Phillips Exeter, and St. Paul's School, were imitated straight across the entire northern tier of the United States. A New Englander familiar with this era can go to a town in Iowa or Oregon and find himself in a familiar atmosphere almost at once. In that tradition, the two men who worked out the patents which largely served as basis for the aluminum industry and who happened to be graduates of a small college thus endowed, Oberlin, left the stock in the Aluminum Company of America they received as compensation as part endowment of that now-famous institution.

This modifier showed its force in the one period in American history when it really threatened to be dominated by the classical conception of capitalist economy. From 1860 on, the era of great fortunes proceeded apace. At its climax—let us say 1890 to 1910—great wealth was the most conspicuous, if not the most important, product of the economic system. This was the era of the Vanderbilts, the Goulds, the Rockefellers, the Carnegies, the Gates, the Fricks, the Whitneys, the Morgans, the Belmonts, the Astors, and the Huntingtons. In his autobiography, Henry Adams observed that the ultimate and controlling principle was that of great wealth, and that the men of great wealth, having the last word, were judges of the system. They could not be judges of themselves because they were the expression as well as the principle of the then society. The statement is too broad; this was not wholly the case. But at this particular moment, the Marxian formula—that wealth increasingly concentrates in the hands of a tiny group of individuals—seemed almost justified.

Marx reckoned without any modifier of transcendental quality. He scoffed at it himself; his experience in Europe led him to believe that no such principle would have any effect; indeed, he thought ethical principles existed to defend and to maintain the class in power. An apostate from his own hereditary religion, he may have been prejudiced against the belief that any religion could affect the actions of men. In contemporary Europe, it is fair to say, there was no great evidence that motives other than those of selfishness dominated the scene. As we have seen, classical economic philosophy justified selfishness, only asking that it be somewhat intelligent.

Under the American system, at all events, the conscription

of profits, legitimate or illegitimate, by the Protestant ethic went steadily on. Andrew Carnegie's fortune was largely spent first in providing public libraries the length and breadth of the United States, and later in endowing universities and providing foundations which would continue this kind of work. The Carnegie Corporation today is the best-known survival nearly two generations later. But as one steps into the library of some tiny Midwestern town, not infrequently one will discover in some not too obvious place that the library was founded by the old Scottish steelmaster who in his days of poverty had profited by having access to books, and wished to make a like opportunity available to others. Most of the great fortunes of that famous and somewhat discredited era are perpetuated now in foundations bearing the names of the families which created them. Many more are concealed under institutional names which are not those of their founders—for even then anonymity was sometimes supposed to be one of the marks of the truly devoted Christian.

Spectacular as were the contributions made by men of great wealth, they aggregated far less than similar contributions made by men and women who had accumulated or inherited a more modest fortune. Individuals who had accumulated very little were nevertheless expected to give from their affluence if their current earnings were substantial. Whether from conviction, or from desire for community esteem, or for other motives not excluding the very pure motive of desire to do good, an appreciable proportion of income accruing to individuals found its way through their voluntary act into noncommercial activity— activities from which the individual concerned could expect no present reward. Later, of course, the tax structure was so organized as to encourage this process; but in its early phases without this stimulus—throughout the whole of the nineteenth century and the early decades of the twentieth—a margin of the product of the economic system was devoted to nonprofit activities. The roster of the great rich of the Mauve Decade, the plutocratic age, and the era of the Four Hundred is perpetuated in the names of great philanthropic foundations, university plants and endowments, and stately museums and hospitals. The contributions, if not the names, of donors great and small now forgotten form the bulk of many endowment funds sustaining modern institutions.

2. Effect on Economic Development

LET US NOT idealize this process, still less be sentimental about individuals. We are discussing a political-economic system, and the impact on it of the philosophical and ethical theory. No one, familiar with the history of the time, believes that either the attitude or the results were ideal. Sensitive though individuals were to the Christian ethic, they were surprisingly insensitive to many of the conditions around them which demanded, even screamed for, change. A Carnegie could build libraries, could endow universities, could argue against inherited wealth, could create great foundations. He was not, and perhaps could not be, sensitive to the hideous results of the twelve-hour day in the steel industry, to the almost animal life imposed on his own workers, and to the fact that the vaunted system of free economy literally devoured the health, the bodies, and perhaps the souls of industrial labor. Owners of the great meat-packing plants in Chicago could and did endow educational institutions; but the conditions in the district dominated by their plants were scandals even then. The best brains of economics and finance assumed that fluctuations would throw millions of men out of work. The writer remembers stumbling over bodies of men dead of starvation or exposure, or both, in Chicago during the depression year 1903.

Labor unions, and indeed labor organizations of any kind, were at law close to illegal conspiracies. They interfered with the free market—whose balances were supposed to be the optimum obtainable in any given set of circumstances. The most elementary devices for assuring the safety of workers, or minimal protection against accidents or the elements, were resisted with a callousness inconceivable today. The ethics of the time did not extend to assuring that the processes of production were humanly decent, or even humanly tolerable. In the interpretation of half a century ago, it achieved results surprisingly like those observable in the Soviet Union, and peculiarly in Communist China, at present.

What it did do was, in effect, to socialize a substantial portion of the profits gained and accumulated during this singularly unattractive phase of private enterprise. And it performed another function, destined in time to be more far-reaching in effect than the conscription of a certain amount of wealth to serve selfless ideals. It maintained and fostered groups of men in clerical, academic, and literary worlds who steadily called attention to and sought cures for the evils which disfigured the face of the economic world. Priests, professors, publicists fought to turn public attention to the waste, wreckage, and cruelty involved in production as then carried on. It took a full generation—say from 1900 to 1930—for them to persuade the United States that, to the transcendental margin provided by philanthropy, there must be added a like margin provided by social organization.

But they succeeded, and the result of their success was a large accretion to the impersonal sector of accumulated wealth and distributed income. The economic residue can be found in a large and growing aggregate of trust funds held for Social Security by the government and by private interests such as pension trusts. Other less spectacular diversions from the stream of individual or private-enterprise profits into the collective margin were attained by other social devices.

The economic effect proved to supply a light to businessmen and to theorists. Diversion for impersonal or selfless ends of a substantial proportion of current income did not prove to be a drag on the economy. On the contrary, it maintained a current of economic activity independent of the profit motive and therefore more dependable. In result, it both stabilized and enhanced the productive process. Failure to anticipate the result is easily explained. The philanthropic uses of diverted income and capital were not motivated by hope of greater production. The objective was humanitarian—to have better schools, better hospitals, more educated children. The drive toward social legislation was not powered by the belief that it would help the national income, but by the belief that it would help human beings. The notion that good human policy might also be sound economic policy only took form as the results began to appear.

During the decade 1950-1960, however, the results were clear enough for any to see. The American political-economic system continued to rely on private enterprise save in certain areas and continued to base operations on the profits of enterprise, the pay of individuals. But, from this total income flow, it diverted three great items to impersonal ends. One of these items, the largest, was the aggregate of federal, state, and local taxes. A second item was the aggregate of contributions, voluntary or involuntary, to Social Security funds, pension trust funds, and similar institutions. The third item continues to be the voluntary donations to private philanthropy and social service—an item that continues to increase both in absolute amount and in proportion to the total national income. All three processes speeded up the formation of capital. All three maintained a distribution process partially, if not wholly, independent of the motives of profit and exchange, and unaffected by their fluctuation. They have proved an invaluable support to the purely self-interest commercial operations which, two generations ago, were supposed to be the entire fabric of a political-economic system.

Probably they did a great deal more than merely give a dependable element of flow to commercial operation. The businessman who today accepts social devices with a certain satisfaction, as "built-in stabilizers," has recognized their least, and not their most important, aspect. Their more important effects, indeed, are probably beyond arithmetic calculation. The private and semipublic philanthropy devoted to medical research has unquestionably freed innumerable man-hours for productive work. Those sums of money, diverted from current consumption through private philanthropy to academic research or through taxation to government and university laboratories, have provided unlimited vistas for future activity, as they have already caused the development of immense new possibilities for production. These created the vast new pool of incorporeal scientific capital whose results are not now measurable, though they are visible everywhere. Hazarding a guess—it can only be a guess—I surmise that the current level of economic activity in the United States—it is the highest level in the world—is due more to the immense injection of theoretical science than to the increase of normal commercial profit-seeking, though the two are, of course, connected in certain areas of economic work.

The point, quite simply, is that a large and growing transcendental margin has been created. The cause for its creation was not search for gain, or personal power. The motive, albeit mixed, transcended the calculable individual interest of the numberless men who contributed the capital. Either through their individual processes of conscience or through compulsion of a social conscience, they were led to recognize and give realization to a range of values arising more out of ethics than out of interest.

3. Theory of the Transcendental Margin as Economic Coefficient

STUDENTS of history have repeatedly been impressed by the fact that economic systems, otherwise comparable, progress at different speeds. One country produces and distributes more, and its income grows more rapidly, than a neighboring country more or less similar in human material and resources. Even more striking, a country will, under certain stimuli, move forward far more rapidly than it did a few years previously—or than, lacking that stimulus, it does a few years later. In every case studied by the writer, the difference appears to lie in the effective value system governing the desires and aims (and with it the action) of most of its inhabitants.

A classic case is that of the two American states Utah and Nevada. They were settled about the same time, by about the same number and race of people. They were comparable in climate, in geographic position, and in natural resources. Utah grew, progressed, and still continues to do so. Nevada, after a few brief spurts due to speculative silver mining, had an unimpressive social-economic history.

The obvious difference lay in their value systems. Utah was organized and its thinking still is dominated by the Mormon church. Theology aside, the organization and philosophy of Mormonism exacted a high degree of effort and expenditure for ends which would not be considered of primary advantage to individuals—at least in the terrestrial world. Specifically, it required dedication of at least two years of a man's life, and 10% of his earnings or gains, for the benefit (as Mormons saw it) of his religion, his community, and his fellow man. Every productive individual was thus required to put more into the economic system than he took out. He provided an excess product to be expended in realizing the value system maintained by the Mormon church, in which he acquiesced, usually with conviction and enthusiasm.

The value system of Nevada has never been stated, but very high on it was satisfaction of the money-making desire of individuals. The mining proprietor, like the Las Vegas gambler today, hoped to take out more from the system than he put in. (A gambler par excellence is a man against the field.) Success means staking a small contribution and, without further work, winning a larger prize. On the cold economic side, this does not add to useful capital, make for great production, or occasion great distribution or growth.

Other examples are not far to find. The phenomenal progress of the state of Israel, as contrasted with the relative lack of progress of adjacent Syria or Iraq, is a forceful illustration of the economic dynamics of the added dimension. Discounting, as one must, the effect of the great contributions received by Israel from outside sources, it still has vastly outdistanced its neighbors. Its value system demanded a high degree of sacrifice and effort over and above that absorbed in the personal consumption or wealth-gathering of its citizens for themselves. No motive of comparable strength has existed in the nearby Middle Eastern states since the days of the early Mohammedan caliphates or perhaps the days of the Turkish sultans of the fifteenth and sixteenth centuries.

Or consider the surprising changes in the effectiveness of the social-economic system in a country swept by the stimulus of a new economic value system. The Germany of the Weimar Republic progressed at a rate far slower than that of Hitlerian Germany after 1934, as evidenced by the careful calculations made (shortly before World War II) by Professor C. W. Guillebaud, of Cambridge University. For good or evil, the value system of Nazi Germany, diabolical as it was in most aspects, did command the assent of most of Germany and engaged the enthusiasm of a good deal of it; and it called forth a high degree of product and effort, for the assumed benefit, not of any individual, but of a strange and mystic Nordic community (to be dominated, of course, by the Nazi-German Reich).

For that matter, most countries engaged in a war in which their people believe also are able to accelerate their economic processes. This has proved particularly true in modern times, when wars have been "national," rather than a product of the designs or motivations of a prince or a feudal group. Certainly this was true when the revolutionary and, later, the Napoleonic wars engaged the enthusiasm of France. It was strikingly true in a number of European countries as well as the United States at the time of World War I, and again of World War II. One feature of such wars is the sudden multiplication of the interest of most individuals in the welfare and defense of their country, and their enhanced willingness to work, pay taxes, sacrifice, and give to bring it safely through.

In all cases, it seems, the motivations transcend the calculable "interest" of the individual. They are, therefore, "transcendental"—not in the religious sense of the term, but in its original meaning of overpassing any intended personal advantage of the individual or his immediate family. Value systems causing an economic system to accelerate differ in all conceivable ways. But they have one factor in common. They engage the willingness of the individuals to labor and sacrifice for ends aside from their private advantage, and for the benefit, as they conceive, of a larger community interest, local, nationwide, or worldwide. That value system calling out a sustained over-all effort for a long period of time obviously has more continuous and lasting results than temporary spurts educed by wartime excitement.

Familiarly, such value systems are part of and are maintained and strengthened by powerful religions. Yet it is entirely conceivable that even without such support a purely terrestrial value system might produce similar economic results.

We have here, it appears, a coefficient, over and above the profit motive, which enhances the effectiveness of any economic system. This coefficient was not allowed for, or at least was considered unimportant, in classical nineteenth-century economic theory. Even R. H. Tawney, who derived much of modern capitalism from the Protestant ethic, did not directly include it, though he, beyond other modern writers, emphasized that an economic system was only a means to an end, not an end in itself. Rather, it was assumed as matter of course that men would always act according to their calculation of personal profit or advantage. Since the open market was final arbiter, whose balance reached the best economic results obtainable under the circumstances, this doctrine in effect deified greed.

Abstractly, the theory was tenable enough. Selfishness, avarice, desire to buy cheap, to sell dear, to take the highest profit obtainable, undoubtedly are widespread and often dominant human emotions. Nevertheless the theory is now untenable as a complete explanation, though valid enough as far as it goes. Perhaps it may have been totally valid in its assumption, when product was never adequate to satisfy elementary human needs. When most of a population went to bed hungry, or feared tomorrow's famine, personal interest in survival was uppermost, and willingness to sacrifice for a social system may have been limited to a minimum. But such a system occasioned little or no advance in the capacities of most men. Still less did it seek to provide for men and women yet unborn, or develop great interest in probing the secrets of the material world or immaterial cosmos, though there were always exceptional individuals or small groups. The personal profit or power motive does not induce great effort to increase the capacity or expand the culture of other men and women, or to increase the human resources within any community, or to develop other than commercial activity. Were an economic system to depend merely on the profit motive, that system would tend to stagnate.

The Theory of the Transcendental Margin can therefore be stated as follows:

The transcendental margin is the product of a value system that causes effort and expenditure beyond that calculated as conducive to the personal advantage of an individual or his immediate family group.

Development occasioned by such a value system does not exclude, but, rather, includes, use of the state and its agencies in mobilizing and applying effort and expenditure. But its effect is never limited to state measures and action.

The aggregate of such effort, expenditure, and sacrifice over and above the aggregate of effort and expenditure for such personal desires is the added coefficient that causes national product to increase beyond satisfying the aggregate effective personal desires of a population.[28]

Let us not be diverted by noting that human motives are always mixed. The Mormon, paying his tithe and spending his two years of mission, may calculate that he will, later, be more prosperous because of that effort. The American philanthropic giver may think that in some unforeseeable fashion the gift will somehow redound to his personal benefit. Such motives may exist along with a desire to please his God or to enjoy the emotional satisfaction of fulfilling an obligation to serve. The exploration is pointless here. Value systems are made effective by a complex range of impulses, hopes, and desires comprised in the fathomless minds of men. Yet the value itself is the mainspring of the motivation.

This coefficient is incapable of being measured accurately by any arithmetic now existing. Yet enough of quantum can be discerned to give it economic (as well as political and spiritual) reality.

The value system exerts itself first by setting up moral imperatives in the individual. These are voluntarily obeyed. Second, it sets up for him defined social imperatives. He is expected to give work, effort, or money, at a sacrifice, by the community in whose presence he lives and of whose fellowship he is a part. Third, the value system gradually crystallizes into established law. It is then enforced by the state so that part of yesterday's

voluntary contribution is required by today's taxation on compulsory service. All taxation, of course, does not proceed from
this fact: much of it is composed of dues required of everybody
for purely utilitarian needs recognized by practically everybody.
But part of it—perhaps, indeed, much of it—is today's legal
formulation of yesterday's voluntarily assumed sacrifice.]

Most schools and practically all universities were originally
supported by voluntary sacrifice and gifts, as are many today.
The value of education as a corollary to the vast value of truth
was generally recognized, systematized, and finally imposed with
general consent. The result is found in taxes to maintain publicly supported education at all levels. Estimating that fraction
of the taxes and civic duties resulting from a codified transcendental objective, as distinct from that part which is utilitarian,
would be difficult, though perhaps not impossible. Add to this
fraction the quantum of voluntary gifts and sacrifice, and we
could reach an extremely crude estimate of the economic size
of the transcendental margin.

Take, for example, the condition of the United States in the
year 1960. Voluntary giving by individuals (including gifts of
foundations and corporations) amounted to just under nine
billion dollars—but 95% of this was made up of individual
contributions. These were uncompelled gifts to philanthropy of
all kinds, for direct relief of need, for schools, universities,
churches, hospitals, for research, museums, symphonic music.
In the case of individuals (that is, excluding foundations and
corporations), their gifts amounted to about 2% of their personally received income. It is true that these gifts constituted a
deduction from their taxable income. It cannot be said that, by
refusing to give, they would have enjoyed 2% more of spendable income.

Actually, they would have been personally richer by about
one half of the nine billion dollars had they refused to give. So
far, we have one element of a quantum here established.

As to taxes required to be paid by the state, we can make
little more than a sophisticated guess. Many items in any budget
can be classified one way or the other. I hazard as a rough
estimate, subject to all manner of correction, that out of the

THE AMERICAN ECONOMIC REPUBLIC

total of the local, state, and federal taxes paid by individuals, at least 25% goes for expenditures essentially altruistic in nature (defense expenditures are here taken as utilitarian). Obviously state and local expenditures include a higher transcendental factor than federal. Schools, museums, libraries, hospitals, relief, child welfare, and the like are supported more by local than by federal taxation. Total federal and local taxes paid in 1960 ($89 billion, federal; $40 billion, local) amounted to about $129 billion. (The figures appeared in the First National City Bank's monthly letter for October 1962.) If our guess of 25% is accurate, the total of voluntary giving ($9 billion) and involuntary tax contribution for transcendental ends would be on the order of $40 billion plus for the year 1960. This would be about 8% of the entire gross national product ($500 billion) for that year.

Yet it would be wholly wrong to accept this (or, indeed, any) arithmetic measure as a measure of result. True, $40 billion diverted from individual satisfaction to serve values conceived to forward the public good is itself an extremely powerful accelerator of economic progress. It creates "effective demand"— that is to say, markets—where otherwise there would be only hordes of beggars. It creates jobs of all kinds. It expands the number of consumers, and by that much stimulates production to satisfy them. On the terrestrial plane it pumps money into the economy at times and points which otherwise would be stagnant. But I consider the financial stimulus less dynamic than the psychological effects.

In the American value system, much of its drive is directed toward education. This increases the level of culture. One result is an expanded and widespread desire for a larger life, inducing more work to satisfy those desires. Markets do not grow where peoples are culturally depressed. Wanting nothing but satisfaction of elementary desires, primitive or uneducated peoples are satisfied at a relatively low level of consumption. Their demands do not greatly rise save with population growth. Though not readily calculable, the education of a population is perhaps the greatest single stimulus to economic desire and consequent industrial growth. Deeper even than that, energy, dedication, and devotion of men and women are unlocked as they appreciate, search, and sacrifice for enduring values. This release of personal effort permeates great areas—perhaps should permeate all areas—of life. As its intensity rises—or falls—the economic speed and growth of the entire productive organization accelerates, or slows down.

Arithmetic does not, and perhaps should not, exist to measure individual affirmations of values. They move in a different dimension, and that probably the determinative one. But, although our economic calculus is too crude to measure the force and results of the aspirations of millions of human hearts, we are aware of their combined power. We can note their effect by comparing the rate of growth of a Utah with a Nevada, of an Israel with an Iraq, of a Netherlands with a Bulgaria. Ultimately, some statistical comparison perhaps can be found. Lacking that, or perhaps even having it, one can observe and admire, rather than measure, comparative differences in tensile strength, in capacity to act, in the beauty of the respective civilizations.

The value system, unmeasured, perhaps unmeasurable, in its effect, is a visible, indeed the most striking, characteristic of any country or community.

America has her own value system. Substantial consensus has been reached on its salient tenets. It has imposed a high degree of accepted and acceptable though compulsory contribution through taxation, and a considerable measure of unimposed, unforced sacrifice and contribution as well. Largely as a result of this, in aggregate, its economic republic has maintained a steady growth for a long period of time. It has attained the highest standard of living ever enjoyed by the population of a large country. Unquestionably, the system can go farther, produce more, progress more rapidly, distribute more widely, and cause to be done many of the things we all know have been left undone.

Historically, the United States is a child of the Reformation. Its value system is the end product of a number of powerful religious movements whose main values are much the same. In their philosophy, the values setting up the American transcendental margin are unlimited, because they are thought to be eternal. Vistas of further action toward their further realization are always open, because they are thought to be infinite. Advances toward their realization automatically increase the transcendental margin. With them comes faster growth of the American economic republic.

The United States has never codified these values. In its culture, indeed, it is almost considered bad taste to exhibit them. Americans refuse for some reason to discuss their personal philosophy even with their closest friends. Each man's value system, his religion, or his philosophy is considered deeply personal and entitled to the protection of privacy. Even at law this is included as a right under the first article of the Bill of Rights of the American Constitution, which prohibits Congress from making any law "respecting an establishment of religion, or prohibiting the free exercise thereof." Yet, were a poll to be taken (as it cannot), the area of agreement among Americans would be found to be surprisingly wide.

Among others, two values would emerge high on the list. One would be the value known in philosophical language as "truth." By this is meant truth in the large, in all aspects, from individual interest in not telling lies and in personal sincerity, to the frontiers of scholarly search for scientific knowledge and understanding of the universe. This value runs the whole gamut of life. It comprises the value judgment preventing the child from being allowed to cheat in school, to demanding that high integrity which must inspire a university mathematician attacking the unconquerable mysteries of space and matter. From that truth value—Americans do have and hold it—came, and still comes, our real interest in education, at all levels, primary to university, prone though we are to justify education on the more sordid pretext that education is intended chiefly to make wage or salary earners more efficient.

The value of truth, charged and accepted with more intensity, would automatically entrain a forceful change in education, in the status of teachers, perhaps also in educational content and educational method. Certainly it would change the relation of schools to communities. We do not have to discard lesser utilitarian goals in education to realize that increased capacity to apprehend and comprehend a larger fragment of limitless truth is one great objective of life itself—as great and joyous for a child in primary school as for the advanced practitioners and pioneers in industrial, governmental, or academic life. An instant effect would be a swift reappraisal of the methods and product, as well as of the budgets, of educational institutions from the grade school to the Bureau of Health, Education, and Welfare in Washington.

A second enduring value is that of beauty. Philosophers have discussed it for millennia. It is one of the cosmic forces in human civilization. Individuals have and hold that value also. The humblest shack owned as a home ordinarily displays attempts, sometimes as pitiful as they are noble, to give it qualities of dignity and beauty. The value translates itself into community opinion. The constant conflict by the more honorable portion of most American communities against sordid murder of the esthetics of an open road by advertisers, or to maintain the dignity of an honorable main street against dollar-chasing real-estate schemes, testifies to that fact.

Suppose, for a moment, an increased dynamic American acceptance of the value of beauty. If, for example, a beginning was made toward realizing the pent-up demand that cities shall be beautiful, the economic effect would be explosive. The task of tearing down and rebuilding a substantial part of the urban construction now in existence would at once increase the construction work load. With it would come occupation and opportunity for many millions of Americans, from city planners, artists, and architects down to workmen and material producers. That demand alone would go far toward ending unemployment in the United States for a decade to come, or (should disarmament be achieved) replace the employment now required for defense.

This is the way in which the coefficient of the transcendental margin works. It engages efforts of individuals and nonstatist groups; but it also demands that the state shall forward the values from which it springs. Progress toward greater realization of the values of truth or of beauty, or preferably both (not to mention others), affords scope for American industrial development to several times its present volume and intensity. As a value system becomes increasingly effective, that is, increasingly engages the effort, expenditure, and the sacrifice of the people holding it, the coefficient of the transcendental margin increases. With such increase, greater demand is made upon the productive organization of the United States. This in turn calls for greater capacity to satisfy the greater demand.

4. The Vital Currents

WITH NATIONS as with individuals, as they think, so are they. The vital current that has brought the American social-economic system to unlimited heights of production and, on the material side, to unequaled comfort for all but a small fragment of its large population was not materialist, but ethical. It does not matter that the body of ethics is differently stated—or left unstated—by the American community. The body exists, and has terrific force.

The conception that the strong should help the weak, that the prosperous should carry a greater portion of the load than the poor, is not an economic conception. It is an attempt to give form to the old socialist maxim "From each according to his capability, to each according to his need." Yet it was that conception that caused the United States to adopt the graduated income tax and to make it the heart of the American tax system. Economic reasoning was only a secondary consideration when the policy was adopted of giving tax exemption to philanthropic institutions. The widespread practice of private philanthropy, developed when the Protestant ethic was more readily understood, carried itself forward into the tax laws of the United States and of most of the American states. As a result, your and my gifts to religious or philanthropic institutions are deducted from the income on which we pay taxes. Even the last stronghold of pure economic motivation—the corporation which operates an enterprise for profit and, in theory, for profit only— in most states now has the statutory power to give to philanthropy a small portion (conventionally, 5%) of its income for philanthropic purposes, and to deduct that income when it pays taxes to the federal government. The law likewise encourages in a variety of ways the setting up of the pension trusts which, as we have seen, are social devices to insulate men from certain kinds of misfortune, notably sickness and poverty-stricken old age. And all of these were preceded by federal, state, and local taxation to support the first great system of free public education, first at the primary, later at the secondary, level, that the world had ever seen.

No one contends that the ideals implicit in this current of American thought have been realized; probably they never will be realized. If indeed they approach realization, new vistas of possibility will have been opened. The pursuit of enduring values can be as long as the span of history. The pursuit of eternal values is, by its terms, unending. With each achievement, however tiny, farther horizons appear. Necessity of action in matters which heretofore went unnoticed becomes obvious, just as the Protestant ethic of the nineteenth century pushed toward wider and deeper education even as it disregarded the economic misery of great sectors of the population.

The point here made is this: the preoccupation of American democracy with selfless goals—that is, goals not related to direct individual advantage on this earth—accounts for the surprising and quite measurable social-economic achievements of the United States. Specifically, it accounts for the fact that this country has the highest gross national product, both aggregate and per capita, of any country (in 1962 this product was running at the rate of 550 billions' worth of goods and services measured in 1960 dollars, actually produced and paid for). Preoccupation with something like a fair, or, at any rate, a very wide, distribution of the benefits was determinative: the job could not have been done without it. A wide distribution of income is essential to a mass market. The American corporate system could not have emerged without this distribution. But wide distribution was not undertaken in order to achieve mass markets so that corporations could be larger. It was the result of the vital, essentially modern, insistence, first, that human beings should not go hungry and unhoused, and, second, as that goal approached realization, that they should have opportunity for comfort and diversion as well. This last, probably, proceeded from an undefined general feeling that any system limiting comfort, diversion, and luxury to a single group was essentially unfair, if not immoral. As in every system, someone looked at his more prosperous or more powerful neighbor and said, substantially, "Why he, and not me?" The prosperous, in fact, asked the same questions of themselves—or at least enough of them did so that there was no invincible resistance.

In part, in the American economic system this was due to a piece of historical luck. Elsewhere in the world—for example, Europe—answers to the question "Why he, and not me?" were ready-made by historical tradition. This king was legitimate because he was descended from Louis Capet or John of Gaunt and he held power by that fact and by the grace of God. The noblemen entrusted with estates and wealth were a class set apart. Too close scrutiny of the historical origins of their entry into that class was not encouraged; at all events, the hierarchic system of rank and fortune, of family position and inherited stance, was accepted. This had its uses in maintaining a degree of order. If the mutual obligations between the classes were well and truly observed, probably it made life tolerable for great masses of people who otherwise would have been in difficulties. But it did not conduce to wide distribution either of power or of wealth. And it certainly did not encourage, let alone assist, any man in the lower class to hope that by merit or ability he or his children could reach an upper and more favored class.

The American economic system never really encountered this, though there are remnants of the old tradition in racial antagonisms and in some of the Southern states. Even in its royalist colonial period, the growing population of America paid little attention to the strata of European civilization. For one thing, when you are struggling with wilderness and weather, you are not preoccupied with social theory. You are thinking of getting a field plowed and a harvest reaped, of making a road passable, of having enough laid up for the winter to see you through. Adam delved and Eve span and so did a gentleman if he expected to survive. Not all, but most of the country grew in the face of that experience. It is of interest to see the same process going on in the Soviet Union today. Communist hierarchy, rank, and ideology are strongest in Moscow and European Russia. But, travelers tell us, in the huge and not wholly clement Siberian portions of the Soviet Union—destined in their time to be immensely more important than European Russia—dogma and hierarchy alike are taken far less seriously.

Whatever the cause, the American colonies indulged the British class system only in mild degree. When the Jeffersonian revolution took place in 1800, the remnants of it were discarded. In economic terms, the result was to set up a powerful political force which caused the American political-economic system to devote a continuous and growing part of its production toward nonindividualist "selfless" ends. This presently appeared as a powerful force in its economic development, and is today a crucial factor both in maintaining balance (avoiding economic crises) and in increasing the distribution and in calling into existence the production which is at present the salient phenomenon of the American system.

Let us not claim that the transcendental margin is peculiar to the American social-economic system. Actually, it can be identified in greater or less degree in most effective economic systems of modern times—and perhaps of ancient times as well. But in the United States the transcendental margin was continuously greater, and expanded more consistently, than in most other contemporary systems. It generated greater productivity, and greater intellectual resources for still further expansion. In the post–World War II period, it has become a decisive influence.

The conclusions may be summarized.

The American economic system and indeed all economic systems are not ends in themselves. Certainly they cease to be so when they have provided for the elementary necessities of the population which created them. They reflect the value system of the community in which they operate.

That value system, and the intensity with which it is pursued, is a coefficient of the productivity of the system. Specifically, it can determine whether the economic system produces, per capita, more or less.

Likewise, the value system will determine the allocation of its product—to education or cathedrals as against automobiles or office buildings, and as between consumption and consumer goods and capital and instruments of production.

Capital is the capacity to mobilize labor, technique, and things to create or add to existing instruments of production. Such capacity may be derived from power or from money, or possibly both. To some extent power may be used in place of money, but at the sacrifice of human life and liberty.

To grow and become more productive, an economic system must devote a substantial portion of its resource and production to achieve ends transcending the calculation of individual material advantage. This is the "transcendental margin."

The ends and the extent of the margin of resources allocated to them are determined by the value system of the community. In the United States, the operative value system is determined by public consensus more or less freely arrived at by the entire community, and expressed through the political mechanism of the democratic state, in association with nonstatist institutions.

CONCLUSION

THE FOREGOING studies permit, perhaps require, drawing certain conclusions. They also indicate certain problems pushing toward the crisis state. As these crises are resolved, they will evidence the next steps in the evolution of the organization of the economic republic.

1. The American economic republic is a guided and managed economy, loosely organized and flexibly administered. It is not the end result of an uncontrolled, automatic free market, but is now the result of state-directed planning. The present free market is maintained by the state. Subject to limits laid down and interventions where required by the political state, it accounts for more than half of the goods and services produced and consumed by Americans.

The fiction that the state does not guide and should not be responsible for the conditions produced must promptly be discarded. The existing fact of continued necessity for and development of state planning ought to be squarely faced, and other planning systems, notably that of France, should be studied for suggestions.

Even in its present partially systematized phase, the American system has proved more productive, and has done more for a larger percentage of its population, than the system prevailing in any great nation of the world. Man for man, every American is better off than any comparable bloc of 185 millions.

This highlights, rather than covers up, the obvious areas where it has proved inadequate. The American "breast-beater"

213

has little right to exist when he compares the United States with any foreign system. He has every right to be heard when he discusses the areas and many details in which the American system should, can, and must work better.

2. The American system has ceased to be dominated primarily by the philosophy or the uncontrolled practice of free prices, free profits, free wages. Its productive results already overpass and are not primarily dependent on the limits or results which would exist in an uncontrolled free-market economy.

3. The theoretical outside economic limit of development of the economic republic is set by the level of productivity practically attainable at any given time. Except in time of war, this limit in America has never been approached. The limit also is apparently capable of great and continuous expansion.

4. The United States, rightly, has preserved in great measure the institution of the free market. But the free market has been retained as a means to an end, and not as a way of economic or political life.

5. The free market is used as an instrument, and, through the antitrust laws, artificially maintained, to prevent unacceptable aggregations of economic power—for example, monopolies—and also to maintain a system in which any individual may enter the free-market sector (and, with state approval, the controlled-market sector) with a new enterprise or a new idea.

The antitrust laws have not, in history, been uniformly enforced. They are, rather, save in certain crude applications such as division of territory and price-fixing, a method of state intervention where concentration of economic power appears to have reached an unacceptable point.

6. Extremes of competition are as unacceptable to the economic republic as are extremes of monopoly or concentration of economic power. Where the state does not regulate prices, it accepts corporations in combinations large enough to maintain a degree of stability. Consequently, it accepts the principle of the "administered price" where such administration makes for full employment and maximum purchasing power, a justifiable price, and an organization of the industry in which there is continuous capacity to compete.

7. Purely commercial (*i.e.,* profit-seeking) avenues of expansion are not the only, and perhaps are not even the greatest, present avenues for further increase of economic activity. It is possible, perhaps probable, that expansion to meet esthetic and knowledge-seeking values (beautiful cities, scientific pioneering, and the like) will play as great a part in future expansion as did commercial enterprise aiming to meet consumers' needs in past expansion.

8. In expanding productivity by the noncommercial route, the economic republic relies heavily, but not only, on the state. Nonstatist institutions of all kinds can be and are used for administration, and to a limited extent for financing. Foundations, universities, philanthropic and cultural institutions are at their best when untrammeled by state bureaucracy and current politics. But they can, within limits, be financed directly or indirectly by the state to attain expansion along noncommercial lines.

"Noncommercial" here means that the services rendered and the results they produce are not distributed merely to users or consumers who can pay, unit by unit, for what they receive, and that the motive behind them is not the desire of some individual or group to collect a profit.

9. The capacity of consumers to consume (being less than the capacity to produce goods and services) is a limiting factor in increasing productivity. Consumers are limited in three directions: by the amount of their spendable income, by the extent of their education and cultural equipment, and by their will to render their value systems effective.

It is an interest of the state to assure that consumers shall have spendable income adequate to pay for production up to the limit of their cultural capacity to consume, after adequate capital formation has been provided for.

Consumers' spendable income may be temporarily increased by making credit available to them. Creation of such credit can be expanded or diminished by the state through the operation of its banking-and-currency system. State operations are limited by a necessary concern for maintaining the purchasing power of money.

10. Capacity of the economic republic to expand its capital goods and permanent equipment—including its technical advances and stock of "incorporeal capital"—depends on its capacity to accumulate adequate capital through "savings" (production not devoted to consumption). Savings can in limited measure be augmented by use of created currency through bank credit.

The distinction between "capital" finance (savings) and credit or currency finance (bank credit) can rightly be overpassed so long as productivity can readily be increased to meet manifest legitimate wants. Bank credit for capital purposes is allowable

(a) when there is substantial unused capacity to produce lying idle, or substantial additional productive capacity capable of being brought rapidly into existence and production; or

(b) when foreseeable savings will be accumulated in the near future, against which bank-credit advance can be made.

Use of bank credit (currency) for capital purposes assumes that goods or services will be increased substantially in proportion equal to the credit or currency created.

11. No one really knows exactly how much capital should be formed annually through "savings." Capital needs should be a subject of thorough study.

12. The present banking and capital-finance systems are, mechanically at least, capable of meeting the problem of expanded productivity. Where they fail to do so, the cause is more probably psychological than economic. The commercial-banking and the capital-finance systems are only barely emerging from the old "moneylender" psychology. The state is only barely emerging into realization that it can make possible to commercial and capital bankers (and borrowers from them) resources of time, guarantee, and rediscount, permitting the banking system to deal adequately with the future as well as with the past and the present.

13. The problem of channeling spendable income into the hands of consumers of all kinds is soluble. The state could do it arbitrarily. But it will not be solved soundly unless a companion problem is solved. What contribution, by way of work,

of effort, or otherwise, must be made by recipients of spend-able income to prevent them from descending into a variety of economic poorhouse, however comfortable? This problem has not been adequately studied. It can only be solved by arranging that no one capable of work or effort shall be involuntarily un-employed.

14. The Western World, and the United States with it, is reaching the threshold of an economic situation comparable to that of 1930. The damage of World War II is repaired. The backed-up wants of individuals during the period of war and reconstruction have been satisfied. A second layer of new wants occasioned by rising standards of education and living exists, but additional productive capacity to meet these is already at hand. In general, supply—that is, productivity—is forging ahead of presently effective demand, and potential productivity is vastly greater than such demand.

In the equivalent situation in 1930, the free-market economy was allowed to dictate conditions in the Western World and in the United States for a period of three years. This will not occur again.

The American economic republic will insist on dominating the economy. Its first line of attack will be the attempt to assure distribution of money sufficient to increase effective demand in the hands of its consumers, preferably in exchange for con-structive work. There will not be doctrinaire resistance, as was the case in 1930. (One of the most conservative monetary theorists, Per Jacobsson, head of the International Monetary Fund, in October 1962 advocated that the United States reduce taxes for 1963—though this would entail an intentional un-balance of its budget.) The resulting expansion of currency and credit as the government borrows to meet the deficit would in-crease the currency credit supply, a risk he was prepared to accept.

Plainly, however, a second line of attack is implied. Not only must the public be in position to buy and consume, but the consumption must actually occur. Or, if the public elects to save, these savings must promptly be invested in additions to public or private plant and equipment. A public-works pro-

gram achieves this, albeit crudely. So also does business investment in plant, though in such times businessmen are hesitant,
and the state may have to arrange attractive credit terms. The
Council of Economic Advisers can prove of inestimable worth
in initiating plans needed to accomplish the result. The certainty is that the economic republic will not sit quiet, as did
the political republic in 1930, hoping that a free market would
eventually rescue the situation.

Finally:

The American economic republic has in hand, available to
it, human and material resources, productive organization, and
political, financial, and economic instruments capable of dealing
justly and generously with all foreseeable social demands and
situations. It merely needs political, economic, and business
brains and imagination to use them.

Moral, cultural, and educational, rather than economic,
forces, as they become part of the American public consensus,
will determine how thoroughly and how well the economic republic under the political state meets these demands. The
United States can do, for itself and with itself, anything it really
wants to do. Its problem now and always will be to determine
what it wants to do, and what it wants to be. Consensus on
these wants is now and will continue to be a result of its system
of values, a value system making every individual a participant
in that consensus. The political-economic system now can and
does make that consensus increasingly effective. As the consensus evolves, it can give effect to that growth.

Morals, culture, education, and their development and expansion are not the product of an economic system. They are the
motives, the drawing power, and causes of its being.

Developing, making real, and forwarding these values is the
work, not of politicians, economists, or businessmen, but of
men to whom economic life is an instrument only toward a
greater end. In ultimate account, for better or worse, teachers
and scholars are the guiding lights. In economics, as perhaps in
all aspects of development, the revelation of Daniel seems valid
in history: "And they that be wise shall shine as the brightness
of the firmament; and they that turn many to righteousness as
the stars."

NOTES

1. The terminology of national income and that of national product have been used interchangeably in sectoral comparisons of this kind, and amount to the same thing for general purposes. In Simon Kuznets' study of changes in the percentage distribution of national income by industrial origin, agriculture accounts for 17.3% of the national income, on an average, over the years 1904-1918. According to data presented in J. W. Kendrick's study, the percentage of gross private *product* originating in the private farm sector works out to an annual average of 17.39% for the period 1907-1911.

The 1960 figure of 3.8% was obtained by dividing the figure for national income in 1960, according to the *Statistical Abstract of the United States* ($417 billion), by the figure for income derived from farms, exclusive of forestries and fisheries ($16.122 billion). The Kendrick data also specifically exclude income derived from forestries and fisheries from gross domestic product originating in the private farm sector.

The extreme similarity of the results obtained in the Kuznets and Kendrick studies is all the more interesting because the Kendrick data are in constant prices while the Kuznets data are in current prices, and because the Kendrick figures allude to gross product while the Kuznets figures are presumably net of capital consumption and indirect taxes.

See J. W. Kendrick, *Productivity Trends in the United States,* National Bureau of Economic Research (Princeton, N.J., 1961), and S. Kuznets, "Long-Term Changes in the National Income of the United States of America since 1870," in International Association for Research in Income and Wealth, *Income and Wealth of the United States: Trends and Structure,* Income and Wealth Series II (Cambridge, Mass., 1952).

The relevant tables by these two authors are to be found in U.S. Bureau of the Census, *Historical Statistics of the United States, Colonial Times to 1957* (Washington, D.C., 1960), pp. 140-141.

2. I have begun this study with analysis of "property" because it is one of the most abused words in the English language. It covers a surprising range of possible meanings and implications, few of which seem to have bothered twentieth-century theorists. Orthodox Communist philosophers (who might have dealt with it) fail to go much beyond the division between goods and services in personal consumption and those involved in production—but then, they consider that private property, beyond a

minimal amount for personal consumption, does not exist in a Communist state and ought not to exist anywhere.

How property is eroded under the American system I endeavored to demonstrate in *Power Without Property* (New York, 1959). Among other things, that essay follows property from its phase of personal ownership and control through the corporation form, and into the extremely attenuated claims which can be held by individuals. They are represented by common stock, rights in pension trusts, participation in mutual funds, and the like.

3. The point here made is that the profit or loss of an American enterprise depends in great measure on its strategic position in the total structure. This is not intended as critical. Businessmen have to take the world as they find it—they did not make it. The system permits them to set up or operate their enterprises in a particular area and at a particular point of time and in the structure then prevailing. Businessmen can and usually do struggle for more favored position. They may ask for higher tariffs (to protect them against foreign competition), for lower taxes (less payment for the service the state provides), or, in those industries which are controlled (like airlines), for a preferred position and better territory—so through the list. Probably a Soviet commissar in charge of, say, manufacturing of raw steel is doing exactly the same thing within the Soviet state apparatus. Whereas the businessman takes his reward by way of profit, the commissar takes his by way of increased prestige and power. There is reason to believe that the commissar's tactics, his lobbying, his "expediting" arrangements by wangling illicit favors from his raw-material suppliers, and the like are far more cutthroat than the American system allows the American businessman. The commissar is fighting the danger of disgrace, destitution, and possibly criminal action for sabotage. The American businessman as a rule has little to fear except retirement—though if he violates the antitrust laws or bribes, he, too, may find himself in a criminal dock.

4. *Distribution of passive wealth.* The estimate of distribution of shares of stock listed on the New York Stock Exchange was made by the New York Stock Exchange itself and published in a pamphlet in June 1962 under the title *The 17 Million, 1962 Census of Shareowners in America.* Their conclusion: In 1952 an estimated 6.5 million Americans owned shares in the nation's publicly held companies. By early 1962 that figure had grown to 17 million. "In addition, an estimated two million more Americans own shares only in *privately*-held companies and are not included in this *Census. . . .* Finally, some 120 million Americans are *indirect* shareowners whose savings are invested for them, in part, in equity securities, by a variety of financial institutions."

Excluding the two million holders of stock in privately owned corporations, where it may be said the corporation is used merely as a method of carrying on personally owned enterprise, the figure of 17 million is impressive enough, even though closer research might shrink the figure somewhat. The estimated number of shareholders does not, however, indicate dispersion of passive wealth. For estimates on that score I have relied on an excellent recent study, *The Share of Top Wealth-Holders in National Wealth 1922-1956,* by Robert J. Lampman, of the University of Wisconsin, a study made for the National Bureau of Economic Research. His figures are not carried beyond 1956 in any case, and most of them end in 1953.

Lampman estimated the total of all personally owned wealth in the United States at about a trillion dollars. He estimated that in 1922, 32% of the total wealth was held by the top 1% of adults, while in 1953, 25% of the total personally owned wealth was held by the top 1% (p. 242). Without separating passive or liquid wealth from other forms, he suggested the possibility that there might be higher concentration (that is, less wide distribution) of corporate stock and liquid bonds than of other forms of personally owned wealth (p. 208).

But he notes (pp. 230-234) that the top 1.4% received 14.2% of all income though they held more than 25% of wealth. He also indicates (p. 244) that the top 1% of adults, though they held 25% of personally owned wealth, are only able to save 15% of all savings. There is, therefore, a steady force eroding this concentration.

Probably this is chiefly accounted for by the incidence of income tax. I suggest that the American economic republic, though it has not socialized wealth, has gone a substantial distance toward socializing income.

5. Source: U.S. Congress, Joint Economic Committee, "Sources of Personal Income," *Economic Indicators, September, 1962* (Washington, D.C., 1962), p. 3. Corporate dividend payments in 1960 amounted to $14.4 billion. Interest payments to individuals amounted to $25.8 billion. Since the total of income received by individuals was more than $400 billion, it is sufficiently plain that the income enjoyed by holders of passive property is marginal to the total picture.

6. According to the New York Stock Exchange *Fact Book 1962,* the following was the value of all shares listed on the New York Stock Exchange at the end of each of the years noted:

YEAR	IN BILLIONS
1954	$169.1
1955	207.6
1956	219.1
1957	195.5
1958	276.6
1959	307.7
1960	306.9
1961	387.8

These figures do not include shares listed on other exchanges and on over-the-counter markets. An extremely rough estimate of the total market value of all shares quoted in all these markets might be $450 billion (as of December 31, 1961).

7. The capitalized worth of industrial enterprises is presumably related to the worth of the product they put out. As gross national product rises, much of which is produced by the industrial enterprises, it is a fair assumption that their capitalized worth rises with it. At all events, the stock-market-price changes suggest that stock buyers think so. The following traces the rise of gross national product for the seven years 1955-1961 inclusive. Source: Bureau of the Census, *Statistical Abstract of the United States: 1962,* Eighty-third Edition (Washington, D.C., 1962), p. 312.

YEAR	IN BILLIONS
1955	$397.5
1956	419.2
1957	442.8
1958	444.5
1959	482.8
1960	504.4
1961	521.3

The aggregate value of shares listed on the stock exchange very crudely parallels the rise in the "value of all shares listed on the exchange."

8. U.S. Congress, Joint Economic Committee, "Expenditures for New Plant and Equipment," *Economic Indicators, September, 1962* (Washington, D.C., 1962), p. 8.

9. Calculation of the exact amount of supposedly liquid property represented by stock alone is subject to all kinds of hazards. In giving the figure of $450 billion I am merely suggesting an order of magnitude. This would be the calculation of the listed value of all the stocks on the New York Stock Exchange plus all the stocks on other exchanges. To this might be added the cash surrender value of life insurance and bank deposits.

But all manner of duplication here enters. Many corporations own great amounts of stock in other corporations. Financial institutions like insurance companies own great amounts of substantially liquid bonds. And so forth. Any figure arrived at does not represent a fair estimate of "value" or "worth"—there are far too many duplications. But even including duplications, it does represent the maximum possible claims on liquidity which may be asserted. The corporation (whose stock is listed on the exchange) may, and many do, own great amounts of stock of other corporations, also listed. Theoretically, the owning corporation can sell for cash their holdings to individuals and others. They have, in theory, both the power and the capacity to do so.

Passive property primarily represents in fact the expectation of a certain amount of income (dividends) plus the assumed capacity to convert into cash. Assumption is made that the securities markets give this capacity, and ordinarily the assumption is true. In the case of emergency, however, there simply would not be buyers unless they could borrow from the banks for the purpose of buying—and the banks were enabled to make such loans because the Federal Reserve banks both permitted them to do so and were willing to lend to the banks the funds which the banks would reloan to the buyers.

10. The steady trend toward translation of personally owned wealth (other than goods in consumption) into liquid form is a remarkable and somewhat disturbing phenomenon. Still more disturbing is the lack of attention given it. *Liquid Claims and National Wealth,* by the writer and Miss Victoria Pederson, was written in 1934. It showed (p. 111) that whereas in 1890 approximately 16% of the then national wealth was "liquid" (bank deposits, cash surrender value of life insurance, domestic stocks and bonds), by 1930 approximately 39% was similarly liquid. This proportion dropped violently to about 31% in 1933 (a panic year), but has since been rising. No one, so far as I know, has bothered to calculate the current figure, and I have not; but I rather confidently expect that currently considerably more than 50% of the national wealth is now assumed to be convertible into cash on demand or on short notice through sale. Obviously attempt to do this on a large scale would either bring on a market crash of catastrophic magnitude or compel an immediate and enormous demand for expansion of our currency-credit facilities. Pretty obviously, too, as soon as strain is apparent, adequate currency-credit expansion will be arranged—as it was not in 1930. But in that case, direct state intervention in banking will necessarily become great. It would probably be accomplished by giving greater powers to the Federal Reserve Board and regional Federal Reserve banks to rediscount or otherwise lend on the substantial "liquid" securities and similar documents which represent this wealth.

This raises the query whether as a result the state would not wind up as pledgee (or perhaps at length owner) of an enormous amount of national passive wealth.

This is why the holder of liquid "wealth," such as stocks and bonds, ultimately depends on the will of the state to expand its currency-credit system for protection in any crisis.

11. I am indebted to Mr. Lewis Galantière (formerly of the Federal Reserve Bank in New York) for a possible sidelight on the proposition that we may have an enforced "leisure class," but at the bottom, rather than the top, of society. He suggests that, in order of their ability and their imagination and their interest, able men and women will seek the most "interesting" forms of employment. This, he suggests, will be true

of the best-trained and ablest minds in the country and of the men
and women of intermediate ability down to the very bottom, where the
least happily employed will seek more interesting jobs immediately
above them.

If, through automation, we develop a situation in which there is,
literally, not enough useful work (in any system) to go around, the
struggle for the more interesting jobs will become bitterer even than
the profit struggle of the nineteenth century. But I do not think it will
reach this point. The "transcendental margin" (discussed later) should
steadily enlarge the horizon and increase the intensity of application of
the American value system. As this proceeds, new areas of desired
results are opened, and new ranges of intensely useful employment will
open with them. There is perhaps more ground for hope in the transcendental margin than in the fields opened by technological development.

12. While asserted with some confidence, this figure of $4 billion is a
rough estimate (and has to be by the nature of the beast). Revenue
annually collected by the federal government from inheritance and gift
taxes alone has doubled in the last seven years, and the upward trend has
been quite constant. Collections from these sources rose from not
quite one billion dollars in 1955, to not quite two billion dollars in
1961, with between 80% and 90% of this revenue attributable to the
estate tax in each year.

YEAR	COLLECTION OF ESTATE AND GIFT TAXES
1955	$ .936 billion
1956	1.171
1957	1.378
1958	1.411
1959	1.353
1960	1.626
1961	1.916

13. Tax receipts from capital gains, over and above inheritance and gift
taxes, both corporate and private, long and short run, apparently net the
federal government two-plus billion dollars a year, although this is
sharply dependent on the fluctuation of the stock market. If collections
from the inheritance and gift taxes are fairly predictable in their amount,
and data easy to come by, the opposite is true of tax receipts from
realized capital gains, first because the level of realized gains in any year
is not predictable, and second because revenue collections from this
source are buried in the income-tax returns of individuals, and have not
yet been sprung out by the statisticians of the Internal Revenue Service.
There exists a three-year lag in official reporting of even the level of

net capital gains and losses for a given year, and the lag for estimates of the actual tax receipts on these amounts is longer.

Estimates exist, however. Dan Throop Smith, Professor of Finance at the Harvard Business School and an authority on the capital-gains tax, states that the estimated yield of the capital-gains tax on individuals increased from $700 million to $1.7 billion between 1953 and 1955. He further states that the tax on corporate capital gains produces about $500 million in annual revenue. This would put annual collections from the capital-gains tax somewhere above two billion dollars, barring a major downturn in the market. (Dan Throop Smith, *Federal Tax Reform: The Issues and a Program,* New York, 1961, pp. 120 and 204 respectively.) It should be remembered that between September 1, 1953, and September 1, 1955, the value of stocks listed on the New York Stock Exchange alone rose from $111 billion to $198 billion, and thus that the grand increase of individual capital-gains-tax payments in this period was the function of a strong bull market.

See Jonathan A. Brown, New York Stock Exchange, "The Locked In Problem," in U.S. Congress, Joint Committee on the Economic Report, *Federal Tax Policy for Economic Growth and Stability* (Washington, D.C., 1956), pp. 369-370.

14. The figures for giving and for the funds held by various forms of charitable, educational, and philanthropic institutions are taken from the seventh compilation of the American Association of The Fund-Raising Counsel, entitled *GIVING U S A* 1962 edition: *A Compilation of Facts Relating to American Philanthropy.* Most of these figures are derived from two sources: the compilation of data from the Internal Revenue Service of the United States Treasury and from the statistics of the United States Department of Health, Education, and Welfare.

In evaluating the economic thrust of the "transcendental margin," note may be taken of the conclusion of the American Association of The Fund-Raising Counsel that assets of philanthropic institutions increased by 170% between 1938 and 1961 (that is, from $20.3 billion in 1938 to $54.8 billion in 1961) and "continued to increase by an estimated 5% annually." This is a greater increase than the increase in population, even after allowing for the fall in the purchasing power of the dollar after 1947.

Obviously all of the increase is not in the form of passive wealth: much of it has gone into buildings and equipment. I hazard a guess, nevertheless, that the larger part of the increase occurred in endowment funds, which are typically invested in supposedly liquid stocks and bonds.

15. The writer knows of no good analysis of "capital" in current economic literature. Realizing the difficulty of analysis, most economists are content to avoid the subject and rest on a general conception of capital as "property in use." Since capital began to be generated with the first primitive tool, it is occasionally referred to as "congealed time"

—but at this point the discussion becomes so academic as to be of little use.

Still worse, the exclusions from "capital" are almost wholly arbitrary. The body of scientific thought, and the formulas for application of scientific principles, being incorporeal, are usually assumed to be incapable of evaluation, and therefore find no place in statistical measurement. Yet, obviously, if all of the scientific knowledge were suddenly deleted from the libraries and minds of men, the capital plant of the nation would lose much, perhaps most, of its utility. Physical assets can be replaced within reasonable time. Incorporeal assets when actually destroyed might require generations. For that matter, the literacy of a population is a substantial addition to its "capital" assets. When the Nazi conquest of Czechoslovakia was complete, a Nazi cabinet minister proposed to destroy its potential by assuring that the next generation of Czech children should be kept illiterate.

"Capital" like "property" shifts meaning as development goes forward.

16. I have stated that the largest single block of "savings" disposable for capital purposes was accumulated by corporations and that a much smaller block was derived from personal savings of individuals, largely accumulated in insurance companies, savings and loan associations, mutual savings banks, and the like. The 1960 figures were: by corporations, $30.8 billion; by individuals, $23 billion.

This requires explanation. All figures given are for 1960.

According to the Federal Reserve figures (*Federal Reserve Bulletin,* 1961), gross total savings in the United States for 1960 were $120.4 billion.

Of these, $30.8 billion were gross savings by corporations. By "gross" is meant that depreciation and depletion were not deducted—this, of course, had been recouped in cash by the corporations through their sales. The $30.8 billion figure represents disposable cash.

Individual savings are more difficult to translate into capital formation.

Individuals accumulated net financial savings of $10.4 billion (S.E.C. figures). Their total savings were $25.9 billion; but they borrowed $15.5 billion. In aggregate, this left $10.4 billion which they could invest. I do not consider the figure wholly satisfactory for analytical purposes. Individuals who saved were not necessarily the same individuals who borrowed, and they may have been able "to accumulate and invest" a rather larger amount than the net. Those who borrowed may have drawn on commercial bank credit. In any case, individual financial savings were very much less than the corporate savings—probably less than half.

Individuals also "saved," but promptly respent a great deal more for what are called "consumer durables" and homes. These figures run large. Individuals "saved" (and "spent") for "consumer durables" (automobiles, television sets, radios, and the like) $44.3 billion. They also spent for homes (other than farms) $18.4 billion—a total of $62.7 billion. I think these savings may be regarded as savings consumed, but some regard them as "investment." It is a question of philosophy. This figure is included in the $120.4 billion given above.

The certain fact about this form of savings, thus "invested" (or slowly "consumed," as it might be put) is that it does not directly produce. It merely adds to the comfort or cruising range of the individual. He has to produce in some other capacity than as car or house owner. This amount of "savings" is not therefore used for investment in direct production facilities. Nor is much of it likely to be available; the individual has little real choice. Theoretically, he could voluntarily refuse to buy a car or home. In practice, he wants the car for pleasure (consumption) or needs it to get to his job—and he has to live somewhere.

Finally, there is a figure (substantial) of "noncorporate construction" and investment in farms: $12.7 billion. A substantial part (perhaps one third) of this is agricultural: farm machinery, barns, and the like. The rest represents savings spent upon small individual enterprises—true capital accumulation by true individual enterprisers—roadside restaurants, individually owned garages, and the like.

Estimating on capital sources and formation and resulting power, I should rank corporate savings ($30.8 billion) as number one; net individual financial savings ($10.4 billion—possibly slightly increased) as number two; and noncorporate construction (excluding farms) where there is no accumulation of power as number three.

I differ with some who regard sums spent on consumer durables (automobiles, etc.) or on homes as readily available for "capital," or capable of being invested in direct production. Some economists like to consider the two large items—individual savings and expenditures for consumer durables and for homes—as "savings," which they are; and that therefore they are available in whole or in part for "capital," which they are not.

Other economists split the difference. In the National Income Accounts, published by the Office of Business Economics of the Department of Commerce in its annual *Survey of Current Business* (for example, July, 1961), depreciation on consumer durables is excluded from gross national capital consumption—apparently on the theory that automobiles and the like are consumer goods. The same service does include depreciation on homes: these are apparently regarded as capital. Just why they do so is matter of institutional preference.

The point depends on how free the individual saver is to make a choice. The aim of this volume has been to get as close to human reality as is practicable. From my own observation I do not think most of these individuals are free not to buy a home, or some sort of car, though the area of choice differs in different localities. Some economists even like to consider as "voluntary individual savings" the amounts one is required to pay under Social Security legislation or union pension funds. Exactly what an individual who does not "choose" to do this can do about it is anything but clear. His only recourse is to go into politics and try to secure a repeal of the Social Security laws, or break up the union system. In other words, his remedy lies not in the choice afforded by the economic republic, but in appeal to the political state. This capacity is precisely what the political state does offer to the economic republic. It is why a free and democratic political state is essential to any modern system of choice.

Some classical economists, for example, Professor Milton Friedman, of Chicago, reverse the reasoning. They believe that a free democratic state is the product of uncontrolled economic machinery. On the facts, precisely the reverse seems more likely. In any event, the reverse system is the American economic system at present.

17. As matter of fact, the ratio of personal to gross business savings has been amazingly stable over the past fifteen years. On an average, *personal* saving has accounted for a shade less than one third of total private saving annually since 1948. *Gross business saving* accounts for the remaining two thirds. In only one year since the beginning of the period did the ratio of personal saving to business saving become more lopsided than 30% to 70%. It was 24% to 76% in 1949. In the fifties, the average of the ratio was 34% personal saving to 66% business savings. (Source: *Economic Report of the President for 1962,* p. 229.)

The true meaning and significance of the saving statistics of this country is well hidden behind a dense and seemingly impassable tangle of conflicting definitions and "conceptual differences." When we say that personal savings equal 30% of national savings, we take into account all national savings (including homes) but exclude consumer durables.

Theorists have difficulty in deciding whether when individuals save to buy motorcars or other household machines the "savings" thus used constitute "capital" or "consumption." I take the view that such expenditures are essentially consumption. Certainly savings so applied do not directly increase production. They have not been—are not—readily (if at all) available for capital. They increase the comfort, the leisure time, perhaps the productive capacity of the individual—a quite different thing (so does a square meal). Expenditures on these amounted to the enormous figure of $44.3 billion in 1960—close to the figure for the entire gross business investment for that year. I exclude them from capital.

Many theorists consider the "savings" thus accumulated—and applied to buy motorcars and other durables—as potential "capital" because individuals might choose not to buy that car but to invest in bonds or stocks to enhance the capital of productive enterprise. This seems to me wholly unrealistic. Individuals must have both transport and equipment. The government, of course, could set up a rationing scheme making purchases of cars and household machines impossible, and could force the saving thus spent into investment channels. It did so in World War II. Short of a major emergency, this is beyond reasonable likelihood.

A final statistical word: if one adds in depreciation on private homes to the figure for personal savings, the percentage of personal to national savings rises from 30% to 37.6%. This would be mere mythology. Home owners do *not* estimate depreciation on their houses, save up an equivalent amount in cash, and invest or otherwise apply it. Business concerns, on the other hand, do exactly that.

18. The greatest Latin-American statesman and educator of the nineteenth century, Domingo Faustino Sarmiento, of Argentina, perhaps estimated American reactions and processes better than any other contemporary observer. On May 5, 1858, participating in the inauguration of an Argentine Methodist chapel, he exclaimed: ". . . Oh, Yankees. If the world were on the verge of tumbling down, they would nominate a chairman, present a project for reconstruction, would vote on it by ayes and noes and would collect the necessary funds in time to stop the disaster." (Edmundo Correas, *Sarmiento and the United States,* University of Florida Press, Latin American Monograph, 1962, p. 15.) No mean prophet, as one remembers organization of the United States of the Marshall Plan, the foreign-aid program, and the Alliance for Progress.

19. The knitting of the American political-economic system into a single, more or less choate, organization, has had far too little attention. Three source studies are important, and all deserve careful study.

(1) *The Economy of the American People: Progress, Problems, Prospects,* by Gerhard Colm and Theodore Geiger (National Planning Association, Planning Pamphlet 115, 1958, 2d ed. October 1961) is outstanding. This is a book by distinguished economists: Dr. Colm served as member of the President's Council of Economic Advisers and also in the Bureau of the Budget; Dr. Geiger has served both in government and as teacher at Columbia University. Of particular interest are the conclusions (pp. 172-174). They state that the American system is "neither capitalism nor socialism" as these words are historically understood. There is a "master"—the national interest of the United States as interpreted by its political process. And "Only a part of the requirements of the national interest have become crystallized into laws. Some are in the form either of 'unwritten laws' and traditions or of the individual choices of men and women who are free to make both political and economic decisions" (p. 173).

(2) The second book, perhaps no less important, is *The New American Political Economy: A Synthesis of Politics and Economics,* by Marshall E. Dimock, head of the Department of Government of New York University (New York, 1962). Dimock comes at a similar synthesis, though he starts less from economic than from political premises. He believes there must be substantial development of government power to organize and to plan. Particular attention is called to Chapters

12 and 13 (pp. 203-236) and to the chart of a proposed federal organization for the leadership of the national economy (p. 230). There is some indication that a grouping and choate direction of the government departments presently without co-ordination is informally happening now. Dimock gives less weight than I would to the possibilities of the Council of Economic Advisers, but perhaps I am unduly skeptical of the efficacy of Cabinet-level committees and councils.

(3) *The Making of Economic Society,* by Professor Robert L. Heilbroner, of the Faculty of The New School for Social Research (New York, 1962). This is an economist's study, with historical background and relatively little emphasis on governmental structure. Heilbroner's approach, like Jean Fourastié's (see note 19), is essentially philosophical. One of his conclusions verges on my own theory of the "transcendental margin." "The central problem which is likely to confront the societies of tomorrow is nothing less than the creation of a new relationship between the economic aspect of existence and human life in its totality." (I should say that the problem is upon us today.) "The danger exists that the market system, in an environment of genuine abundance, may become an instrument which liberates man from real want only to enslave him to purposes for which it is increasingly difficult to find social and moral justification" (p. 233).

This is not a danger; it is a present condition. It is this that causes novelists like Aldous Huxley (*Island,* p. 235) to suggest that the United States pampers and supplies its youth so that they can buy in sufficient quantities to keep the factories running—the consumer has no other significance. I think Huxley underestimates the American consumer. The quantum of the transcendental margin he provides (see Chapter 13, Sec. 3, *post*) attests with solid evidence that it is an underestimate.

20. There is some division of opinion among economists as to whether a budget deficit corresponding to expansion of credit tends to increase business activity and expansion. The Commission on Money and Credit assumed that it did, or at least could be made to do so. (See *Report of the Commission on Money and Credit,* 1961, Chap. V, p. 121.) Professor Milton Friedman, in *Capitalism and Freedom* (Chicago, 1962, Chap. V, pp. 75-84), is doubtful, and especially doubtful if the deficit is created by additional government expenditures instead of by lowering taxes. He suggests that the evidence is not conclusive one way or the other. The Council of Economic Advisers both in the Eisenhower administration and at present seems to have believed that a government fiscal deficit does aid expansion of activity and, conversely, a surplus would tend to curtail it. I myself believe that they are right, but that much more work needs to be done to determine detailed methods of using fiscal policy as a stabilizer or stimulus.

Politically, the question is clear. Whenever there is poverty, or substantial numbers of unemployed men on one side of the economic machine and adequate piled-up goods or unused readily available productivity on the other, the state will be required by political pressure to find some way of connecting the supply with the need. Currency and credit can do that, certainly temporarily, and probably over a long term. If not overdone, it should be possible to make the process adequately safe. The demagogic appeal merely to print money and distribute it has to be resisted—as does the "hands-off" policy, leaving human costs to redress the balance.

Probably the political synthesis is this. In the case of widespread distress, state intervention is a certainty. Wise handling of fiscal policy is the least drastic of the possible interventions.

21. For those interested, comparison must be made between the American practice and the system prevailing in France. There, flexible economic planning has been carried on for a number of years with an extremely high degree of success. The power of the state to plan is ascribed by Pierre Massé, at present the president of the French Planning Commission, to the fact that the French government invests rather more than 50% of all capital invested in France. It can do this because it owns or controls a large proportion of economic enterprise in France. Through its direct buying power, it can give business to the private-sector enterprises and corporations which conform to the plan, denying business to those which do not. In addition, of course, it can give preferred credit conditions to such enterprises. Whether the United States would accept so high a degree of power in the federal government is questionable, certainly at present. Yet the advantage of being able to assure industrial development in areas of the United States presently not industrialized and of decentralizing industry so as to remove the growing pressure on great cities is obvious. Another generation may well see a shift in sentiment. Actually, we have little direct knowledge of what American sentiment is now.

22. The power of the national government to redistribute economic activity through use of its direct power to purchase, lend, and organize is best illustrated in the Area Redevelopment Program legislation (42 USCA 28, §2501 ff.).

This legislation sets up an area-redevelopment administration in the Department of Commerce. It is headed by an administrator, working under direction of a policy board, namely, a committee of Cabinet ministers together with the administrator of the Housing and Home Financing Authority (FHA) and of the Small Business Administration. (For practical purposes, the Cabinet committee does not intervene much.) A companion national advisory board is set up, though it is probably scenery more than influence.

The Secretary of Commerce is authorized to designate "redevelopment areas" where unemployment has been for some years 6% higher than the national unemployment average, or has been, respectively, 50%, 75%, or 100% more than the national unemployment average for four years, two years, or one year, respectively. Unemployment is thus the criterion for action.

When an area is so designated, the Secretary of Commerce after making appropriate studies (one hopes he has done so in advance) may "make loans for development projects including establishment of new industries." In practice, this amounts to lending money at low rates of interest up to 65% of the capital cost of such new projects. He may also steer and accelerate public works and federal purchase orders into the area. For this sort of activity $100 million have been allocated.

That amount in any substantial area is, of course, a drop in a bucket. Relatively little has been done under this scheme because programs have not been appropriated for and tackled on a really massive scale. Yet the conception and the organization is a beginning, capable of great expansion. It could meet major problems, some of which may arise at any time. Were a shift in defense-munition needs to cancel further need for military aircraft, two great areas—Southern California and Connecticut—would fall abruptly into economic blight.

Disarmament would, of course, end the flow of many billions of government orders in diverse parts of the country with ensuing cessation of employment, commercial operations, and contributing economic activity. Were this to happen (one wishes this were an imminent possibility—it is not), the logic of the situation should require devoting approximately equal amounts of money to redevelopment of the areas hit hardest. The writer believes this is exactly what would happen. Assumption that the economy of the United States would collapse on disarmament is nothing more than a widely repeated Communist canard. Wide use of the area-redevelopment device, enlarged in scope, plus (one hopes) a good many other activities, would promptly be forced on the American economic republic. The voters would compel this if its politicians did not act of their own accord. Lack of advance planning —a present fact—would not mean temporary economic collapse. It would merely increase vastly the ultimate cost by making necessary unemployment allowance for a more prolonged period than would be necessary with adequate advance plans. Obviously a country which can afford expenditure for armament could afford a like expenditure for nonmilitary purposes (of which there are plenty crying for attention) without substantially changing the current tax take or other revenue operations of the government.

23. If one wishes to indulge in economic science fiction, this is one field where it can be gratified without doing great violence to sensibilities. Let us note particularly the field of "consumer credit." A large sector of the American public already knows what it is to buy on the installment plan, or to have a credit card handy, making it possible to purchase practically anything, from a meal at a restaurant or a summer holiday, to gasoline, a car, or a set of furniture. No one has yet realized that a central credit-rating bureau, determining whether these

cards should be given or withdrawn, could have a violent impact on the life of a dedicated credit-card holder. One could imagine a political tyrant arising out of such a system.

Or one could imagine a day coming in which every child reaching maturity would be automatically entitled to a credit card entitling him to education, food, and shelter; and on attaining, say, age twenty-six, to buy an automobile or perhaps a house. (Veterans have had somewhat similar privileges in respect to home buying for the past several years.) Behind these, there must be a banking system able to advance cash to the sellers—and a collection system able to collect in installments or otherwise from the holders. The Federal Reserve Board could make this possible.

The fiction writer of the future may assume that credit is as much a natural right as the right to vote. Only gradually would it become politically understood that capacity to supply production, or, if need be, to limit consumption would become necessary companion measures. But if technological development makes productive capacity virtually unlimited, the arrangement would be economically manageable.

No one (so far as I know) has yet brought action in the courts to compel granting of credit to him, or has alleged that its denial would deprive him of his constitutional rights to "life, liberty, or property, without due process of law," or, more likely, to "equal protection of the laws." A generation hence, however, such an action will be by no means unthinkable. In fact, it is rather likely.

24. In 1920, 42.2 million persons were reported as part of the labor force. Of these, 11.4 million were then occupied in agriculture—27% of the total. In 1960, the employed labor force was reported as 66.7 million, but only 5.7 million were employed in agriculture.

The 1920 figures are taken from the United States Bureau of the Census, *Historical Statistics of the United States* (Washington, D.C., 1960), pp. 74 and 140-141 respectively. The 1960 figures on agricultural employment are taken from the United States Bureau of the Census, *Statistical Abstract of the United States: 1962* (Washington, D.C., 1962), pp. 226 and 317.

25. Most economists think and write of the free market as though it were a normal, inevitable, natural phenomenon. Factually, the "free market" is an artificial, delicate, and precarious affair. It is, and can be, maintained only by sedulous and continuous state intervention (sixty-odd major antitrust prosecutions annually). In the American economic republic the "free market" is a state-supported instrument or device, used or laid aside as national interest may dictate.

Were continuous state protection to be eliminated, the free market as it is conceived by most theorists would cease to exist in a very few years. It almost ceased to exist in great areas of industry in the first decade of the twentieth century, although the Sherman Antitrust law had been on the statute books since 1890. President Theodore Roosevelt and his successor, President William H. Taft, undertook to re-create it by applying the Sherman law. When that machinery proved inadequate, President Wilson increased state intervention by causing the passage of the Clayton Antitrust Act and the organization of the Federal Trade Commission.

This was because the free market, unregulated, acted quite normally. The strong and powerful eliminated or absorbed the weak and undefended, and monopolies proliferated. This phenomenon was not due to the designs of evil men interfering with it. It occurred because they acted as men in a free market could be expected to act. They used competition not for the purpose of keeping prices down, but for the purpose of putting their competitors out of business, and becoming monopolists. They fixed prices and territories where they could. They required buyers, as a condition of purchasing goods or services they did need, to buy other goods and services they did not need or want or at prices they did not wish to pay. Where they could not drive out competitors, they consolidated with them. If unable to do that, they made agreements for common action. This is what happens in the free market.

Except for state intervention, I hazard the guess that inside of a decade three quarters or more of the free-market sector would be dominated by monopolies or cartels. The immensely long list of antitrust prosecutions, civil and criminal, and of Federal Trade Commission proceedings sufficiently evidences the steady, persistent, and uninterrupted drive of the productive units of the free market to eliminate competition in it.

In practice, the United States, with all its machinery, does not maintain a classic free market now. It has settled for oligopoly—the modified competition of large units. On the whole, it finds this satisfactory, or at least acceptable.

This was inevitable from the moment when corporations were allowed unlimited scope and size—and they were given this privilege because great scope and great size were needed to achieve production.

If anyone really wishes a free-market system (and no one does), it can be achieved. A law might be passed prohibiting all corporations, and requiring that anyone entering the market do so on his personal credit and personal responsibility for all debts incurred. This would compel (relatively) small-unit production and marketing, and would tend to limit any marginal operation to the lifetime of a man, or perhaps a man and his sons. The result would probably be to decrease the productivity of the United States by perhaps one third or one half. Almost no one in the United States would care to pay this price. The fact is that the economic republic, despite lip service to past abstractions, does not want the abstract free market so dear to current theorists.

While we are at it, I suggest that there is no solid historical evidence that the free market ever did exist as a general phenomenon aside from agricultural products. Probably it has appeared as a natural phenomenon in certain trades and for limited periods of time. It has remained for the American economic republic, and its counterparts in Europe, to endeavor by artificial government action to construct a free market precisely by eliminating certain wholly predictable results of free-market operation. This, I think, is the real answer to arguments made, brilliantly, by men like Professor Milton Friedman. Friedman does not, to be sure, attempt to define "freedom" or "free society" in great depth. He says, "Historical evidence speaks with a single voice on the relation between political freedom and a free market" (p. 9). I do not think that historical evidence exists. Many of us can file an excellent brief for the proposition that an uncontrolled free market is one of the quickest ways of producing economic coercion of individuals and of eliminating the condition Friedman considers basic—"that transactions are bilaterally voluntary and informed."

26. In 1933, membership in labor unions amounted to 2.9 million. This was a decrease from a high point of 3.6 million in 1929. The increase began after the passage of the Wagner Labor Act as follows:

YEAR	UNION MEMBERSHIP (*in millions*)
1934	3.2
1935	3.7
1936	4.2
1937	7.2

In 1961, union membership amounted to 14,957,054. In addition there are a substantial number of smaller independent unions (under 25,000). The membership of the largest single group—the American Federation of Labor and Congress of Industrial Organizations (AFL-CIO)—amounts to about 13 million.

27. In describing the "Protestant ethic," I have discarded secondary statements. I have drawn heavily on the statements to me personally by my grandfather, G. Frederick Wright, whose memoirs perhaps give a fair picture of the economic as well as the theological doctrine. Born at Whitehall, Vermont, pastor of the Congregational Church at Bakersfield, Vermont, and later of the Free Church at Andover, Massachusetts, he spent most of his life as a professor at Oberlin, teaching in the Theological School while becoming more widely known as pioneer in glacial geology and Fellow of the Royal Geographical Society than as Doctor of Divinity. From him and from my father (also a Congregationalist clergyman) and from familiarity with Protestant colleges established straight across the northern tier of the United States, one can perhaps reach a rather deeper understanding of the scope of the Protestant ethic than from the familiar statements of economists and

secondary students. They, naturally, give greatest weight to the fact that the Protestant Reformation eliminated many restrictive Catholic rules carried down from medieval thinking. The Reformation permitted lending money at interest, whereas medieval Catholic doctrine considered any interest as sinful "usury." Protestant doctrine did not attempt to control prices by maintaining the conception of a "just price," as Catholic schoolmen had done. Unquestionably, the Reformation played a great part in bringing into existence the "free-market" conception dominant in the nineteenth century. But it also set up moral limitations on its operation, and those have been largely ignored.

So far as the United States is concerned, the Protestant ethic might be called the "Judeo-Christian ethic." I find no doctrinal difference, at least in America, between Protestants and other religions on this point. In many ways, the Jewish ethic imposes obligations more stringent in actual effect than the Protestant ethic. Historically, of course, the phrase is justified. Jewish and Catholic influence attained strength in the United States only after the turn of the twentieth century, while the Protestant doctrine was regnant in the eighteenth and the nineteenth centuries.

For a layman's statement see *The Gospel of Wealth and Other Timely Essays,* by Andrew Carnegie, edited by Edward C. Kirkland (Cambridge, Mass., 1962). Carnegie in some aspects went far beyond the normal thinking of the Protestant ethic—for that matter, far beyond the thinking of today. Believing as he did that poverty had moral values, he concluded that hereditary wealth was essentially a curse to the children receiving it (p. 63). While the millionaire ought to increase his revenues (p. 72), he ought to distribute the bulk of his wealth before death. "The day is not far distant when the man who dies leaving behind him millions of available wealth, which was free to him to administer during life, will pass away, 'unwept, unhonored, and unsung,' no matter to what uses he leaves the dross which he cannot take with him. Of such as these the public verdict will then be: 'The man who dies thus rich dies disgraced' " (p. 28). This goes far toward imposing a moral capital tax of 80% or 90% on any man whose assets warrant his being called "rich." Carnegie based this not only on social grounds, but on the welfare of the children (p. 56): "I should as soon leave to my son a curse as the almighty dollar," as well as on straight religious grounds. He advocated a graduated inheritance tax as early as 1889.

Carnegie practiced what he preached. Most of his wealthy contemporaries did not agree with him.

For an acid and hilarious contemporary comment, see Mark Twain's *Letters from the Earth* (edited by Bernard De Voto, New York, 1962), especially p. 117: "Letter from the Recording Angel to Abner Scofield, Coal Dealer," giving him highest honors for praying for a monthly income of $45,000 and at the same time actually contributing fifteen whole dollars to a poor widow. St. Peter, the recording angel noted, would welcome him with a torchlight parade. Heaven would be glad when he went there. So would hell.

Mr. Clemens seemed to suspect that the motivations of the Protestant ethic did not yield adequate results.

28. Direct relationship between the intensity of a transcendental margin (as here defined) with the economic progress of the state to me seems established. The evidence is sufficiently compelling to accept it as a "constant," that is, that where there is such a margin, there is a measure of progress, and the larger the margin, the greater the factor of progress. This has nothing whatever to do with whether the inspiration for it is "good" or "bad." The Utah-Nevada contrast is obvious. Less well known is the fact that Nazi Germany achieved a burst of progress between 1933 and 1938: see *The Economic Recovery of Germany from 1933 to the Incorporation of Austria in March 1938,* by C. W. Guillebaud (London, 1939). Guillebaud was not sympathetic to German National Socialism and endeavored to be objective. He did not lay German gains to the transcendental margin (the theory had not then been propounded). He considered the remarkable German economic progress as due to the remarkable increase in gross investment (p. 48), to rationalization of that investment under the successive four-year plans, and to increase in the credit and guaranteeing facilities. The underlying fact, nevertheless, was that much of the increased gross-capital investment went into plants to produce or capable of producing armament. It was stimulated by a rising tempo of nationalist aspiration, made acceptable by Nazi internal propaganda, that the Hitler regime was building a future empire in whose benefits the children of every Nordic German would share.

The word "transcendental," I repeat, has no religious significance. (Even when transcendence is diabolical in concept, as has happened, one remembers that the devil was a fallen angel. At all events, he is said to have inspired quite a number of followers.)

The case of Israel in comparison to surrounding states is a plainer illustration. Figures on Israel's increase are given in the recent volume by Jean Fourastié, *La Grande Métamorphose du XXe Siècle. Essais sur quelques problémes de l'humanité d'aujourd'hui* (Paris, 1962, Deuxième Edition. Augmentée).

Fourastié is a rare combination: an economist and also a philosopher. His work has scored a remarkable influence on French thought. It deserves to be much better known in America. Fourastié's first work, *The Great Hope of the Twentieth Century,* outlining some of his ideas, has had an amazing success in Europe since publication in Paris in 1948. Fourastié's fundamental thesis is that an economic system must include not only the material needs of the men in it, but must also move toward the realization of their picture of themselves in the foreseeable future and of their relation to the universe.

Some of Fourastié's conclusions closely approach those of Marshall E. Dimock in *The New American Political Economy*. For example, Fourastié's insistence that great problems are philosophical rather than economic. "The problem . . . far exceeds the false problems we have been considering up to now. These dealt only with a part, a sector of human activity; the real problem includes the entirety of human personality and even of human life" (p. 48, translation mine).

The integration of economic organization with human will is essential to a democratic economy. It has been, I think, better achieved in the American economic republic than anywhere else. This necessarily implies some philosophical questions: "What is the good life? What is the good society? What is the fully developed man?"

Robert L. Heilbroner comes close to the fundamental theory here given. He points out in a remarkable book, *The Making of Economic Society,* that as a result of the "Protestant ethic," Protestant countries, with their Puritan's creed of work and thrift, forged ahead in the economic race, and that in our own time state planning has been introduced to "off-set inherent goal-setting weaknesses" (p. 230). And again, "Thus the danger exists that the market system, in an environment of genuine abundance, may become an instrument which liberates man from real want only to enslave him to purposes for which it is increasingly difficult to find social and moral justification" (p. 233). The "motivation base" (Heilbroner's phrase) underlies all economic activity. Obviously, as it becomes increasingly social and moral, it progressively transcends calculation of individual advantage.

The motivational base in the United States demonstrably transcends the aggregate of calculations of individual advantage. I suggest that the American value system indicates probability of its further expansion, and that the level of productivity will rise as that expansion takes place.

INDEX

Academy of Moral and Political Science of France, 19

Adams, Henry, 193

Adams, Walter, 155

Administered price. *See* Price administration

Advertising, 151-152

Affluent Society, The (Galbraith), 6

Agricultural Adjustment Act, 97, 141

Agriculture: and McNary-Haugen Act, 96; as a controlled market, 140-144; decline of in U.S., 12; employment in, 233n; investment in, 134, 227n; numbers engaged in, 233n; reorganization of credit activities, 97

Alliance for Progress, 229n

Aluminum Company of America, 103, 153, 193

America in Mid-Passage (Beard), 88

American Association of The Fund-Raising Counsel, 225n

American Commonwealth, The (Bryce), 88

American Economic Republic: and economic and intellectual freedom, 41; birth of, 91, 95; effectiveness of industry in, 161; faster growth of, 206; governmental structure of, 100-116; integration of economic organization with human will, 238n; introduction to, 3-16; legal structure of, ix; organization of, 95-185, 213-218; responsibility of the individual in, 176; role of Congress in, 108-109; social-ized sector of, 176-185; success of, xi, 3; value system of, 189-212

American Federation of Labor— Congress of Industrial Organizations, 165, 235n

Antitrust policy, 41, 152-155, 160, 163-164, 173, 214; Clayton law, 90, 102, 145, 152, 153, 234n; Sherman law, 86, 90, 96, 101-104, 105, 106, 145, 152, 233n, 234n; Special Committee on, 152

Area Redevelopment: Act, 113; Program, 231n-232n

Automation, 66, 154, 173, 174, 224n

Automobile industry, 83, 123-124, 150

Bank of England, 127

Banks and banking: as the prerogative of the modern state, 27; credit and the interest rate, 121-124; failure as result of the free market, 86; failure of 1933, 97, 118-119, 126, 178; function of commercial, 124-127; investment of capital, 132; taken control of by government, 97; state intervention in, 223n. *See also* Credit, Federal Reserve

Beard, Charles and Mary, 88

Berle, Adolf A., 27, 220n, 223n

Bituminous coal industry, 156, 160

Black, Justice Hugo, 101

Bleak House (Dickens), 183

Brown, Jonathan A., 225n

Brown Shoe Company v. *United States,* 153

Brüning, Heinrich, 80

Bryan, William Jennings, 86
Bryce, Lord, 88
Budget, 109-112, 120, 230n
Bureau of Mines, 157
Bureau of the Budget. *See* Budget
Bureau of the Census, 150
Businesses, semicontrolled, 155-159

Campbell Condensed Soup Company, 57
Capital: accumulation of, 127-136; analysis of, 225n-226n; "created," 68-73; formation of, 62-67; incorporeal, 60-61, 65-66, 73-75, 197, 216, 226n; investment of, 127-136; sources of, 60-75
Capitalism: classical, 8; obsolescence of, 16. *See also* Nineteenth-century economic system
Capitalism and Freedom (Friedman), 230n
Carnegie, Andrew, 194, 195, 236n
Carnegie Corporation, 194
Cartels, 145, 234n
Catholic ethic, 192, 236n
Chicago, conditions in, 195
China: conditions in, 196; economic system of, 10; steel production in, 39
Civilian Conservation Corps Act, 98
Clayton Antitrust Act. *See* Antitrust policy
Colm, Gerhard, xi, 86-87, 229n
Coming of the New Deal, The (Schlesinger), 99
Commerce, Department of, 227n, 231n
Commercial enterprise in the U.S., organization of, 31-35
Commodity Credit Corporation, 142

Communications industry, control of, 137-140
Communism: and labor, 167; and property, 219n-220n; banking under, 127; control of production under, 129; equalitarian basis not maintained under, 52; industrial organization compared with U.S., 161; obsolescence of, 16; power elite of, 23. *See also* Soviet Union
Communist Manifesto, The (Marx), 8, 20, 21
Competition: and economic stability, 159-162; artificial, 152-155; extremes of, 214; market, 81-84; small-unit, 154, 155, 160
Concentration of economic power: argument against, 155; degree of as an acceptable balance, 161, 214; in industry, 146-152
Congress of the Hundred Days, 99
Congress, participation in economic policy, 108-116
Corporations: accumulation of capital by, 63, 65; allowed unlimited size, 234n; and delegation of power, 37; and investment of capital, 130-131; and philanthropy, 208-209; and price administration, 83; and small private enterprises, 30-31; and the political state, 15; classified, 160-161; concentration of, 150-151; expansion of, 154; diminish power of individual owners, 26-27; growth of, 12-13; in industry, 146-152; Larousse on, 20, 21; legitimacy of, 43; mergers of, 152-155; outlawed, 82; Supreme Court decisions on, 89, 101. *See also* Antitrust policy, Concentration of economic power, Monopolies
Correas, Edmundo, 229n
Council of Economic Advisers,